ACTS OF READING
teachers, texts and childhood

Edited by
Morag Styles and Evelyn Arizpe

Trentham Books

Stoke on Trent, UK and Sterling, USA

Trentham Books Limited
Westview House   22883 Quicksilver Drive
734 London Road   Sterling
Oakhill   VA 20166-2012
Stoke on Trent   USA
Staffordshire
England ST4 5NP

© 2009 Morag Styles and Evelyn Arizpe

First published 2009

British Library Cataloguing-in-Publication Data
A catalogue record for this book is available from the British Library

ISBN: 978 1 85856 438 8

The author and Trentham Books would like to thank the Publication Assistance Fund at Dublin City University which contributed to the cost of publishing this book.

Designed and typeset by Trentham Print Design Ltd, Chester and printed in Great Britain by Page Bros (Norwich) Ltd.

Contents

INTRODUCTION
Acts of Reading – from Nursery Libraries to Digital Screens
Morag Styles and Evelyn Arizpe

Acts of reading

Acts of reading conjure up theatrical metaphors and the reader of this volume should expect a script of some depth and variety with the different chapters as constituent parts of the performance. Indeed, the audience is invited to embark on a wide-ranging and dramatic journey into some of the roots and byways of the history of reading, reaching a long way back in time to Aesop, the medieval period and the beginnings of printing in some of the chapters, while pausing for a while in the eighteenth and nineteenth centuries in others. The book is also, however, bang up to date, with the final section taking account not only of developments in reading of recent times, including the digital technology revolution and what that means in terms of texts and readers, but also gazing with plenty of optimism into the likely future of literacies.

The scope is wide in terms of genres and topics – stories, novels, picture-books, poetry, the Bible and other sacred texts, fairy tales, fables, maxims, pictures, films, commonplace books, reading primers, grammar primers, scrolls, children's writing, government documents and directives, research evidence, questionnaires and myriad screen-based texts, plus scenes and dramas of every description including texts in galleries. When speaking of all these texts, we tend to use the word 'read', and yet, as soon as we consider any of them in particular, it becomes evident just how tenuous this commonality really is. In fact, as reader-based and post-structuralist theorists have argued, the act of reading is determined not only by the reader's interaction with the text but also by the historical and socio-cultural context in which this act takes place, giving rise to some of the dichotomies we mention later on.

The 'teachers' of the title refers not only to classroom educators, such as those for whom we have fascinating new evidence about their own reading habits (see Cremin, Bearne, Goodwin and Mottram) but also to the many people all of us encounter as we engage in acts of reading from early childhood onwards. Then there is the learning that comes out of the internal conversations readers have with authors and artists as they make meaning of the books they read; and the texts themselves which teach important reading lessons (Meek). We also pay attention to some texts that were specifically produced to teach reading, in one case highly visual scrolls for poor Irish children (Coghlan and O'Connor) and, in another instance, eighteenth century primers where reading was directly linked to formal grammar (Navest).

Jane Johnson's inspirational archive

The inspiration for bringing together scholars from all over the world to talk about acts of reading was the Jane Johnson archive. This exceptional archive contains not only her Nursery Library but also her 'Pretty Story' for children and her commonplace book, among other fascinating documents. There is no room here to describe the whole of Johnson's domestic oeuvre, so we remit the reader both to our book, *Reading Lessons from the Eighteenth Century*[1] (Arizpe and Styles, 2006) and to the primary sources themselves.[2] However, for those who are as yet unacquainted with Jane Johnson and who will read about her in some of the chapters in this book – particularly those in the first section – we offer some background.

Johnson was a genteel Englishwoman who grew up in London and then moved with her husband, a vicar, to Olney in Buckinghamshire where they raised their four children – Barbara (1738), George (1740), Robert (1745) and Charles (1748). Soon after her husband's death in 1756, she moved to Witham, in Lincolnshire. Had it not been for Jane and her family's penchant for keeping family documents, she would have remained one of the many unknown mothers who wrote down her thoughts and verses in private and who created materials to help teach their children to read – little scraps and jottings of ephemera of the kind normally lost to posterity. As it turned out, since the initial discovery of the Nursery Library in 1982, more documents have come to light which have confirmed she was a woman who had the intellect to conceive a clear theory of learning from her own reading and the artistic skills to transfer this theory into objects both beautiful and practical to engage her own children (and now scholars from all over the world) in the act of reading.

Setting the stage

Rather than summarise what each chapter contains, which seems to us an exercise in tautology, we plan in these introductory remarks to highlight certain key commonalities, redundancies and dichotomies which the book explores, in order to provide a context – or, if you like, to lift the curtain on what follows.

We start with a range of important questions posed by Margaret Meek Spencer. How do children read? What do children read? What makes children into readers? What role do adults play in acts of reading? Despite years of research and discussion, the debates remain open and always will, given that the answers will change along with historical, cultural and technological developments. In response to such questions, there are certain key themes that recur throughout the book, however diverse the subject-matter of different contributors – the imagination, play and storytelling, visual aspects of reading, change and transformation, collaboration and community, the nature of childhood.

Reading these contributions, we have marvelled anew at the power of narrative to move us, teach us, and encourage us to use our imaginations. The great written stories of the past still draw us under their spells, like fables which show us how to live (Graham) and fairy tales which are often our earliest and most deeply loved texts (Tosi). Today, however, new stories are being told using novel and interactive technologies with their clever voices off, providing ironic comments on the way we live now. These popular screen-based texts often make rich, subtle, intertextual allusions to many other texts, requiring what Victor Watson has described elsewhere as sophisticated, multilayered readers – the kind of readers that most children are today. Anouk Lang reminds us that what was previously private has become public in the digital age, though there are new 'rules of social engagement' and she highlights the radical potential in the 'democratisation of online spaces'. Eve Bearne talks about the need to trust children to cope intelligently as critical readers of a wide range of texts, extending our reading repertoires to 'embrace screen-based texts while continuing to value print'.

Forever young

David Whitley, reminding us of Wordsworth's famous dictum that 'the child is father of the man', argues that 'the acts of reading implicit in Wordsworth's poetry shape the way we now perceive childhood'. He suggests that Wordsworth was one of the earliest writers to present children as recognisable people. Many contributors urge us to trust children with their intuitive delight in creating and shaping their own acts of reading, and to follow Virginia Woolf's advice in *The Common Reader* that readers should use their common sense, follow their own instincts, and avoid literary prejudices. In the words of Francesca Orestano, 'when reading, we must stay forever young'. Links are also made between the literacy of the past and present by Vivienne Smith, who shows that Kevin Crossley Holland's hero of *The Seeing Stone* (2000) trilogy set in Arthurian Britain faced some of the same sort of problems with literacy as boys do today – including the lack of effective role models for reading.

Adults, usually with good intentions, have always agonised about children's reading and one issue worth drawing attention to is the instinct of the old to control and, at worst, censor what the young may read and how they may read it. However, history shows us that the healthy reaction of the young is to resist such constraints and that a goodly proportion of young readers have always defied attempts to impose conformity and limit their freedom to reach out and read as and what they please.

And to be fair to those of the past and present warning children of the dangers of reading, most have wanted young readers to experience pleasure as well as knowledge from the texts they read. Locke's 'easy pleasant book' recommended for inexperienced readers in the late seventeenth century struck a chord with millions of adults over many generations. The many editions of Aesop's fables (Graham) and of Newbery's books, as well as the borrowing that took place between writers and publishers (and even parents such as Jane Johnson), are evidence that the idea of bringing play, verse and image into reading pedagogy was a success (Arizpe and Styles, 2006). Reading was further liberated for children in the Victorian and Edwardian periods with fiction dominated by memorable characters who knew their own minds and often went against the grain of dominant adult morality codes.

The central role of the imagination is taken up by many contributors. Janet Bottoms draws attention to William Godwin's belief that if the imagination is to be cultivated at all, then the process must begin in youth. Peter Cook explores relations between children and adults in Edwardian novels by Nesbit, Grahame and Saki where the authority of adults, limited by conformity to the moral and social codes of their day, is often juxtaposed with the imaginative wisdom of children. Nowadays, books are gloriously played out as drama in the Seven Stories Centre for Children's Books (Hammill), where authors can orchestrate further acts of reading with stages, sets, costumes and designs which invite young readers to get involved in playing with text in new ways.

All the contributors to this book share a belief in the worth of young readers' capacity to launch themselves into flights of imagination which take them from local events to fly-away destinations. Shirley Brice Heath reminds us that Jane Johnson's seminal reading lessons encouraged 'linguistic, visual, and gestural congruencies, along with the all-important uses of imagination and embodiment, [to] take place in meaningful ways'. Jane Johnson embedded the words and pictures of her teaching material within narratives of the children's everyday worlds to offer familiarity yet also invite them into 'performative modes to re-enact and to embody characters and stories'. Again and again, Heath shows how the links work between the visual, verbal and dramatic, arguing that verbal fluency goes hand-in-hand with attention to visual focus and dramatic role-play which, in turn, enables children to explore being inside someone else's character in thought, voice and action.

Dichotomies and redundancies

What also struck us forcefully during our reading as editors were the number of dichotomies, which recur like *leit-motifs* in successive chapters. These include past and present; adults and children; the relationship between dead and living minds; boys and girls; regulation and freedom; teaching and learning; comparing and contrasting; premises and consequences; home and school; expert and apprentice; word and image; older forms of reading and writing and new, more visual technologies with screen-based texts; heaven and hell; public and private; readers and writers; stage and page; continuities and changes.

At the same time, we were struck by the number of redundancies within the chapters – 'redundancies' in the sense of 'truths', highlighted by Meek as she borrows Heath's words. They are the truths about the act of reading that emerge again and again: the importance of allowing child readers to find their own ways through texts, the valuing of readers' experience and participation, the need to trust children's creativity and their capacity for both delight and intellectual understanding. Meek and Heath agree that these 'redundancies' are in fact 'good evidence' which we would do well to attend to.

These dichotomies and redundancies remind us that nothing about reading and young readers is ever simple, though many wish it were so! The acts of critical reading in this book make one wary of common sense views of teachers, texts and childhood. Instead, we stress the importance of taking an exploratory approach, remembering that for every argument there is always a counterargument and that the pendulum of reading culture and its pedagogy continually swings from one direction to another over time. *Acts of*

Reading brings to the fore the value of sound evidence and research and the need to keep questioning the current trends but also the need for constructing ever more solid arguments – so that we do not slip backwards into fearing the power of the act of reading but move forward into giving all children the opportunity to experience this power.

The final act

This volume began life as an international conference[3] where we took delight in each others' research into reading. Since then, the contributors to the book have practised many different acts of reading as they prepared their chapters for publication. As editors, we have engaged in a different kind of reading in an effort to ensure consistency and correctness. Readers of this volume will make their own idiosyncratic readings by skipping sections they are less interested in and giving close attention to chapters that chime with their own viewpoints or which take them on new journeys. If the chapter is reread at another time, it will, of course, be a different reading. All of which reminds us of the multitude of possible acts of reading and how near and yet so far we are from comprehending what seems such a simple performance once the technique has been mastered. Watson sums it up nicely when he says that 'we bring the whole of ourselves to our reading and the way we read reflects everything that is important about our reading culture'.

This seems as good a place as any to end this preamble. The stage is set, the play is cast, roles taken up, lines learned, gestures practised, rehearsals over, curtain up. As with all good drama, we hope you will enjoy the show.

Notes

1 We are in the process of organising an online version of *Reading Lessons from the Eighteenth Century.* Please check the Lilly Library website for the link.

2 The archive is divided between the Lilly Library, Indiana University, Bloomington, which holds the nursery library – http://www.dlib.indiana.edu/collections/janejohnson- and the Bodleian Library, Oxford, which holds 'A Pretty Story', letters and Johnson's commonplace book.

3 *Acts of Reading: Teachers, Texts And Childhood from 18th century to the Present Day*, Faculty of Education, University of Cambridge, 19 And 20 April 2007. For more information go to http://www.educ.cam.ac.uk/events/conferences/past/readingconf2007

The editors are grateful for the generosity of the Lilly Library, University of Indiana, in providing the image for the cover free of charge. We should like to thank Elizabeth Johnson and Breon Mitchell most warmly for their continued support throughout our years of research into the Nursery Library of Jane Johnson.

1

Old and New Protocols of Reading

Margaret Meek Spencer

Protocol: 'the first leaf of a volume; a fly leaf glued to the case and containing an account of the manuscript' (*Shorter Oxford English Dictionary*, 1972, 1606)

'an original note or minute... a factual record of observations' (*Chambers Dictionary* 1993, 1379)

The Jane Johnson archive

There is no doubt that the hand-made materials discovered in a hat box on the top shelf of a small closet in an empty house in Muncie, Indiana in 1982 and later identified as Jane Johnson's manuscript Nursery Library, are now recognised as a distinctive contribution to English social history of the eighteenth century, to studies of children learning to read, and to children's literature. The box contained 438 small pieces, mostly cards, most backed with Dutch floral gilt paper, all exquisitely made. The textual variety is amazing: traditional verses, stories, pictures, word lists, Bible quotations, a book for Jane Johnson's son George. This list scarcely touches the diversity of the extraordinary, miniature hoard. I can imagine that, attracted by the materiality of the gift and having watched their parents read, the Johnson children would play at reading. Before long they would discover that the pictures and the words are the same at each glance, the alphabet is constant as are the sentences, sometimes with pictures, about good behaviour.

When I first saw these unusual visual aids on film brought to a conference in Cambridge in 1994 by Shirley Brice Heath, it was difficult to believe that such small objects could be as the experts claimed. My reaction changed when I thought about the time it must have taken her to create these miniatures by copying (often with subtle changes) contemporary literature for children by

John Newbery and others and from recollections of her own entry into literacy with its rhymes, sayings, tales and poems. The Nursery Library materials are now housed in the Lilly Library at the University of Indiana. Details of the contents and other findings are set out in two books by a group of scholars, whose shared interests in the history of childhood include children learning to read and the role of women as educators.

The first book, *Opening the Nursery Door* edited by Mary Hilton *et al*, focuses on fitting the new evidence from the Johnson collection into the pattern of what is already known about reading and writing in childhood. Hilton's preface explains

> the extent of the overlapping and complementary fields of enquiry about the nature of childhood within British cultural life over three centuries: the debates that have surrounded the texts written and read to children, the multifarious ways childish consciousness has been considered, shaped and schooled, the emotional and moral investment that has been placed in children by adults; and, most centrally, the hitherto neglected role of women educators in early childhood. (1997, 1)

An unexpected discovery was the unpublished story Jane Johnson wrote for her children. In it she cast them as 'good' characters and thus ensured their repeated reading about themselves. Although the narrative follows a common pattern in children's stories of the time, Jane weaves together, unconventionally, both realism and fantasy. The socio-historical actualities behind this and other texts in the collection led to the second book: *Reading Lessons from the Eighteenth Century* by Arizpe and Styles with Heath (2006). Here the details bring readers close up to the life and activities of the remarkable woman who helped her children to grow through imaginative childhood literacy into well-informed adulthood. Patient, careful research in the archive and the generous display of the results now show 'what it meant to be a reader in the eighteenth century'. Following the discoveries and listening to the comments of the expert witnesses were pleasures that, at the Cambridge conference on which this book is based, accompanied those new revelations of children reading.

What was it that claimed the close attention of the learned readers and writers beyond their obvious delight in the socio-historical importance of the *ephemera*? The word is Heath's: 'the bits and pieces of temporary use' (1983, 17). As anthropologist, she recognises in Jane Johnson's words and pictures 'much more than their surface appeal'; no strategy of a children's picture book illustrator is ever without purpose, and authors of work for children know that their greatest strength is in the ambiguities of their language and pictures, allowing imagination to take their readers to a host of possible interpretations. There is evidence in Jane's work and in that of the most celebrated authors and illustrators of children's literature, of the 'power of role and performance combined' (2006, 202). They confirm that effective reading is never a passive affair; what counts as evidence in acts of reading is bound to be complex. Even so, Jane Johnson's library is the kind of present that literate parents would want to give to their children.

The Johnson archive makes plain that the study of reading, from children's earliest efforts to their specialist competences, is bound to include the culture of both readers and texts. Jane brings together contrasting experiences to make patterns of 'text-based and life-referenced conversation'. Her Library reflects protocols of learning derived from John Locke. Here are some:

- when children have mastered the alphabet they should read for pleasure

- understanding is better than rote learning

- parents have an obligation to prepare their children for their future lives as adults

- children can begin to read early once they have learned to talk

- children should be read to. This is important for their view of the task of learning and performance when they read out loud or on their own

In setting out the details of Jane Johnson's teaching, Arizpe and Styles also find 'some continuities in the way reading is taught in the twenty-first century'. They suggest she understood that 'children find their idiosyncratic ways into reading' and approved interactive learning where the text does the teaching (2006, 92). When Jane Johnson was helping her children to learn to read, published texts, including newsprint and *The Spectator*, were increasing in number, kind and availability. The grip of the spelling book was loosening; anthologies of literary texts were becoming more common. These changes are a far cry from the almost instantaneous access to the multitudinous textual kinds we now take for granted, but the comparison of the nature and effect of these changes is apt.

Jane knew that her children's future lay in the world outside home. She saw their literacy competence as a way to 'prestige, sociability and cultural expectation'. When the Headmaster of Uppingham school failed to 'abate' the school fees for her son, Robert, Jane sent him 'two pairs of good new sheets, two silver spoons and one dozen of good new towels instead of the entrance money to the House' (2006, 42). Behind this lies her concern that Robert, home-taught in his early years, should have at school the same standing as his contemporaries and match them in self-confidence.

New protocols

Between Jane Johnson's time and ours there has been a fairly general belief amongst the literate in the power of literacy to change lives, and that individual children's success in becoming readers increases their understanding of the contemporary social dynamic; how their world works. Within a circumscribed social context, Jane's teaching was both pragmatic and personal, useful and relevant. It is still the same when parents read with their children and encourage them to extend their skills to different kinds of books. Nowadays the classroom is the place where most children have to demonstrate their progress.

The best account we have of children closely observed in classrooms is *Inquiry into Meaning, an Investigation of Learning to Read* where detailed child studies carry conviction and hard evidence. This six-year long investigation of children's different reading styles was designed by teachers and researchers together, with the intent of finding out what has to be included when we try to understand what counts as evidence of children's reading progress. At the centre of the project are the 'personal meanings' of the learner. The collection of relevant data, the vivid portraits of the children, the systematic observations of their learning and the quality of the results remain unsurpassed. These are the only longitudinal studies from classrooms that present in great detail what the children did and what researchers analysed and documented. Reading is defined as 'the act of *orchestrating* diverse knowledge in order to extract meaning from a text while maintaining reasonable fluency and reasonable accountability to the information contained in writing' (2001, 44). Any serious account of children reading is bound to refer to these studies. The link with Jane is the desire to discover what children do when they read and how they talk about the process of reading itself. One of the observer's firmest convictions is that children *differ* as readers, an idea that Jane Johnson also held dear.

Our current view of reading is complicated by the belief and the evidence that we are experiencing a digital technological revolution, which extends to reading in a variety of media, notably websites. In David Buckingham's view, 'young people need to be equipped with a new form of digital literacy that is both critical and creative'. He continues, 'there is little evidence that children's reading of print has actually declined, although they may well be reading for different reasons or in different ways' (2007, 79). The digital age technology has, visibly, great potential for new kinds of communal literacy and different kinds of texts, especially those that have pictures instead of words. In Buckingham's world, 'computers convey images and fantasies, provide opportunities for imaginative self-expression and play, and serve as a medium through which intimate personal relationships are conducted' (151). This seems a long way from the Johnson family literacy, but digital media are cultural forms, as are the contents of the Nursery Library. Ironically, contemporary children's progress as media users comes from engagements with technologies bought by their parents for use at home. Alongside this, we are told that there has been a marked increase in home-tutoring, extra lessons in school subjects, notably reading, after school.

New protocols of reading from research reports sometimes seem to beget confusion rather than clarity about the nature of children's reading progress. At the heart of the matter is an important, continuing search for accurate descriptions of how children come to make sense of written language, pictures, plans, maps and other intricacies of meaning making. Recent reports have identified the construct of 'sedimented identities' in children's earliest efforts in writing and drawing, 'forged at home through their familial practices' (Rowsell and Pahl, 2007, 388). A time-line from Jane Johnson is there.

In school, children's reading progress is monitored in accordance with government-approved norms. Methodology is discussed at length as a matter of national importance. Children's difficulties in reading aloud are still counted as mistakes, despite their more favoured redescription as 'miscues'. Where teachers gather to theorise their practice and confirm their professional skills, they include children's *desire* to learn to read as part of a more general curiosity to explore what happens in the world. But reading lessons often neglect this. It is easy to forget that reading begins as different kinds of play and that children give themselves private lessons when they turn the pages of a picture book on their own (Meek, 1988).

Despite a long record of investigative research, schooled reading in the UK is still a matter for concern. New case studies of individual children learning to read are fewer than in the days when close observation was the standard research practice in classrooms and elsewhere. Roger Mills, a psychodynamic counsellor, has been observing significant points in the reading growth of his son from early childhood and recording them in *Books for Keeps*. Hal is now seven, at school, meeting the vagaries of the English spelling system. He doesn't like to make mistakes when he reads aloud, so he shows his frustration when he miscues a word he thinks he should know. Hal's father believes his son's frustration is like his own, showing how family traits repeat themselves. Longitudinal studies like this one provide selected evidence of progress. More elaborate records are difficult to fund and don't fit in with the demand for a quick national fix.

The research evidence that has provoked most comment lately comes from the Progress in International Reading Literacy Study (PIRLS). It reports that UK children have high marks for their attainment in reading, but very little pleasure in reading itself. The part played by children's books in their literacy growth has been widely acknowledged for the last decade (and probably longer), but there is no obligatory study of children's books in the professional studies of their teachers. There is an endorsement of 'high quality children's literature' in the Primary National Strategy (2006), but no consistent policy thereafter. Who will endorse an inquiry into 'The right book to the right child at the right time'? (This is the title of work in progress by Kimberley Safford and Fiona Collins.)

Electives

An interesting comparison with Jane's teaching comes in what we know of children who are being taught out of school. On February 24 an article appeared in *The Times*: 'Three Times More Children Taught at Home' (24.2. 2008). It was an account of a feasibility study for the government about 'The Prevalence of Home Education in England'. The report emphasised the difficulties in obtaining exact details of children in Elective Home Education because 'there could be significant numbers of home educated children who are not known to a Local Authority'. *The Guardian* took up the topic and proposed that the number of 'electives' – parents who chose home teaching – was between 7,000 and 21,000. The known reasons for taking children out of school have definitely increased: dissatisfaction with discipline, standards, arrangements for children's safety, bullying, school phobia, and a view that the present system is overly bureaucratic and assessment-driven.

Elective children are usually put back into school to take reading tests. According to *The Times*, most of them do better in tests than their age group in school. The National Curriculum is said to be consulted by parents and tutors, but not imposed. For a more detailed account, *The Guardian* chose a case study of a family where two boys had been medically diagnosed as having learning difficulties. They had separate individual tutoring; computers and web-sites contributed to their progress. The comment was: 'a key principle seems to be that the boys learn what life presents to them rather than their lives being organised round a pre-determined programme' (14. 4. 2008). The unclaimed evidence is elsewhere, in the boys' thought and language.

Redundancies

In search of reading details from individual learners, I found that, of all the official or informal ways of looking at children's growth as readers and writers, the Primary Language Record has been the most convincing. The Record was designed at the Centre for Literacy in Primary Education to provide a framework for documenting a child's progress and development between the ages of three and eleven. A substantial part of the record keeping was devoted to the expressed views of both parent and child. In conversations with the teacher, parents came to understand the details of the learning in their child's school, and teachers became aware of the opportunities, or the lack of them, that children had for reading and writing out of school. Each child's reading and writing were 'sampled' and recorded in terms of growth. The Report was first used in London in 1985, with remarkably effective results which were later replicated in New York and San Francisco.

After a change of government, the Record was considered too expensive in money and time, too detailed when compared with tests and the search for one way to teach all children how to read in school. What remained at CLPE was a commitment to the continuing experience of teachers as researchers concerned to link their work in the classroom with theorising their observations. Jane would have approved the attempt to record the individuality of each reader. CLPE is still renowned for its forward-looking literacy research and teacher education.

Individual Learners

The time-line that stretches from Jane to the latest revisions of the National Literacy Strategy in UK (now known as the Primary Strategy) has a sturdy list of undertakings to assess children's progress. Why is it, I wonder, that very few references are now made to the evidence of individual teachers and parents whose observations and interactions with children were made available for scrutiny by the arrival of the tape-recorder. It made possible the collection and analysis of children's developing language. In 1962 Ruth Weir wrote *Language in the Crib*, about her child's pre-sleep monologues. What she had hitherto regarded as his infant babble proved, by listening and transcription, to be practice attempts to intone words he had heard as names of things and events. Eight years later, two teachers on an advanced course that included the study of children's early language repeated Weir's investigation with their own children. They were amazed by the clarity of the child's self-instruction. This was a time of serious longitudinal exploration; the evidence is now part of classical linguistics. Similarly Nigel Halliday, son of the famous linguist,

Michael Halliday, provided enough early talk to fill a handsome volume with his exact words and his father's transcriptions and insightful commentaries (see Halliday, 2006).

In 1983 my colleagues and I were reading Heath's seminal *Ways with Words: language, life and work in communities and classrooms* with wonder and thoughtful delight. We were following the argument that 'in Roadville and Tracton the different ways children used language were dependent on the ways in which each community structured their families, defined the rules that community members could assume, and played out their concepts of childhood that guided child socialisation' (1983, 11). We tried to be 'learning researchers' as Londoners were facing the realities of diversity at that time. Alongside our student teachers we were challenged in classrooms and looked for practical help as well as ethnographic wisdom. Heath joined us in discussions. Her encouragement to our students was not a series of practical tips; instead she let them know that they were nearest to the evidence of children's needs and so they knew what counted as help. Since then she has turned those responsible for children's learning away from the lure of simplicity and made plain the inevitably complex nature of learning that includes play and imagination.

In 1986 Gordon Wells published the results of his fifteen-year longitudinal study of children in Bristol: *Language at Home and at School*. The later book version is: *The Meaning Makers: Children Learning Language and Using Language to Learn* published in Toronto in 1986 as a 'story'. He followed 32 of the original representative sample of 128 children 'through to the end of their primary education'. The intention was to 'identify the major linguistic influences of children's educational achievement' (1986, xii) and to make sense of evidence he collected.

The problems posed by children who simply make no moves towards reading, independently or with help, have been addressed by a successful publishing endeavour, Barrington Stoke. It brings together a number of consultants, teachers, speech therapists, parents and successful young readers, whose tasks are to ensure that the text of the original author has 'accessible language, a fast-moving and unambiguous plot and clear presentation' for the target audience, The format and the print are given the same consideration. This top quality publishing has proved successful in encouraging young readers to feel the power of reading. They share with their contemporaries other kinds of reading with increased confidence.

These snippets of serious research undertakings, and others mentioned earlier, may not do justice to their intentions but they act as indicators of the complexity of children's learning to read. Teachers are close to what children are seen to do and what they think they are doing. Parents are anxious to help in the early stages of school. They also want to know all about the reading tests and the results, and why classroom drama is seen as relevant to their children's understanding of the ideas behind the words of the set book. Secondary school children are expected to understand how continuous texts, books, are examined for *comprehension.*

Where does our interest in Jane Johnson fit into modern reading? This is exactly what Heath explains: 'Certain 'truths', 'discoveries,' or 'theories' (note that educators use all these terms often to refer to the same concepts) seem to have been discovered and rediscovered. Such truths have to be newly announced and claimed every few decades. What appear to be redundancies across centuries, are in fact good *evidence* of the sustained importance to human beings of the learning of the young and the role adults can and must play in promoting this learning in the best possible ways' (1983, 11). There you have it: *redundancies* in its new, protocol meaning from dictionaries in our technological age: 'the presence of components which improve the reliability of a system'.

The powerful protocol: books

In the UK literacy is a core problem in education and a matter of social concern. Too many adults and children are unable to read and write well enough to be at ease in a culture where these skills are common and necessary. Their needs are recognised, but still it has proved difficult to encourage inexperienced readers to enter into reading and then to read enough with expectations of success. In some schools there is evidence of a link between reading failure and children's troublesome behaviour in classrooms. Early school reading has aspects of political control in what and how children have to learn; compulsory phonics is an instance. But if we are to have confident readers we must consider them as creative, imaginative individuals. Good teachers want their pupils to have the best of what is available to read. They need lots of books, different kinds of texts to demonstrate acts of reading and a chance to talk about reading as something both important and pleasurable.

We know what makes children's reading better: it has to become a habit where the dominant feature is *interest.* Stories can become explorations, ways of knowing different people, finding out what happens next. Readers own books and re-read them to discover something about the author. They link up book versions of a tale with the film and the DVD. When teachers read aloud a whole story, the 'tune' of the text stays with the readers who hear it in their inner ear when they meet the written version on their own. At this point children who are taught at home are privileged. Reading can happen more informally and more often.

The particular reading paradox is this: while we worry about literacy as a social problem and treat it as a pedagogic puzzle, we acknowledge at the same time the unmatched production in the UK and elsewhere of children's books of artistic and literary merit. For every conference called to remedy illiteracy there is another, often a prize-giving to celebrate authorship, art, publishing and parental upholding of children's *literature*, with its world-famous creators and sponsors, and the kind of reading that Daniel Pennac (2006) demonstrates as a personal right. How, then, can we unite these two main concerns about literacy to ensure that the young people who know little of the pleasure and the power of reading are helped to read the books that make a difference? If we are to 'recover' the young people who have turned away from reading at any stage of their development as readers, it may be time to reconsider what counts as evidence of each child's *potential*. The shadow of Jane Johnson lurks in our discussions as a distinctive protocol of the important evidence that comes from individual readers.

Bibliography

Arizpe, E and Styles, M with Heath, S B (2006) *Reading Lessons from the Eighteenth Century: Mothers, Children and Texts*. Lichfield: Pied Piper Publishing

Barrs, M, Ellis, S, Hester, H, Thomas, A (1988) *The Primary Language Record*. London: Centre for Language in Primary Education

Buckingham, D (2007) *Beyond Technology: Children Learning in the Age of Digital Culture*. Cambridge: Polity Press

Chittenden, E, Salinger, T with Bussis, A (2001) *Inquiry into Meaning*. New York and London: Teachers' College Press

Halliday, M (2006) *The Language of Early Childhood*. (J Webster, ed). London: Continuum

Heath, S B (1983) *Ways with Words: language, life and work in communities and classrooms*. Cambridge: Cambridge University Press

Hilton, M, Styles, M, Watson, V (eds) (1997) *Opening the Nursery Door: Reading, Writing and Childhood 1600-1900*. London: Routledge

Hopwood, V, O'Neill, C, Hodgson, B (2007) *The Prevalence of Home Education in England: A Feasibility Study*. York: DfES Publications

Locke, J (1693/1968) Thoughts Concerning Education. In J A Axtell (ed) *Educational Writings of John Locke*. Cambridge: Cambridge University Press

Michael, I (1987) *The Teaching of English, from the sixteenth century to 1874*. Cambridge: Cambridge University Press

Mills, R (2008) Hal's Reading Diary in *Books for Keeps* 169, 1 March

Rowsell, J and Pahl, K (2007) Sedimented identities in texts: Instances of practice. *Reading Research Quarterly* 42 (3) 388-404

Pennac, D (2006) *The Rights of the Reader*. (S Adams, tr) London: Walker Books

Stannard, J and Huxford, L (2007) *The Literacy Game*. London: Routledge

Weir, R (1970) *Language in the Crib*. The Hague: Mouton

Wells, G (1986) *The Meaning Makers: Children Learning Language and Using Language to Learn*. London: Hodder and Stoughton

2

Iluminating Shadows: Jane Johnson's Commonplace Book

Victor Watson

A commonplace book is a particularly complex kind of text, made more so because it is impossible to know precisely how it should be read – especially when it is about reading, and a response to reading. There is an excellent account of Jane Johnson's commonplace book (Oxford, Bodleian Library, MS.Don.c.190, fols 72-102) and of the sources of her extracts in Chapter 5 of Arizpe and Styles (2006),[1] and I was especially struck by something that the authors say towards the end that the apparently 'passive' task of copying another writer's words is actually a self-conscious and interactive working through of meaning.

This is very true, and I want to use it as my starting-point.

Jane's commonplace book mainly comprises quotations dutifully copied out. Some of these are quite long – one, for example, is an extract from *The Spectator* which is so extended that it amounts to a miniature essay on the nature of Discretion. Such extracts give the impression of a painstaking, slow and deliberate activity, operating mainly in a receptive and perhaps contemplative mode. And yet this commonplace book is nothing of the kind. It is dynamic, dramatic even, and mostly in ways which we can never entirely understand.

Perhaps my interest in Jane's commonplace book arises because I once kept one myself. It was written almost forty years ago and I still have it. It went on for about two years. I don't remember why I started it, nor why I stopped. It was very like Jane's, consisting largely of quotations which I felt I wanted to record, to share with others perhaps, to comment on, or just to keep for reference. It also had original thoughts of my own. Some of those thoughts were eccentric in the extreme, even a bit crazy at times. And I think I see the same characteristics in Jane's commonplace book – usually in the form of brief *jeux d'esprit*, little bursts of mental excitement, sometimes rapturous, sometimes savagely sharp or satirical, sometimes reflective.

Jane's quotations are mostly indicative of an orderly mind – a rational and Augustan mind, seriously devoted to matters of good conduct, with a liking for the epigrammatic, and a tendency to compose balanced sentences with a caesura in the middle. Her commonplace book *seems* to have hardened under an Augustan crust of orderly extracts dutifully copied out and reflected upon; but beneath or within that crust an intense and dynamic mental drama was taking place.

There are several unanswered questions. Was she writing for an intended reader – Woolsey, her husband, perhaps, or one of her children? Were there other commonplace books preceding or following this one? How often did she have to change or sharpen her pen? And where did she do her writing? It is unlikely that she carried her notebook about with her as she would also have to have taken her pen and her inkwell too. It is more likely that she retired to her room for periods of reading, thought, and composition, where there would be a supply of ink, a penknife, and spare pens. We cannot be sure; but everything – including the manner of her writing – suggests periods of private and unhurried reflection.

So how should we read it? Especially as it was not written for us at all? It is tempting to read it as if it were a novel, or as if it might tell a story. But it is neither a novel nor a journal, and there is no orderly progression of thought, no predictable flow from one emotional state to a related one, nothing con-structed or connected in its inherent rawness. There is no narrative shaping, no climactic epiphany. Here are some examples. (I have retained Jane's spell-ing and punctuation – except for the long s, which she used consistently according to the practice of her time. It is not always possible to know whether she intended a capital initial letter or not; I have sometimes had to decide for her.) Many of the quotations are from *The Spectator*, often aphoris-tic, urbane comments on conduct or morality. But once, after three of these, Jane abruptly shifts ground and quotes

> The Goddess of Persuasion with all her Charms dwells on his Lips
> (Labelle Letters) [This source remains unidentified. Eds]

This is quite different. Why did this perception suddenly seize her? Did she know someone for whom these words seemed particularly apt? Or was she responding to the imagery, or the musicality of the phrasing? Immediately afterwards she turns soberly back to *The Spectator*. Elsewhere she quotes from Dryden's translation of Persius' 5th Satyr:

> For this a hundred voices I desire,
> To tell thee what a hundred tongues would tire;
> Yet never would be worthily exprest,
> How deeply thou art seated in my Breast.
> (Aulus Persius Flaccus, John Dryden, tr, 1693)

Did she have someone in mind? When she came across this, did she think 'Yes! That is how I feel about Woolsey'? Or perhaps she privately transformed it into a personal prayer, and it was God who was in her heart. Or one of her children, perhaps. Or perhaps there was no-one at all. Hard on its heels comes an extract from Swift. Jane clearly had a love of sharp epigrammatic satire.

> God shows the value he has for Riches by the Fools he gives them to.

Many of her quotations or observations are like that; they have a considerable satirical charge in them – this for example:

> When Old Batchelors Die they will be Changed into Jack-Asses to carry the Whores to Hell. +

This, like many of Jane's entries, is marked with a plus-sign [+], used as an asterisk throughout, apparently to indicate a composition of her own. She almost certainly gained additional pleasure from the knowledge that it was also a cross.

One or two of her entries are scary:

> To a Sturdy Beggar, that said it was better to beg than steal, No, I'd rather you steal than beg, for then you'd have a chance to be hang'd, & we should be rid of you. +

and immediately following that:

> To a man that wish'd I would ride to Hell, No, I assure you that's the last place I'll ever choose to go to, because 'tis the most likely one to meet with you again. +

Even when she is not intending to be satirical, she naturally composes her sentences with the weight and balance of aphorisms, as if they were heroic couplets in prose.

> An ununinterrupted [sic] series of ~~self~~ applause is too great a feast for a mortal, therefore 'tis necessary to play the fool sometimes by way of mortification. +

She frequently takes possession of her extracts by personalising the pronouns. She quotes from *The Spectator*:

> Every thing that is false, vicious or unworthy shall ever be despicable to him, though all the world should approve of it.

But in her version, it is:

> Every thing that is false, vicious or unworthy shall ever be despicable to *me*, though all the world should approve of it. [my italics]

She quotes *Proverbs*:

> Avoid it [the path of the wicked], pass not by it, turn from it, and pass away.

But she re-writes it:

> Avoid *him*, pass not by *him*, turn from *him*, & pass away. [my italics]

Why did she do this? A change like this is unlikely to have been a mistake. Was there someone she'd come in contact with who in her view should be avoided at all costs? Or is she perhaps referring to the Devil? Her alterations are not always as straightforward as simply changing a pronoun. She writes:

> There is nothing in the World so beautiful as Virtue! It is the greatest Ornament any body can put on! It is more becoming than Rich Silks, Trimmings, Lace Embroidery, & Brilliants, It makes even Deformity pleasing, & Stupidity amiable. Who does not love those that are Adorn'd with Truth & Virtue, even tho' they are Deform'd in Body & Weak in understanding? +

This extract is followed by a quotation from *The Book of Job*, but more heavily adapted this time:

> I put on righteousness, and it clothed me: my judgement was as a robe and a diadem.

which in her words becomes:

> Put on Righteousness as a Robe, & Truth as a Diadem.

Had the biblical quotation prompted the preceding rapturous lines on the beauty of virtue? Or did she turn to it afterwards as a fitting coda to her own words? And why did she change it from a narrative expository statement to an immediate commandment? A simpler explanation is possible, of course – that she did not always have a Bible to hand and wrote imperfectly from memory.

Not all her extracts are attributed, and in some cases it is not clear whether it is a quotation or an original composition of her own. Take this, for example:

Good men <u>do</u> at last obtain what their Virtue hath deserved. But Evil Men shall <u>never</u> arrive at any tolerable degree of Happiness.

The way to Happiness, (which every one covets) is Plain & Easy, For what can be more comfortable to the mind than Calmness? What more troublesome than Passion? What more at rest than Clemency? What so full of Business as Cruelty? Modesty & Chastity enjoy a perfect Leisure, whilst Lust is ever tired with Laborious pursuits. The possession of Virtue stands us in little cost or trouble, but Vices are all chargeable to be kept. He that acts unjustly really injures himself the most.

To Do as we would be done by is the Law of nature & nations, & if strictly practiced in every nation, no man could do amiss, How Good was God to the Sons of Men to write this Plain this Intelligible Law in the Heart of every one of them, from the world's beginning.

If these are her own words, how perfectly she has captured the music of generations of writers on this subject, from the King James Bible to Bunyan. The rhetoric of the pulpit can also be heard in her words – so that it is hard not to wonder if she talked to Woolsey about his sermons. Did they feed each other ideas, phrases? Were they like Dorothy and William Wordsworth, so intimately inside each other's minds that they could never be sure where a new thought originated? We can never know the answer to these questions, but it is clear that this is a vigorous mind at work, not one that is just transcribing.

At one point Jane read the 'Song of Deborah' from *Judges*, which tells the violent story of Jael the wife of Heber the tent-maker, who – after a great military defeat when her enemy Sisera came to her tent – drove a nail through his head.

24 Blessed above women shall Jael the wife of Heber the Kenite be, blessed shall she be above women in the tent.

25 He asked water *and* she gave *him* milk; she brought forth butter in a lordly dish.

26 She put her hand to the nail, and her right hand to the workmen's hammer; and with the hammer she smote Sisera, she smote off his head, when she had pierced and stricken through his temples.

27 At her feet he bowed, he fell, he lay down: at her feet he bowed, he fell: where he bowed, there he fell down dead. . .

31 So let all thine enemies perish, O Lord: but *let* them that love him *be* as the sun when he goeth forth in his might. And the land had rest for forty years.

There is much here that might have interested Jane – especially, perhaps, verses 24 or 25; or the last verse; or even the dramatic climax of the story, verse

26. But no. It was verse 27 which she copied out, faithfully getting the repetition right, sandwiched between dutiful quotations about sincerity and female virtue.

> At her feet he bowed, he fell, he lay down: at her feet he bowed, he fell; wher [sic] he bowed, there he fell down dead.

There it is, that single verse, almost the least likely for her to select from that biblical account. Why? Equally puzzling is why on one occasion she transcribes the same observation three times, each slightly differently phrased:

> Gratitude & Friendship are things much talk'd off, but very little Practiced. +
> Gratitude & Friendship are more talk'd of than Practiced. +
> Gratitude & Friendship are things much talk'd off, but never practiced. +

Was she trying out the wording? Seeking the most stylistically felicitous version? We can never know.

She quotes two couplets from Pope's translation of Homer's *Odyssey*; one of them is:

> And every envy'd Happiness attend,
> The man who calls Penelope his friend.

A few extracts later, she tries one of her own:

> Who ever Breaks the Holy Sabbath Day
> Unbless'd shall pass the other six away.

She must at about this time have read both of Pope's great translations, for she quotes a long speech by Agamemnon in its entirety. Her mind was never still. She quotes twice from *The Spectator* on the superiority of virtue to beauty. 'There is no charm in the Fair sex that can supply the Place of Virtue,' she writes. And then: 'Without Virtue Beauty is unlovely, and Quality contemptible.' But – in a spirit of intellectual irony perhaps – she immediately follows these two observations, mischievously perhaps, with a double-edged quotation from Sir Philip Sidney: 'I Love to find Virtue in a fair Lodging.'

There is one extract which is particularly interesting and curiously moving. She attributes this to *The Arabian Nights Entertainment*:

> Do you sit on this hand, & you on that, & then let me turn my eyes on which side I will, they will meet with an agreeable object.

What appealed to her here? The phrasing? The melody? The idea of loving community? The thought of her family gathered together with her? It must have meant a great deal to her, because a few pages later it appears again, slightly different this time, and unattributed:

> Do you sit, three on my Right hand, & three on my Left, & then as the table is round, which way soever I turn my Eyes they will be saluted with agreeable objects.

It seems possible that the extract stayed in her mind and later resurfaced in her own words, as her own thought. Or perhaps they are both an adaptation of a familiar much-loved quotation. [According to Malcolm Lyons, an expert on *The Arabian Nights*, this quotation is not from this source; we are grateful to him for this information. Eds] But that is all we can know about it; scholarship can take us only part of the way. After that, either we may use our imaginations to speculate or we have to stop thinking about it. With such insights into Jane everything is illuminated, but little is exposed. New shadows are cast, new areas of mystery. The meaning of these matching extracts is not to be found in the text; it worked only in the elusive moment-by-moment stealth and intimacy of Jane's thoughts.

I suspect that Jane's Bible was her constant companion. She refers to it repeatedly. And we know from her other writings that she hated drunkenness and debauchery. So it is no surprise to find that in the commonplace book she writes:

> With what difficulty shall they that have Riches inherit Eternal Life! The Force of Custom, the Charms of Women, Wine, & Gay Company are very strong; Pray God Preserve my Sons from the common Vices of a Gentleman's Life, & Grant that they may be as Chaste as Joseph, & as Temperate as the Descendants of Jonadab the son of Rechab. +

The abrupt shift from the language of eighteenth-century England to the phrasing of the Old Testament almost certainly occurred because Jane had just been reading *Jeremiah*, chapter 35. Here the Rechabites testify that they intend always to obey their father's command to live as nomads, sowing no seed, planting no vineyards, and living always in tents. None of this interests Jane ; what she remembers are verses 5 and 6:

> 5 And I set before the sons of the house of the Rechabites pots full of wine, and cups, and I said unto them, Drink ye wine.

> 6 But they said, We will drink no wine: for Jonadab the son of Rechab commanded us, saying, Ye shall drink no wine, *neither* ye, nor your sons for ever: . . .

Jane extracts that from the rest, and applies it evangelically to her own children.

The entries are not precisely dated but in spite of that it is possible to see which were made at the time of Woolsey's illness and death.

> I gave a strong proof of my Courage, made a Bold Stand against Vice, but my forces were weak, & the Enemy soon got the better & drove me out of the Field. May Virtue for the future have a more powerful, & more successfull Advocate.

We can only speculate upon the moment of weakness and distress that led to this admission. It is immediately followed by four lines of writing crossed out with such painstaking determination that it is impossible to decipher her words. These were, almost certainly, observations about which she had second thoughts. On Woolsey's death, she writes:

> Doubtless XXXXX Woolsey is immortal & happy, let us congratulate the Time of his Decease as the Day of his Nativity; & leave mourning to the crowd of mortals, who do a thousand things, without ever thinking what they are about. They tread in the Steps of others, never examining, Whether they be right or wrong: Custom & Education have almost banish'd Reason from the Earth. (XXXXX)

Immediately following she writes 'Our Friends, are as troublesome as our Enemies. 'What *could* she have meant? – especially as it is apparently a quotation but she has, again, erased the attribution. Perhaps she could not endure the endless callers coming – in our bland phrasing – 'to pay their respects'.

As Arizpe and Styles point out, Jane's handwriting becomes uncertain and shaky at this time. She has trouble with her pen, and there are uncharacteristic blots and smears of ink. She quotes from Young's *Night Thoughts*, 'Death but intombs the body; Life the soul.' She also composes a small couplet of reassurance, written in thick unlovely handwriting:

> Make God Your Friend,
> & /(Things) times will mend. +

There is a longer entry at about this time:

> Thou art God is my Strong Hold, where unto I Will always resort, He has promised to help me, for he is my House of defence & my castle. My Strong *Rock*, my Saviour, my God, & my might, *in whom I will trust, my Buckler, the Horn also of my Salvation, & my refuge.* He shall deliver me from my strongest Enemy, & from them that hate me. For I have an Eye unto All his Laws, & will not cast any of his commandments from me. [my italics]

This is an imperfectly recalled (or deliberately paraphrased?) version of the first few verses of Psalm 18. Only the words I have italicised are exactly quoted and the final clause is an adaptation of a later verse of the same Psalm: 'and I did not put away his statutes from me'. I think we can take for granted that the devout wife of an Anglican clergyman would also have been familiar with the famous passage from Ephesians, Chapter 6, 13-17, in which Christians are exhorted to arm themselves against the onslaught of Satan. This, too, was probably in her mind as she wrote:

> 13 Wherefore take unto you the whole armour of God, that ye may be able to withstand in the evil day, and having done all, to stand.
>
> 14 Stand therefore, having your loins girt about with truth, and having on the breastplate of righteousness; . . .

***

It is tempting to venture into guesswork about Jane's emotional state as she worked on this section of her commonplace book. But little can be said with any certitude except that there are indications that she was disturbed and distressed. However, I think we can also see here evidence of the mysterious and private ways in which words can provide consolation. That adaptation of the 18th Psalm is a case in point: it was not only that the words provided a meaning which she needed to hold on to at that moment; it is also that they handed over to her a posture and tone of resolution and faith. This is achieved by the biblical use of the first person ('where unto I will always resort; *My* Strong Rock, *my* Saviour ...') so that Jane was not just copying out a reassuring aphorism but privately (perhaps even physically) bracing herself and stiffening her resolve.

It is helpful to bear in mind that privately reading and studying the Bible was central to the English Protestant tradition, especially in the seventeenth and eighteenth centuries. This activity brought the word of God directly to any believer. It would not only give light and understanding but would also be a prompt to self-improvement or self-appraisal, and lead to moments of joy and illumination, or provide consolation and reminders of God's unfailing support. It is my belief that, when Jane came upon *any* book that she found interesting, she read it in the same way that she read the Bible. Before the proliferation of novels, people read fewer books, but read them intensively and attentively – reacting, responding, even re-writing. Words are important, Jane would think. They carry life, especially if you believe them to be – literally – the words of God.

That is why her commonplace book is so dynamic and dramatic. At the back of any of her quoted extracts there might be a sharp reflective turn of the mind, a shift of mood, a small longing, or a burst of joy and promise. It was an instrument in the moment-by-moment drama of her mental, spiritual and emotional life.

We should not be surprised by this. People such as Helen Arnold and Margaret Meek have consistently told us that when we read we bring the whole of ourselves and the whole of our lives to the reading; and the way we read reflects everything that is important about our reading culture.

Note

1 Arizpe, E and Styles, M (2006) *Reading Lessons from the Eighteenth Century.* Lichfield: Pied Piper.

3

Bringing 'Wisdom into the Hearts of Young Persons': Aesop, Watts and Newbery as sources for Jane Johnson's fables and maxims

Evelyn Arizpe and Morag Styles

There is much to be said for this Way of instructing People in good Moral Truths by the Way of Stories and Fables: The first Consideration that deserves to be taken notice of, is the Perspicuity and Easiness and Pleasantness of this Way of Instruction [...] the Ancients therefore wisely contriv'd Stories of this Nature, that they might insensibly insinuate Wisdom into the Hearts of Young Persons, and work as it were into the Soul betimes. (Anon, 1711, np)

This chapter is based on further research into the Jane Johnson archive. It discusses the influence of John Newbery on Johnson's Nursery Library but it also discloses and analyses two further discoveries about Johnson's sources relating to Isaac Watts of *Divine Songs* fame and the anonymous writer (above) of a version of Aesop's fables. Our discoveries may shed light on the publishing history of some key early items of children's literature and on the ways in which popular texts were copied and modified in both commercial and private contexts.

Jane Johnson and Isaac Watts

Jane Johnson (1706-1759) created her lesson cards and other materials for her children during the decade of the 1740s. Although her Nursery Library is evidently the result of her own unique creativity and talents, it is also influenced by the educational ideas of scholars and authors such as John Locke, Fénelon (the Archbishop François de Salignac de La Mothe), Charles Rollin, Joseph

Addison and Samuel Richardson, as well as by the primers published by John Newbery and Thomas and Mary Cooper, among others. We know this is the case as Johnson followed their advice in the making of her reading materials and mentions some of these writers in her commonplace book (Oxford, Bodleian Library, MS.Don. c.190, fols. 72-102).

We assume that Johnson must have also known the work of Isaac Watts. By 1753 his editors could confidently claim that 'there is no man now living of whose works so many have been dispersed, both at home and abroad, that are in such constant use' (quoted in Hoyles, 1971, 143). *Divine Songs* (1715) was the best-selling book of poetry for more than a century. A representative figure in the English Enlightenment, Watts' work argues for the social and religious compromise of the extremes of Puritan and polite thought. He was influenced by Locke, whose ideas were common currency at the time, and admired Addison for his finely balanced reason and feeling, wit and piety – views shared by Johnson as is evident in her letters and commonplace book.

It is possible to see the influence of Watts' musical hymns on Johnson's religious verse, but his pedagogical ideas may have also had an impact on her educational project. For example, in 1741, in order for teaching to be more effective and pleasurable, Watts suggests 'some little tablets of pasteboard be made in imitation of cards' (Watts, 1741/1859, 342). Johnson's lesson cards are, indeed, made of layers of paper pasted together. Watts links literacy, and poetry in particular, with the development of virtue, arguing that the use of rhyme and metre will make lessons more entertaining to children as well as more easily remembered. Johnson had some facility with poetry herself and chose to put many of her moral and didactic texts into verse. Johnson actually copied a whole set of Watts' verses onto her cards. These maxims come from his book, *The Art of Reading and Writing English* which was first published in 1721 and continued to be reprinted throughout the eighteenth century. Finally, Watts advises on including images to help learning, as these are likely to appeal to children's senses and curiosity (Watts, 1741/1859, 301). Johnson's lesson cards include a multitude of stimulating and engaging images.

In his preface, Watts expands on his educational purpose which is to provide a book that will aid the teaching of reading and writing by correcting common mistakes and perfecting the learner's knowledge of English. In addition to tables of words and syllables, he suggests adding

> easy Portions of Scripture collected out of the Psalms, and Proverbs, and the New Testament, as well as other little Composures, that might teach [children] Duty and Behaviour towards God and Man [as well as] some Pages of short Sentences to

> discourage the Vices to which Children are most addicted [and] some well-chosen, short, and useful Stories, that may entice the young Learner to the Pleasure of Reading [...] (Watts, 1721, xiii)

Johnson's lesson cards and her books for George offer similar features as they not only include lists of syllables and words, but also portions of scripture and 'short and useful' stories, such as the fables which will be discussed below. The 'short Sentences to discourage Vices' she simply takes, verbatim, from Watts himself. The 'Last Table' is entitled 'Copies containing Moral Instructions, beginning with every Letter of the Alphabet'.

Watts was not the only author to include an alphabetically ordered verse in his 'spelling-book'. The primer published by Thomas and Mary Cooper, *The Child's New Play-thing* (from which Johnson borrows some of her word lists), also includes a set of maxims, beginning with each letter of the alphabet. However, these are wordy and convoluted while Watts' have the benefit of simplicity which characterises all his work. Words and phrases are short, the iambic pentameter is musical and the rhyme makes them easy to remember.

Johnson had evidently recognised the merits of these maxims, as she copied them onto a set of six cards (Set 24; these and the other cards mentioned below can be seen online at the Lilly Library website mentioned above). The advice they contain refer to many of the vices Johnson held in particular contempt, such as stealing, lying, cursing and swearing, and the Johnson children could have easily linked them to their own experience of trying to 'keep their books without blot' or not 'be sullen when chid'.

The only difference is at the end of the table, when Watts adds a note about the letter 'X': 'The Letter X begins no English Word, so that we must begin that Line with Ex, unless the reader will chuse this instead of it'. What he proposes instead is a verse which reveals a sense of humour as it gently mocks his educational intentions: 'X is such a cross letter, Balks my Morals and Metre' (Watts, 1721, 151). Johnson has chosen not to include this, perhaps because it would not fit easily on the card and might spoil the neat pattern of four verses.

We have discussed Johnson's use of images in detail in our book: sometimes they correspond to the text, sometimes they provide an ironic comment on the text and at other times they seem to have nothing to do with the text at all. Like the other images, these were probably cut out from a lottery or printed sheet sold by booksellers, precisely for the purpose of amusing children. In this set, Johnson used one side of the cards for text and the other for pictures; the images are cut-outs in black and white which do not seem to be particularly relevant to the verses. Two of them show magnificently dressed kings on horses on a background which suggests they are two of the wise men (the third king is from another set of cards which we'll discuss later). Another two presumably represent the Biblical episode of Herod's massacre of the innocents. In contrast to the previous violent scenes, the last pair of cards contain images of tranquillity populated by shepherds and domestic animals. All six images appear to be part of the same lottery sheet, some more of which we will see later. While not directly related to the content of Watts' maxims, they do reflect religious themes and were probably intended by Johnson to lead to meditations on virtue and wisdom.

Although contemporary literature for children has eliminated these sorts of moral maxims (except, perhaps, in religious textbooks) there is still a widespread belief that instruction is better learnt by children if it is put in verse form, to include humour if possible, and to be relevant to children's experiences. Proverbs are still used with children, although they survive mainly as an oral form. However, there does exist in children's literature one didactic and moral form that is still popular – namely, the fable.

Fables from Newbery

It is not surprising that, along with maxims and scriptural admonitions, we find fables on Johnson's lesson cards. Fables had been well-established as pedagogical tools since before the eighteenth century and they were respected because of their antiquity and wisdom. In 1711, Addison wrote in *The Spectator* (which was one of Johnson's favourite reads) that 'Fables were the first Pieces of Wit that made their Appearance in the World, and have been still highly valued, not only in Times of the greatest Simplicity, but among the most polite Ages of Mankind' (*The Spectator* 183).

However, they were still part of the corpus of popular literature and many of them included obscene and scatological material. At the same time, because of their use as rhetorical devices in public debates, they also carried political and ideological messages for adults. As David Whitley remarks 'Far from being safe for children in any morally worthy, unproblematic way, then, the Aesopic fable stood at the centre of some of the most heated political, social and religious debates within the seventeenth-century culture' (Whitley, 1997, 66).

Locke pointed the fable in the direction of the nursery when he wrote that the animal fable was the only form of literature suitable for young children because they provided both 'easy and pleasant' texts, and thus would entice them to read, while also being instructive. Fénelon and Rollin expanded on this advice in their writing, stressing that fables are short, instructive and amusing. Many authors and editors of fables took up Locke's idea and adapted them for children in several ways: such as selecting the less ambiguous ones, putting them into verse, composing morals suitable for young readers or adding illustrations (see Judith Graham's chapter in this book).

By the time Johnson was creating her nursery library in the 1740s, there were many versions of Aesop available for children, among them Richardson's 1739 edition (see Whitley, 1997). In his own novels, Richardson uses fables to convey subtle meanings (Lewis, 1996, 29-31). For example, Pamela indicates that fables were among the texts that Lady B lent her to 'improve herself' and at one point she applies the fable of the hungry grasshopper to her own situation. We know that Johnson read *Clarissa* and almost certainly *Pamela*; the evidence suggests that she read Richardson's fables too.

There are thirteen fables written on the cards in the nursery library (all but one can be found in Set 14), some of which may throw light on the early publishing history of *A Little Pretty Pocket-book*. Johnson did not give them titles, but what follows is a list of the fables she included, using the titles which are most commonly used in Aesopian collections:

> The Wolf and the Kid
> The Bee and the Bear
> The Clown and the Flies
> The Cock and the Precious Stone
> The Dog and his Shadow
> The Farmer and his Dog
> The Snake and the Hedgehog
> The Lion and the Mouse
> The Squire and his Dogs
> The Dull Schoolboy
> The Stork and the Crane (or The Husbandman and the Stork)
> The Boy who cried Wolf (or The Shepherd's Boy)
> (Set 14)
> The Old Man and Death (Set 16)

'The Wolf and the Kid', 'The Husbandman and the Stork' and 'The Shepherd's Boy' are certainly copied from Newbery's *Pretty Pocket-book* which went through several editions in the eighteenth century; the earliest extant copy is the 'Tenth Edition', according to the title page, from 1760 (held at the British Library) and the next copy is from 1763 (held at the Lilly Library). The first edition of *A Little Pretty Pocket-book* was advertised in 1744 in *The Daily Post* and *The Penny Morning Post* but neither a copy of it, nor of the supposed other nine editions, have ever come to light (claims for the number of editions were notoriously unreliable in this early period of publishing). Johnson's cards provide evidence of the existence of at least one of these earlier editions, because she was making her cards during the early 1740s. Additionally, in 'A Pretty Story', 1744, Johnson mentions that the children 'Read so well that they were the admiration of all the Gentlemen and Ladys [sic] that lived near them' (Oxford, Bodleian Library, MS.Don.d.198: 20) in a very similar style to the caption under one of Newbery's images: 'All Good Boys and Girls take care to learn their Lessons, and read in a pretty manner; which makes every Body admire them' (*A Little Pretty Pocket-book* 1760, 75).

One of the questions raised by the presence of Newbery's fables in Johnson's Nursery Library is why she bothered to copy them if the family had access to the book: did someone lend it to her and did she decide to copy what she thought were the best bits for her children? Another question is why she left out the fourth fable, 'Mercury and the Woodman'.[1] Perhaps that particular card got lost or damaged or the text was simply too long for the card, but it is also possible that Johnson did not like this fable because of the presence of the pagan Greek god.

Unlike Watts' maxims which Johnson copies verbatim, she has altered a few words of Newbery's fables here and there, seemingly to please her own sense of rhyme. Here are the changes Johnson made to the 1760 edition (the original fables can be seen in Set 14 at http://www.dlib.indiana.edu/collections/janejohnson).

'The Wolf and the Kid':

- the tense throughout is changed from past to present with the exception of the last line
- first line: 'brouse' to 'browzed'
- fourth line: 'nobody' has been capitalised
- fifth line: 'hearing this' to 'over-hearing'
- seventh line: capital 'N' in 'No' changed to lower case

'The Husbandman and the Stork':

- second line:'Trepanned by a Crane' to 'Was trapanned with a Crane'
- second line: comma to semi-colon
- third line: 'Was pleading' to 'He pleaded'

'The Shepherd Boy':

- the capital 'D' in 'Danger' has been changed to lower case
- third line changes, including punctuation, 'Cries out to his neighbours,' to a stronger 'Bawls out Help!, Neighbours, help'
- fifth line: 'and' changed to 'but'
- fifth line: semi-colon changed to colon
- sixth line: comma added after 'roars'
- eighth line: 'But his Cries are in vain' to 'But he roars out in vain'

Most of the changes seem to have been made for the sake of either textual clarification (such as the reference for the verb), greater impact, better metrification or, of course, appeal to young readers.

After each of the fables, Newbery has included a 'letter' from Jack the Giant-killer (the supposed author of the book) to Master Tommy and Miss Polly, which comments on the fable and reveals its moral. Summarised, the morals of these three fables are: obey your parents (or the wolf will eat you); take care with whom you associate (such as wicked children) and never tell a lie (or Jack the Giant Killer – and other adults – will be very angry). It is easy to see that these morals would have appealed to Johnson as we know that obedience, truth and good behaviour were very important to her. All of these morals are stressed in her *Pretty Story*: Master Tommy is a thief and a liar and because of his wickedness is finally removed from the story altogether, as if he might have an adverse influence on the other good children.

As Whitley suggests, the whole point about a fable is that it contains a moral which 'evaluate[s] human conduct' (Whitley, 1996, 98). The inclusion of a moral at the end of a fable was one of the reasons why they were thought suitable for children (it also made it clear to the readers that these were just stories and animals did not really talk or behave like humans). However, Johnson does not copy the giant's letter nor does she include any moral for these or any other fables in her collection and we will discuss a possible reason for this further on.

Aesop Naturaliz'd

But what of the other ten fables in the Nursery Library? We were able to trace these to a little-known edition of Aesop called *Aesop Naturaliz'd: in a collection of fables and stories from Aesop, Locman, Pilpay, and Others*. Although it is mentioned in some of the histories of Aesop, we have found almost no information about this version. The printer is D. Midwinter who was based 'at the Rose and Crown in St. Paul's Churchyard' in London at the turn of the eighteenth century. Among the books he printed was Fénelon's *The education of young gentlewomen*, which influenced the upbringing of many young girls. He also printed a French/English dictionary and books on the art of glass, on the art and history of 'physick' and various other 'how to' books. He may have been the author of this little collection but we haven't found any evidence to support this.

As the title notes, these fables and stories are not only from Aesop but also from 'Locman, Pilpay and Others'. Locman (sometimes Lokman, Logman or Luqman) was supposed to be an oriental fabulist; many think however that he did not really exist and was really Aesop himself. (Locman apparently lived about the same time as Aesop and was also described as 'an ugly black slave'.) Pilpay or 'Bidpai' was supposed to be an Indian sage who used the stories in the education of a rajah's children. These stories can be traced to the *Panchatantra*, an Indian text believed to have been written in 200 BC although the stories come from much earlier oral traditions. In 1709 the Persian version was translated into French under the title *Les Conseils et les Maximes de Pilpay*, which appeared in English as *The Instructive and Entertaining Fables of Pilpay* in 1699. Like many other readers in her time, Johnson was fascinated by the oriental and this may have led her to select this particular book.

Whatever the real sources, most of the fables from our anonymous edition are clearly based on ancient texts. However, some of them, like the 'The Dull Schoolboy', with its mention of the criss-cross row, must have been composed nearer Johnson's time. The criss-cross row was another name for hornbooks and referred to the cross that headed the text or to the pattern formed by letters. Under the title 'The Naughty School-Boy', a similar verse appeared in Thomas Harris's *A New Playbook for Children* in 1749. The same lines also formed part of a longer poem called 'A Description of a Naughty Boy' in Newbery's *Pretty Book for Children* (not to be confused with the *Pretty Little Pocket-book*). The earliest extant edition of Harris' book is the fifth edition, from 1751, which suggests that he borrowed his version from Newbery rather than the other way round. Johnson certainly copied her version from Newbery rather than Harris.

Returning to Aesop, the third edition of *Aesop Naturaliz'd* was published in 1711, but we have not found an extant earlier edition. There is an earlier book, from 1697, which has a similar title *Aesop Naturaliz'd and exposed to the Public view in his own Shape and Dress*, also anonymous, printed by John Hayes. Our 1711 author has copied some of the shorter fables from this book for his edition, making a few changes such as cutting out part of 'The Old Man and Death'. Although many of the fables in the two versions of *Aesop Naturaliz'd* are the same, Johnson's texts show that she used the one published by Midwinter.

The Midwinter collection of fables seems to have been popular as it went through several editions in the eighteenth century: 1711, 1727, 1743, 1756 and 1771. Johnson may have had the 1711 edition from her childhood (she would have been the right age for this) or she may have used the 1743 edition, published closer to the time when she was creating her library. One of the interesting aspects of this volume is its preface, which Johnson is almost certain to have read. Although scholars have pointed out the importance (and similarity) of the prefaces to the various *Aesops*, it is curious that none of the scholars who have worked on fables have chosen to comment on this one in any depth. While the author is clearly influenced by the school of Locke, he seems to have his own particular view of his mission; he uses various visual and medical analogies and tries to aim his fables at both younger and older readers. It is interesting to consider this preface in detail, as the description of the benefits of reading fables would have justified their inclusion in Johnson's Nursery Library.

To begin, the author modestly describes his writing as 'scribbling' and says that he was not aiming at 'Inmortality'. Instead, echoing Locke, he stresses the entertaining element of the task as he wishes 'to see if he cou'd give some little Pleasure to others as well as he had diverted himself' (Anon, 1711/1743, np). He mocks readers who may think the stories are trivial and easy to write and challenges them to try and 'make a fable' themselves. He then sets out various benefits of this sort of instruction: first, following Locke's dictum, they are 'easy' and 'pleasant' and (like Watts) even more so in verse. He writes of stories as 'impressions', similar to images which become 'fix'd in their Memories' at an early age, so that they 'insensibly insinuate Wisdom into the Hearts of Young Persons, and work it as it were into the Soul betimes' (Anon, 1711/ 1743, np). Another benefit of fables is that they are 'innocent' and thus offend no one in particular while those who see themselves in the tale will accept the Truth 'if gently and nicely' put to them. He compares this to a good physician softening the effect of a strong drug, 'coloquin' (a purgative also known as 'colocynth' or 'bitter apple'), which might be too harsh on the stomach, with a medicine of a 'milder nature'.

Another medical comparison is made to illustrate the subtle, persuasive power of fables:

> Man is gently convinc'd almost before he is aware, and brought to pass sentence upon his own Folly before he reflects what he's a doing; 'tis like a Physician's conveying a Lancet in his Handkerchief, and letting a timerous [sic] Patient Blood, before he perceives it, and while he imagines he's only gently stroking the Place. (Anon, 1711/1743, np)

The final benefit of fables according to the preface is more practical: they are usually short and to the point. He compares the fable to a visual form, a 'well painted' or 'miniature' portrait which 'at one view' describes a man better than if he used 'a great many Words' (Anon, 1711/1743, np), using the story of Menenius Agrippa, whose brief fable quickly pacified a dangerous crowd. Another medical analogy highlights the speedy effects of 'Chymical Drops' which are preferred to a prolonged treatment of a weak patient. The preface ends with the author apologising for those fables that are not as well told as others but he hopes that 'Humour' will make up for his faults.

Also in verse, the morals in this book are quite long and seem rather contrived and convoluted. As Whitley points out, during the eighteenth century the fable began to lose its ideological, controversial nature as it was turned towards the nursery, becoming 'a more benign introduction, later an *aide memoire*, to a set of universally acceptable maxims that constitute the moral certitudes of respectable adulthood' (Whitley, 1996, 96-7). The fact thar Johnson included the fables, but not the morals, from Midwinter's *Aesop Naturaliz'd* suggests that she was selecting them with her particular audience of children in mind. It is possible that Johnson encouraged her children to discuss these texts or, perhaps, to write their own morals, guided, of course, by their mother's 'moral certitudes'.

The question here is why Johnson selected these ten fables out of about 150: did they correspond more closely to some particular virtue she was trying to instil in her children? What are the morals of the particular fables she chose? Some of these fables have different morals in different collections, but if we take the simplest lesson from them we have the following: revenge is not always sweet; being annoyed by small things can make bigger problems worse; what is important to each one of us is different according to our nature; by being greedy about what we don't have we risk losing what we do have; take care whom you invite into your house; don't rush into making judgements; weak creatures can help more powerful ones; harmless innocents pay for others' folly. All of them relate to positive or negative traits of human beings although the protagonists are usually animals.

Johnson also chose fables with familiar, rather than exotic, characters and animals: bees, bears, clowns, flies, cocks, dogs, farmers, snakes, hedgehogs, lions, mice, goats, wolves, shepherds, cranes, storks. Although some are quite violent, like the farmer and the squire who kill their dogs, some contain humour, like the old man who asks Death to help him carry his burden, or the snake who can't get into his house because of the hedgehog's prickles. This mixture of the dramatic and the satirical is characteristic of much of Johnson's own writing.

With one exception, Johnson does not make any significant changes to the fables she copied from *Aesop Naturaliz'd*. This exception is the fable of 'The Cock and the Precious Stone'. The original fable ends with 'One Barley-Corn I'd rather view,/ Than all the Treasures of Peru' (the *Aesop Naturaliz'd* from 1697 refers to 'the Indies' instead of Peru.) Johnson has eliminated the reference to Peru and changed the ending to 'One Barley Corn I had rather see/For what are Diamonds to me'. Was this because she felt the reference to Peru was too alien for her children? Did she wish to bring it closer to them by adding a more familiar reference? What is interesting is that Richardson's edition of the same fable mentions diamonds and includes the phrase 'to me' which is not in the other versions. Although we could not find any other evidence for this, given Richardson's intention of making the fables suitable for children, it is probable that Johnson read his fables but preferred the shorter, versified forms for her cards.

Aesop illustrated

After Comenius, many educationalists emphasised the importance of including images to support and stimulate children's learning. Locke's edition of Aesop's fables included woodcuts, as did Richardson's later versions. Newbery includes an illustration for each of his fables but, curiously, neither of the two *Aesop Naturaliz'd* contain images. However, this was not a problem for Johnson who added her own visuals on the other side of the fable cards. As we have noted with the other cards in the Nursery Library, sometimes the image she chooses is relevant in some way to the text, as in the case of 'The Squire and his Dog' where on the verso of the card we have a Christ-like figure who may represent the squire and a younger person with a dog. The image on the verso of the 'Naughty School-Boy' is more ironic, as it shows a group of people reading and discussing a book, illuminated by a large star. For 'The Cock and the Precious Stone' there are two cocks which seem to belong to a set of images about birds, two of which illuminate other fables.

As we saw above, several cut-outs seem to be part of a set of Biblical images: the three kings, the massacre of the infants and the Christ-like figure. Four of the other fables contain images that seem to be from a different set, on court-ing and fashion. The fable of 'The Old Man and Death' has a grand classical pavilion in colour, almost like a theatre stage set, on the verso (see book cover) which is very different from the black and white oriental city shown on the back of 'The Lion and the Mouse'. Neither of these seem to have anything to do with the fables, although the oriental one could be part of the Biblical set.

Conclusion

The texts and images Johnson placed on her cards and other teaching arti-facts are a reminder of the importance of 'imagination, creativity and ex-periential learning' (Heath in Arizpe and Styles, 2006, 201) that characterises Johnson's project. Text and image are used to stimulate talk, writing and role playing with the interests and experience of the learners at the centre. John-son's borrowing from other authors was not unusual in her time and, as we have argued in *Reading Lessons* (2006), both in her lesson cards and her commonplace book she made the texts her own, through modifying some of them but also through placing them in a domestic, social and personal con-text which gave them new meanings.

In letters written in 1772 by Johnson's son Robert (who was then 27 years old), he tells his brother George (then 32) that he has ordered and obtained several volumes from the bookseller. (All her children grew up to be enthusiastic and knowledgeable bibliophiles, as well as kind, generous and moral people.) Among the list of books are the fables of La Fontaine. As Locke wrote, Aesop's fables 'may yet afford useful Reflections to a grown Man; and if his Memory retain them all his Life after, he will not repent to find them there, among his manly Thoughts' (Locke, 1693/1968, 259). Did the brothers remember the little cards with fables which their mother so lovingly copied and illustrated for them? We will never know for sure, but it seems likely that Jane Johnson's attempt to 'bring wisdom' into the hearts and minds of her children, through her own words and a careful selection of the literature of others, proved to be successful.

Note

1 The 1760 edition at the British Library only includes three fables (the Stork, the Shepherd Boy and Mercury and the Woodman (which is numbered as 'Fable IV') but does not include The Wolf and the Kid. There is a BL note stating that this edition is incomplete, but it is possible that the first editions of *Pretty Pocket-book* did *not* include all four fables. The 1763 edition has all four fables, again, with only the fourth one numbered. By the 1770 edition, all four fables are numbered.

Bibliography

Anon (1697) *Aesop Naturaliz'd and exposed to the Public view in his own Shape and Dress, by way of Essay on a hundred Fables*. Cambridge: Printed by John Hayes for Edward Hall

Anon (1767) *A Little pretty pocket-book intended for the instruction and amusement of little Master Tommy and pretty Miss Polly*, London: Printed for J. Newbery, at the Bible and Sun in St. Paul's Church Yard

Anon (1749) *A New play book for children, or, An easy and natural introduction to the art of reading*. London: Printed for Thomas Harris

Anon (1751) *A Pretty book for children, or, An easy guide to the English tongue* Vol. I. London: Printed for J. Newbery, J. Hodges and B. Collins

Anon (1711) *Aesop Naturaliz'd: in a collection of fables and stories from Aesop, Locman, Pilpay, and Others*. The third edition; with the Addition of above 50 New Fables. London: Printed for D. Midwinter, at the Three Crowns in St. Paul's Church-Yard

Anon (1743) *Aesop Naturaliz'd: in a collection of fables and stories from Aesop, Locman, Pilpay, and Others*. The fifth edition; with the Addition of above 50 New Fables. London: Printed for D. Midwinter, at the Three Crowns in St. Paul's Church-Yard; and A. Ward at the Kings Arms in Little Britain

Anon (1743) *The Child's New Play-thing: being a Spelling-book, intended To make the Learning to Read, a Diversion instead of a Task*. London: Printed for M. Cooper at the Globe in Pater-noster-Row

Anon (1760) *A Little pretty pocket-book intended for the instruction and amusement of little Master Tommy and pretty Miss Polly*. London: Printed for J. Newbery, at the Bible and Sun in St. Paul's Church Yard

Addison, J (1711) *The Spectator* no. 183, Saturday, September 29

Arizpe, E and Styles, M with Heath, S B (2006) *Reading Lessons from the Eighteenth Century*. Lichfield: Pied Piper Press

Hoyles, J (1971) *The Waning of the Renaissance 1640-1740*. The Hague: Martinus Nijhoff

Johnson, J. (1744/2001) *A very pretty story*. (G Avery, ed). Oxford: Bodleian Library, Oxford University

Lewis, J E (1996) *The English Fable*. Cambridge: Cambridge University Press

Locke, J (1693/1968) *Some Thoughts Concerning Education*. (J A Axtell, ed). Cambridge: Cambridge University Press

Noel, T (1975) *Theories of the Fable in the Eighteenth Century*. London: Columbia University Press

Richardson, S (1740/1991) *Pamela* Vol I. (M Kinkead-Weekes, ed). London: Everyman's Library

Richardson, S (1740/1984) *Pamela* Vol II. (M Kinkead-Weekes, ed). London: Everyman's Library

Richardson, S (1753) *Æsop's fables: with intructive morals and reflections*. London: Printed by S. Richardson for T. and T. Longman

Watts, I (1715/1971) *Divine Songs*. Oxford: Oxford University Press

Watts, I (1721/1972) *The Art of Reading and Writing English*. Menston: Scolar Press

Watts, I (1741/1859) *The Improvement of the mind to which is added A discourse on the education of children and youth*. Halifax: Milner and Sowerby

Whitley, D (1996) Aesop for children. In M Styles, E Bearne and V Watson (eds) *Voices Off*. London: Cassell.

Whitley, D (1997) Samuel Richardson's *Aesop*. In M Hilton, M Styles and V Watson (eds) *Opening the Nursery Door*. London: Routledge

Main Manuscript Sources

Manuscript Nursery Library: Johnson, J. mss. Lilly Library, Indiana University, Bloomington

Papers of Jane Johnson of Olney, Buckinghamshire and of her family, 17th-19th centuries: Bodleian Library MSS. Don. b. 39-40, c. 190-6, d. 202, e. 193-200

4

The Deeper Game: Intuition, imagination, and embodiment

Shirley Brice Heath

These letters were but the vehicle for gallantry and trick. It was a child's play, chosen to conceal a deeper game... (Austen, 1971/1815, 319)

Epigrams give authors license to take even the hint of an idea and run with it. The opening quotation to this chapter is no exception. This epigrammatic detail from Jane Austen's novel *Emma* captures key aspects of the scholarship of those who have mined the archives and artifacts of the seventeenth and eighteenth centuries to understand the 'world of imagination, fiction and fantasy' (Spufford, 1981). Why is it that we look back to centuries past and search for everyday bits of evidence of the human capacity for mental flights of fancy through play?

An easy answer is that we know today that reason, logic, science, and technology have come to dominate the late twentieth and early twenty-first centuries. Everywhere, critics and pundits speculate about the loss of literary arts and their readers, the trivialisation of visual arts, and the temporariness of installations and exhibitions in museums and public spaces. The dumbing-down of instructional materials and programmes for teaching reading shuts out texts about dreams of the extraordinary and the impossible. Rarely do public and commercial forces seem to respond to pleas for imagination and its power to instill cognitive moves away from the seeming fixedness of reason and logic.

This chapter could be interpreted as a lament, for it looks back to the hand-made children's library of Jane Johnson. But the goal here is to use the past not only to suggest our own shortcomings, but also to understand underlying universal principles of engagement in learning to read.

Recounted elsewhere in this volume (see also Arizpe and Styles, 2006; Hilton, Styles and Watson, 1997), are the life and work of Jane Johnson, a remarkable creator of materials for teaching her own children to read. Her body of work (created circa 1740s) includes dozens of sets of cards and other materials, along with small chap-like books and a short story. Though many of these creative pieces echo the religious instruction materials created for children in earlier decades, much of the work urges flights of imagination and takes the children from local events to flyaway destinations. Many of the cards come in sets that reflect a single genre (poem, declarative statement plus question, or short narrative). Close examination of these materials reveals that their creator layered imagination with potentially boring cognitive skills, such as categorisation. This chapter considers ways that Johnson made possible the 'deeper game' of play in learning to read. The proposal here is that she holds much in common in her production means with today's most awarded children's book illustrators and authors. In spite of having to struggle for ample audience, this latter group shares many of the intuitions we see evidenced in the ways Johnson embraced imagination and embodiment in her work.

Three primary features mark the materials of play and games of Johnson's handmade children's library. These features are: 1) the imperative of linking the cognitive and social; 2) the integration of scientific observation and mathematical understanding with language and literacy; and 3) demonstration of the fact that verbal fluency goes hand in hand with attention to visual focus and dramatic role-play.

This reading of Johnson's work comes through the anthropological lens of studying artifacts, analysing their components, and looking at how the separate pieces add up to a story greater than the sum of its parts. Her work merits close analysis of its language, illustrations, and patterns of visual and verbal representations. The analytical lens used here comes from research on language socialisation and work in the neurosciences on visual and verbal learning. The particular theoretical label for the work of this young mother is *ephemera*, artifacts made of highly expendable materials, reflecting both functional and ideological roles within their particular setting – in this case the family home. As artifacts, ephemera are rare; they are not drawings on palace walls, tea cups used by royalty, or archives of consciously preserved materials. They simply get left, and usually they are tossed onto the rubbish heap. Anthropologists relish ephemera, for they often give the concealed, hidden, or deep stories of families, organisations, and societies.

Johnson's ephemera allow us to see how this eighteenth-century artist embeds the words and pictures of her reading material within narratives of her children's everyday social worlds. From this familiar terrain, her visual art and her written words lead the children to imagine and extend their everyday worlds and their presumed capacities as humans. 'Imagine yourself as a dove, able to soar above the earth. Where would you go, and what would you do?' As her materials suggest such cognitive stretches for the children, Johnson seems to follow a line of thinking that posits the young as curious little scientists, keen observers, and readers willing to envision beyond the images of the immediate text. She uses concrete experiences familiar to the children in some materials, and in others, she mixes the remote, decontextualised, and abstract with the messiest of the ordinary. Consider, for example, item 29 (Set 17):

> O! had I wings I would
> Fly like this Dove
>
> [dove in flight appears pasted on the card]
>
> To Visit Miss Wrighte
> Who so dearly I Love.

Beneath these lines is written in careful printed letters: 'George Johnson'.

Here she imagines wings for herself (and her young son George), but the resulting capacity for flying would enable a flight to a known friend – close by and familiar.

Throughout her reading materials, Johnson lays out premises or starting points and then asks the children to look ahead to consequences. If they eat 'sugar and Plumbs', then they must live with the consequences. In many card sets, she engages the children with levels and divisions of categorisation by providing a 'mixed' but certainly carefully chosen list of vocabulary items. Take, for example, the items included in a set of cards: *plate, dish, fork, knife, spoon, salt, meat, beef, veal, mutton, lamb, pork, bread, cheese, pudding, table, cloth, mug, cup, glass, wine.* Carefully considered, these suggest in their listing the sequence of their use in setting a table and taking part in a meal. Yet they also suggest the opportunity to explain the relationship between meat, on the one hand, and *veal, mutton, lamb*, and *pork* on the other, or for that matter, distinctions between *mutton* and *lamb*.

Neuroaesthetics and the visual and verbal

For centuries, intuitive teachers of young children have searched out materials that blend the verbal, visual, and dramatic. Children hear stories, see illustrations, and sometimes act out roles with gesture, occasional song and dance, and direct engagement to invite listeners and viewers to enter into the act. Today this very mixture of seeing, saying, and acting draws the attention of neuroscientists who want to understand how visual, verbal, and embodied learning co-occur. In particular, how do they co-occur with advanced learning or gains in learning?

We know that Johnson's work is richly complex in terms of genres (aphorism, maxim, fable, short story, street cries, etc), and the materials within some of her cards suggests that she had more than a passing knowledge of the world of acting and of English drama in the first half of the eighteenth century (Arizpe and Styles, 2006, chapter 7). This was a world of market entertainment throughout England, where travelling entertainers (such as harlequins, acrobats, and strolling players) performed in open spaces in front of public buildings and commercial establishments. These entertainers were not bound to the proper and moral or the socially critical. Their material often veered toward the scatological. Johnson occasionally revealed that she had been a witness to such occasions. For example, in a few of her cards, she mentions 'Monkey Man', a notoriously crude and naughty character, whose appearance and language double the suggestive power of linking 'man' with lower-order primates (Set 22, item 27).

Johnson's work frequently links stage and page, and she was, no doubt, influenced in this aspect of her art by her knowledge of the early eighteenth century public stage. Her placement of illustrations – character facing character, each precisely cut from two different sources so as to illustrate the narrative behind the card's intention – imitate what she saw on the public stage in actors' and entertainers' uses of their bodily postures, facial expressions, and backdrops to tell the stories. Moreover, many of her illustrations are themselves of the strolling players and the assorted entertainers who accompanied them: acrobats, dancers, musicians, etc. Throughout, Johnson's materials are both direct and indirect references to eighteenth century 'readerly theatre' (Fishman, 2004).

Moveable scenery entered the public stage only in the second half of the seventeenth century. From that point on, stage effects and complements to the mainpiece plays spread throughout the provinces from the British playhouses in London. For a five-act play, the occasions between scenes and even after the main play allowed for all sorts of new characters (see, for example, Bevis, 1970). These newcomers were just that -characters often in the sense of caricatures and not real persons playing the parts of real people whose speeches had been scripted. These entertainers were jugglers, pantomimists, dancers, singers, harlequins and contortionists. Plays became the vehicles of 'gallantry and trick '- both highly entertaining.

On stage, during the plays, actors took on new forms of silent expression. All these innovations moved away from the auditory entertainment orientation of the early modern stage (which often existed in small enclosed spaces rather than open markets and public spaces). Audiences for public performances could no longer depend upon hearing the actors, and the stage shifted to accommodate onlookers as spectator-readers. The facial, gestural, emotive expressions, and person-centered role interpretations of characters had to be read rather than heard. Long scenes in which an actor said little or nothing often centered in that actor's body movements and facial expressions. Interpretation depended on onlookers reading his intentions, motives, and backgrounds of actions (for more on this phenomenon, particularly through pantomime, see Sawyer, 1990). Pantomime depended on visual elements that also had to be read in an actor's body for a performance to be interpreted in the context of the ongoing script, realised only partly in the words of other actors. Moreover, with pantomime and greater focus on indications of motive and intention through gesture and facial expression, actors had to attend to one another on the stage, creating what came later to be called 'the fourth wall' between the stage and the audience.

In many of her cards, Johnson takes her cue from the mix of the between-acts and after-play characters along with the core narrative. Entities within this mix need not be all on a central theme or even related in their purpose; each has its entertainment value. In similar fashion, good teachers often go off-lesson to pursue the development of their children's own dramatic enactments of where their learning is taking them.

In some ways, Johnson also creates her children as part of a 'home stage' and the dramas of that place. They perform, play roles, and act against backdrops within her cards. As they do so, however, they create not just for entertainment and general education, but as young scientists thinking, contrasting, and categorising. Jane Johnson brings the eye, hand, body, and imagining powers to work in pursuit of the acts of the scientist thinking as well as the performer reading.

What are we to make of the multiple and complex ways in which Johnson mixes the verbal and visual in her reading materials? And what are we to think of the number of times her work invites children into performative modes to re-enact and to embody the characters and stories of her writings? Most of the time, her visual models are either adults or non-humans acting in ways unacceptable to socially responsible human communities. These invoke emotional response and ask for affective reactions, whether humorous, scornful, or reproaching.

Since the early 1990s, researchers in the neurosciences have had the technological means to examine human brains during task performances and learning situations that involve emotion, envisionment, and embodiment (cf Damasio, 2003). One area of this work examines visual artworks from the past in relation to responses of viewers today. The goal is to link brain function (what some term 'the mind's eye') to external stimuli upon which visual artists depend in their representations. For example, neuroscientists have shown that depth cues come through shading, texture, and linear perspectives that trigger particular areas of the brain's visual system (Vinberg and Grill-Spector, 2008). Researchers in neurology link the techniques of artists to these evocations of specific brain functions (Zeki, 1999). The uniqueness of viewer responses that paintings by certain old masters and modernist artists evoke is explained through dual examination of brain function and characteristics of the paintings. It may well be that certain artists intuited human capacities for aesthetic interpretation and took these intuitions into their visual art. The goal of neuroaesthetics is to probe techniques within the artworks themselves and juxtapose these with current knowledge of the actual working of the brain now available through fMRI (Magnetic Resonance Imaging) technologies.

Neuroaesthetics is often described with exaggerated claims of being able to 'unveil the laws of being human' and of understanding how humans 'see' and 'hear' beauty as well as how artists inspire positive emotions in viewers, listeners, and readers. The field has many critics (cf Tallis, 2008). Yet it is the case that advances in neurobiology and neurophysics, as well as imaging technologies, indicate the neuronal bases of what artists, then and now, may have sensed. Their highly sensitive tuning capabilities may well have led them to create and assess their work and that of others in terms of roused emotions and pleasurable sensations. Perhaps the heart of their exceptional artistry rests in this sensitivity that some interpret as their 'seeing deep' into the actual workings of the brain.

Intuition among educators, and particularly among those whose words and images work together in their mind to create particular kinds of responses from young learners, may be explained in similar ways. The claim here is not that Johnson qualifies as an exceptional artist or literary writer. Instead, the idea behind this chapter is that she (as well as many other children's experts, including mothers and fathers, nannies and teachers, pediatricians and dentists) developed a certain sense of how to bring several aspects of human abilities together to increase learning by the young.

Neurologist Semir Zeki points out that 'art has an overall function which is remarkably similar to that of the visual brain, is indeed an extension of it....' (1999, 8). Zeki claims that art enables the brain to search for essentials; art demands selection, connection, and projection. The visual and memory capacities of humans, astonishing as they are, have their limits. The visual system looks for critical features or details and stores and links these so that we can navigate the world. This same kind of sorting and selecting goes on in visual aesthetic reactions. We view a visual item, select those properties or features that further mental work, connect what we see with memory, and cast ahead from the visual artifact into our own ability to create narrative and analogy. At a visceral level, these combined actions enable us to re-embody the work of artists, or, in the case of combinations of visual and verbal materials designed for our learning, we re-enact and envision for ourselves the content of the materials before us.

Embodiment

It is common to hope for young learners that they can learn to think like a scientist (artist, mathematician...). To do so means to enter into a sense of being the source model and developing a theory of mind of that model. Johnson's ability to cast her children ahead into decision-making positions as problem-solvers portends the late twentieth-century 'discovery' of the power of embodiment for children's learning. Her artifacts tell us how she understood the acts of reading as the foundational basis of learning to think like a scientist. For her, the book, and all the related materials she created to illustrate what went into books, had to be the home or the grounding of some of the most challenging aspects of later learning – that of learning to be a scientist, a problem-solver, a strategist. Her short narratives repeatedly provide details and lay open for interpretation and analysis a range of possible conclusions that the child might reach. Several of her large word charts carry as their subtext a role the child might play – gardener, hunter, naturalist – in sorting out just what the connections between the words on the chart might be.

Learners have to imagine and learn to embody ideas. Previously talked about much more in connection with humanistic thinking than with scientific reasoning, imagination within the sciences has received mounting attention in the past few years. Two factors account for this relatively recent development. First is the dramatic increase in attention to vision as a strong contributing factor in the creative inspiration of scientists. Also accounting for current interest in imagination is the work of cognitive scientists who have, through experimental work and modeling or 'mindware', shown the extent to which imagination works in the 'extended mind' (Clark, 1996, 2007ab).

The scholars who have both been influenced by and helped to shape these factors point to the fact that imagination is socially acquired and that it is a social process that both needs and benefits from association and/or immersion with other socialisation patterns. Games and sociodramatic play as socialising forces allow children to explore being inside someone else's character in thought, action, and voice (Sutton-Smith, 1997).

Perhaps most significant about the home aspects of imaginative play is its contribution to learning language. Linguist Catherine Snow and others point out that reading with a child provides twice as many words of input per minute as does ordinary interactional talk. But the benefits of this input come from not only quantity but also quality; that is, the words have not only to 'say something', but also to enable the learner to image-in (imagine) or 'see something'. This envisioning or imaging in the head lays the groundwork for key patterns of discourse necessary in problem-solving.

As socialisers at home, Jane Johnson and parents across the ages take advantage of the possibility of entering children as agents into narratives in which they play roles. The appeal of these stories lies in their ability to please us, make us laugh, disturb us, and entice us to want to know more. But stories – some would say the best of stories and storytelling – leave gaps, allow us to go further, to know more than the story tells. What is remarkable and quite peculiar about stories, however, is that when we know we are hearing a good story told well, we put our analytical faculties aside. But stories leave contrails, like the jets that speed through the sky. And after stories, we wonder, ponder, and try to figure out or answer questions we wish we had asked during the story (though every good storyteller, like every team of dramatic actors, insists that listeners hear the story through). There are reasons for these gaps, and they have to do with the ways that stories set loose the imagination to go right along with the analytical faculties. In our imagination, we enter into the characters and scenes of the stories.

Imagination is helped by embodiment. Neuroscientists and cognitive scientists in the early 21st century have therefore emphasised the interconnectedness of envisionment, narratives, and embodiment in book titles such as *How the body shapes the way we think: A new view of intelligence* (Pfeifer and Bongard, 2007; see also Embodiment and cognitive science, Gibbs, 2006). Teachers and parents, who know the value of engaging bodies in learning, relish songs and stories that allow listeners to embody the feelings, sensations, and even the movements of the characters in the narratives they hear. Moreover, close visual observation is intimately linked with narrative formation and recall. Scholars working to understand embodiment in learning stress the fact that particular patterns of thinking, such as those associated with the sciences, depend upon the ability to imagine beyond the present and to envision what it takes to follow the imagined path ahead. Such imagination depends on *roles* envisioned as well as the *personae* associated with each of these roles. Many roles are possible, and these need not only material but also symbolic practices to help the imagination enact these roles.

Jane Johnson put her children into roles – both directly and indirectly. Her children, Barbara and George, are named actors in a few of the brief tales on her cards. Their friends are too, and so are the familiar animals and adults of their world (for more on this point, see Arizpe and Styles, 2006). Today those working in science education, as well as in the learning sciences, point out that any future work within science laboratories, graphic design, or computer modelling will be most likely to come from those who in their youth have had extensive practice doing what cognitive scientists term 're-imagining' the life of the work or text at hand. Facility for figuring out what an adaptation to an existing theory or practice could mean under certain conditions of change depends on envisioning ahead through a web of circumstances past and present. Exploitative problem-solving, a central practice of scientific thinking, depends upon being canny about considering all factors within a context in terms of potential action and bringing into play several cognitive and physical resources linking body and brain in learning. Though we may only speculate on exactly how Johnson could have used her materials to challenge her children, it is difficult not to see within the designs and juxtapositions of words and images her cunning way of inspiring her children to think about factors within a given context and their potential for different courses of action (Set 17, item 25 is only one of her cards that makes consequences obvious, while far more of her illustrations hide the obvious within complex features of context).

One specific finding from recent neuroscientific research is especially rich in its suggestive power for the value of linking what is observed visually with what we can recapture verbally and remember in our meaning-making through symbol systems. Neuroscientists have shown how important it is for young children, when they come across a new word, to acknowledge *they do not know what it means.* To teachers, this point may seem counter-intuitive, for we often encourage children to believe they *do indeed know what a word means.* But neuroscientists want to know the differences in brain functions when one sees the self-as-not-knowing as well as the self-as-knower. They want to understand how searches for verbal meaning link with visual attentiveness. Their experiments show that children who say they do not know the meaning of a word are those most likely to be close visual observers. These children appear not only to want to see themselves as participants in reading, but they also have a propensity toward learning by observing the scene, whatever that may be – page, page plus illustration, or the entire book.

Children who both admit *and* observe try to figure out what unfamiliar words mean by searching about for both visual and verbal cues that might improve their understanding. Much of this work on close looking suggests that sustained attention to visual representation carries over into metacognitive processing linked with verbal behaviour such as reading or drawing the meaning of a word from associated visual stimuli (see Merriman and Marazita, 2004, on links between visual perception and awareness of one's own lexicon).

Johnson's materials seem to insist on the verbal and visual attentiveness of her children. The aesthetic qualities of the Nursery Library stand out as the most obvious evidence on this point. However, numerous other aspects of her work underscore her sense of not only the visual supports to the written word that come through illustrations, but also the need for reading illustrations or finding a way on the page or in the local context or within memory *to see and to be.* The latter relates directly to the conversational prompts contained in most of her card sets. It is impossible to imagine that she did not create those illustrations to provoke conversations of interpretation that would depend on seeing and linking details within the art as well as tying the entire visual illustration to the written words on the single card within the set.

Take, for example, the case of Johnson's ways of including within her materials references to both the wealthy and the poor. However, within her materials, and often through cards that portray either the rich or the poor, Johnson also inserts in quite distinctive genres certain sub-texts that reflect other levels of awareness. Primary among these are her references to women (and tradesmen) in their work. Tasks and obligations range from stopping fights in public places to women having to beg for food for their children (illustrated in a street cry: 'Give some Bread to my Children I beg and I pray. Or they will be starved having had none to day' (Set 17, item 25)).

Often within these cards, her sub-texts are layered. For example, in the beggar's street cry, the illustration is composed of two separate pasted cut-out pictures, one of a woman richly clothed responding in a haughty manner to a separate but facing illustration of a poorly dressed woman with two children by her side reaching out toward the woman of wealth. Johnson's unspoken commentary through her selection of illustrations points to the needs of wealthy women as well as those of the poor. Jane Johnson seems to be saying in her illustrations: see the evidence of attitude, mental state, background, and need of these individuals. The woman of poverty lacks material goods, while the wealthy woman lacks empathy and compassion.

The aesthetic matters

At this point, after seeing so many of the exquisitely detailed illustrations of Jane Johnson, we may find it unnecessary to say that the aesthetic matters. Good teachers have for centuries valued the aesthetics of illustrations within children's literature, used art to prompt creative thinking by children, and found visual and musical representations to be optimal stimuli for verbal participation by children. Details within visual illustrations that lie embedded within and expand the narrative story will facilitate children's language acquisition of syntactic structures that they otherwise have little opportunity to practice or perform in everyday or pragmatic social interactions. Performing in the role of others puts into the mouths of children vocabulary items, stylistic features of talk, and syntax they do not use in their mundane worlds (cf Wolf and Heath, 1992).

Every scientist thinks and expresses 'what if?' 'what about?' and 'under which conditions?' as well as 'I think I may be able to figure that out.' An orientation to what could be and what can be known lies behind the sciences. Scientists begin early with opportunities to think, act, and talk along these lines and have or find opportunities along the way to continue to practise and develop their ideas. Yet very little research attention from developmentalists or linguists has gone to studying the linkages between language socialisation before and within learning to think like a scientist.

Aside from the extensive attention that goes to vocabulary, studies of learning in the sciences rarely focus on the extent to which both early and later language socialisation matters for taking up the role of science-thinker. In John-son's materials, we see the multiple and interlocking cognitive, visual, sym-bolic, and behavioural demands of being a young scientist that she brought to bear through the aesthetic qualities of her work.

Behind all her pretty pictures, Johnson set out some tough linguistic demands. She visually created calls for categorisation, hypothetical proposals of 'what if?' and comparative analyses. A distinction that is vital in the world of problem-solving and thinking like a scientist is that between *comparing* and *contrasting*. Consider the description of two restaurants. If someone asks us to *compare* A with B, we will be inclined to offer judgments 'Oh, I really liked A much better than B. Maybe that's because I had my favorite kind of sauce/meal/music there.' But if someone asks us to contrast A with B, we will be much more likely to offer comments such as 'Well, A certainly has more ambience, and the menu is much more varied than B.'

Jane Johnson's cards ask (implicitly) for contrasts and not comparisons in the majority of cases, aside from those sets dedicated to religious teachings. Johnson does this by including the natural and the odd in card sets that also portray such mundane activities as lying down on the ground, watching robins, commenting on the coaches of the rich, and remembering street cries of the milkmaid. There is a constant back-and-forth movement, compare-and-contrast, see-and-remember quality to the game sets of Jane Johnson's materials. In one set (Set 17), item 27 is of a milkmaid, while item 26 is of a linnet and thrush, and item 30 is of a peacock:

> # 26 A linnet, and a
>> Thrush. Sitting in a Bush
> [a pasted colour cut-out of two birds sitting in a tree]
>> For three Months in the Spring, They
>> most sweetly do Sing.
> # 30 Of all the fine Birds
>> that fly in the Air,
> [a pasted peacock in full display and painted over in part as well]
>> None can with the
>> Peacock, for beauty
>> Compare.

In many of her card sets, Jane Johnson builds opportunities for meaningful integrative roles likely to evoke rare vocabulary items, sentence-structure variation, and use of both declaratives and interrogatives. The children have ample opportunities with these artifacts to move ideas collaboratively among themselves and, with their mother as expert, to hold possibilities and pro-babilities up for inspection and contradiction as well as clarification.

Gesture

A final word on Johnson's wisdom about 'acts of reading'. As noted above, some of her cards call for scrutiny of the facial expressions and gestures of the actors. She intricately cut and coloured the illustrations so as to ensure details of both. Recent research on gesture demonstrates ways that language and gesture work together in communication and, in particular, within problem-solving. In experimental work, neurolinguists have shown that when learners' gestures match or go along with what they are saying, their level of under-standing exceeds that of those whose gestures are less expressive of the meanings of the verbal material (Gentner and Goldin-Meadow, 2003; Goldin-Meadow, 2003). Ineffectual public speakers often gesture excessively while talking. Only later will audience members be aware of the incongruities and confusions in the verbal text. Listeners, when asked for summaries after such talks, have difficulty remembering content but they have no trouble describ-ing the speaker's behaviour. Research now shows that language and gesture must match for listeners to grasp meaning coherently. Johnson, in her use of details of gesture and commentary on attitude, emotion, and action of indivi-duals pictured, moves her children along toward attending to gestures and their congruence with the meaning-making of the narrative.

So what?

At the end of any process of artifactual analysis and historical research, arduously and painstakingly carried out, often over thousands of miles and with piles of correspondence, the ultimate question of 'so what?' has to be asked. Those 'possessed' by the process of historical inquiry understand per-fectly well why the pursuit of bringing back to life an historical figure, period, or item can occupy scholars for years. Others never caught up in such pur-suits may, however, deserve some explanation of the stories of Jane Johnson, her children, and their writing, reading, and playing with ephemera.

The British novelist, A. S. Byatt, explained the inspiration for her prize-winning 1990 novel, *Possession*, in a way that sums up the intent of all his-torians and, most certainly, of those involved in bringing Jane Johnson's tale together. Byatt recounted the naming of her novel and its core purpose as follows:

> The beginning of *Possession*, and the first choice, was most unusually for me, the
> title. I thought of it in the British Library, watching that great Coleridge scholar,

Kathleen Cobun, circumambulating the catalogue. I thought: she has given all her life to his thoughts, and then I thought: she has mediated his thoughts to me. And then I thought 'Does he possess her, or does she possess him? There could be a novel called *Possession about the relations between living and dead minds.*' (emphasis not in the original; Byatt, 1990).

It is just this relationship – that of minds across the years engaged in similar activities with surprisingly common materials and means – that explains possession by an historical figure and his or her time. (Coincidentally, Byatt as author weighed in on the topic of neuroaesthetics in 2007, arguing the potential of the field for improving understanding of aesthetic responsiveness in readers and viewers; see Tallis, 2008 in response.) For in no search of an individual's history can a scholar avoid being drawn into the social and cultural activities of the period.

This chapter has continued my own anthropological and artifactual engagement with Jane Johnson's materials – reading their patterns and linking the stories behind these patterns to findings from recent neurological evidence on the specialised integrative verbal, visual, and performative work of the brain. The particular interest here has been to consider the primacy in art of engaging what neurobiologists call 'cortical seats' and 'mirror neurons'. What is it that we see in representations through art that enlist particular neurological interactions? My ethnographic research in recent years has been with young people learning in laboratories, rehearsal spaces, and studios. Little difference marks the fundamental nature of the key processes of learning and working in these places. The sciences and arts inextricably entwine now as they have across the ages.

Through Johnson's materials, we see this intertwining. In the case of seeing and interpreting art, we all engage our brains in fundamental processes of science; we learn to be hypothesisers, scenario builders, and jugglers of multiple variables or contextual clues. This then is a key aspect of the 'deeper game' that Jane Austen attributes to our play with art forms.

It is in the very nature of all play, and most markedly within literacy supports in play, that the linguistic, visual, and gestural congruencies, along with the all-important uses of imagination and embodiment, take place in meaningful ways. No strategy of a children's book illustrator is without purpose, and authors of works for children know that their greatest strength is in the ambiguities of their language and pictures, allowing imaginations to take their readers to a host of possible interpretations. Children outstrip most adults in their powers to fantasise, parody, and riddle in wild and unpredictable directions. It is precisely their engagement in play that fuels the imaginations of the young and that allow them to embody roles they will take on in the future they are learning to project for themselves.

This idea and others that became prominent in child development, school reform, science learning, and literacy studies in the twentieth century appear evident throughout the Nursery Library of Jane Johnson. In many ways, Johnson's Nursery Library reflects theories of learning that came to prominence only in the twentieth century.

Yet most of these truths must be re-discovered and newly announced and claimed every few decades. Such is the case for much within the socio-historical work of Lev Vygotsky and his teachers as well as his followers. The case is the same for imagination, creativity, and experiential learning, as well as many other ideas in education that became current in recent decades. John Dewey, Howard Gardner, David Perkins, and the educators in Reggio Emilia would all understand that what appear to be redundancies across centuries are in fact good evidence of the sustained importance to human beings of the learning of the young and the role that adults can and must play in promoting this learning in the best possible ways.

Note: Portions of this piece have been adapted from Chapter 7, Child's Play for Private and Public Life, in Arizpe and Styles, 2006.

Bibliography

Arizpe, E and Styles, M with Heath, S B (2006) *Reading Lessons from the Eighteenth Century*. Lichfield: Pied Piper Press

Austen, J (1971/1815) *Emma*. Oxford: Oxford University Press

Bevis, Richard E (ed) (1970) *Eighteenth-Century drama: Afterpieces*. London: Oxford University Press

Byatt, A S (1990) *Possession*. New York: Vintage.

Byatt, A S (2007) Observe the neurons. *Times Literary Supplement* (September 22).

Clark, A (1996) *Being There: Putting brain, body, and world together again*. Cambridge: MIT Press.

Clark, A (2007a) Magic words: How language augments human computation http://www.nyu.edu/gsas/dept/philo/courses/concepts/magicwords.html.

Clark, A (2007b) Embodiment and the sciences of mind. Lecture, Brown University 2/5/2007

Damasio, A (2003) *Looking for Spinoza: Joy, sorrow, and the feeling brain*. New York: Harcourt

Dehaene, S (2007) *Les neurons de la lecture*. Paris: O. Jacob

Fishman, J (2004) *Active literacy: Performance and writing in Britain 1642-1790*. PhD dissertation, English Department, Stanford University

Gibbs, R (2006) *Embodiment and cognitive science*. Cambridge: Cambridge University Press

Gentner, D and Goldin-Meadow, S (eds) (2003) *Language in Mind: Advances in the study of language and thought*. Cambridge: MIT Press

Goldin-Meadow, S (2003) *Hearing Gesture: How our hands help us think*. Cambridge: Harvard University Press

Heath, S B (2006) Child's play for private and public life. In E Arizpe and M Styles (eds) *Reading lessons from the eighteenth century.* Lichfield: Pied Piper Press

Hilton, M, Styles, M, and Watson, V (eds) (1997) *Opening the nursery door: Reading, writing and childhood 1600-1900.* London: Routledge Press

Merriman, W E and Marazita, J M (2004) Awareness of lexical ignorance. In D Levin (ed) *Thinking and seeing: Visual metacognition in adults and children.* Cambridge, MA: MIT Press

Pfeifer, R and Bongard, J (2007) *How the body shapes the way we think: A new view of intelligence.* Cambridge, MA: MIT Press

Sawyer, P (1990) The Popularity of Pantomime on the London Stage, 1720-1760. *Restoration and eighteenth-century theatre research* 5 (2) 1-16

Spufford, M (1981) *Small books and pleasant histories: Popular fiction and its readership in seventeenth-century England.* Cambridge: Cambridge University Press

Sutton-Smith, B (1997) *The ambiguities of play.* Cambridge, MA; Harvard University Press

Tallis, R (2008) The neuroscience delusion. *Times Literary Supplement* (April 9)

Vinberg, J and Grill-Spector, K (2008) Representations of shapes, edges, surfaces across multiple cues in the human visual cortex. *Journal of Neurophysiology* 99 (13) 1380-193

Wolf, S A and Heath, S B (1992) *The braid of literature: Children's worlds of reading.* Cambridge, MA: Harvard University Press

Zeki, S (1999) *Inner Vision: An exploration of art and the brain.* New York: Oxford University Press

5

Five Centuries of Illustrating
Aesop's Fables

Judith Graham

We know very little about Aesop other than that he was born, in all likelihood, in the sixth century BC and that his clever stories (not written down until centuries later) brought him fame and perhaps punishment. Because humans and animals lived closely together in the past, it is likely that all early tales had animals in them and that animals were given human characteristics, such as being able to talk. Aesop's fables, with his cast of animals and birds, share characteristics of tales (which we could describe as narratives, either based on true or imaginary facts) and of parables (which suggest a hidden message or secret meaning) but he wants his fables to do more than that. He wishes the listener to detect a moral, understand what is socially acceptable or recognise a political truth. In Caxton's words, from the preface to his Aesop which he printed in 1485, the fables 'shewe al maner of folk what maner of thing they ought to ensyewe and folowe. And also what maner of thing they must and ought to leve and flee'.

The fable obscures these intentions so that no overt moralising seems to be going on yet the messages are conveyed and the reader or listener is suitably sympathetic, outraged or amused. Whilst we may sometimes find the moral which follows the tales absurd, quaint or even curiously irrelevant to its fable, for the most part the sly fox, the proud lion, the vain crow, the devious wolf, the boastful hare, the strong bull and the patient ass successfully teach their lessons about the virtue of hard work, the perils of greed, the importance of loyalty and generosity. So successfully are the lessons taught in fact that we hardly think of the extent to which fables have coloured our language and

Figure 1: Unknown illustrator in *Aesop* (1484) printed by Caxton

thinking so that sour grapes, look before you leap, crying over spilt milk, more haste less speed, crying wolf, necessity the mother of invention and many other phrases have become everyday sayings.

Hand-scribed versions of the fables are thought to date from the fourth century BC but only fragments remain and those date from the early AD centuries. Hand-scribed versions of the tales, particularly in Latin and Greek, were used in schools and monasteries and some of these, as well as hand-illuminated versions, can be found in museums. Fables have also been found decorating pieces of pottery and woven into textiles. The Bayeux tapestry of the eleventh century has the fable of the fox and the crow woven along the bottom of a section. However, it is only from the invention of the printing press in the mid to late fifteenth century that the history of Aesop's fables, and especially of their illustration, can be charted with any certainty.

The first known printed version of fables attributed to Aesop came from the printer Zainer in Ulm, Germany, in about 1476. The text was in German and was translated from those early Latin and Greek hand-written versions by the author Steinhöwel. This is one of the first texts ever to be printed and the first with illustrations (wood-blocks), though the artists are unknown. However, it is certainly because of the illustrations that Steinhöwel's Aesop became the standard European text in medieval times and the illustrations were copied or adapted in countless subsequent versions, right up to the nineteenth century. Steinhöwel's text was translated into many languages and one French translation (by Macho) was used by the printer Caxton in 1484; it was this Aesop – the third book that Caxton ever printed – that English-speaking children would have known. The unacknowledged illustrators in Steinhöwel appear here too, slightly adapted in some instances.

The importance of illustrations in these early printed books cannot be underestimated. We are some two hundred years before Comenius' *Orbis Sensualium Pictus* (1658) with its 150 small pictures illustrating the whole of the 'visible world' and from *Some Thoughts Concerning Education* (1693) in which Locke echoes Comenius' belief in the use of pictures for children. Locke recommended that children be given pictures to encourage 'enquiry and knowledge' by linking learning with the senses, and particularly with visual experience. But, without necessarily expressing the theory, here are Steinhöwel and Caxton and their unacknowledged illustrators providing their readers with visual support and delight right at the beginning of printing.

Since Caxton, there have been hundreds of versions of Aesop's fables. The written texts have not simply been reworked; a tradition developed that writers should compose their own versions of the fables, or perhaps, as in Caxton's case, translate them from another language. But with illustrations it seemed that there was no such expectation of originality. To some extent this was due to the woodblocks being available for endless re-use. In fact, the use was not quite endless – deterioration is visible in some cases and well-used woodblocks would ultimately have been re-cut or amended. From 1484 until the nineteenth century one sees a fascinating array of illustrators who seem to be more or less copying from one another.

However, 500 years of illustrating Aesop has not been a question of 400 years of no change with only the last 100 years producing varied and non-standard responses; the copying is seldom simple copying and small differences prove intriguing. Of course, printing processes became ever more refined – etching on metal for instance produced a sharper image – but one can suppose that changes come about, occasionally, when illustrators respond more personally to the fable. They may want to create a beautiful picture complete with landscape and other detail; they may wish to inject humour; they may feel they can aid their readers' appreciation of the narrative and the drama by the composition and focus of the picture. In what follows, I shall discuss the ways in which illustrators have chosen to support the meaning of the text, the decisions they made about the number of illustrations required, and the relevance of detail, originality and humour. I shall use examples as far back as Caxton right up to the twenty-first century.

How the picture supports the text

Perhaps a basic requirement in illustrating Aesop's fables is an image that relates to the written text. For children struggling to learn to read, maybe in Latin or Greek, a little image that crystallised the story, must have been a life-line. And it is perhaps important that the image be accurate. So if the text asserts that a thirsty fox repeatedly jumps up to reach a tantalisingly distant bunch of grapes it behoves the artist to show those grapes to be well out of reach. (I will refer later to those illustrators who do not show key moments of the fables and whose visual response avoids the obvious key moments.) For two or three hundred years after Caxton, one can imagine children exclaiming in exasperation that 'the fox could easily reach those grapes' as illustration after illustration, across the centuries, shows a fox who, for instance, could climb onto a little wall shown nearby (Passarotti (or Titian) in Faerno, 1563/5) or stretch his hind legs a little more (Osius, 1574) and have his heart's desire. It is likely that early illustrators (or more specifically their printers) would not have been confident to leave a large area of white space to suggest distance. They had, after all, only a very small woodcut to play with. Rackham, in his 1912 *Aesop*, by inserting the written text between fox and grapes, can skillfully suggest how high up those grapes really are. A child with *Baby's Own Aesop* (Crane, 1887) on his or her lap would have been delighted to see that this fox really cannot get the grapes. The way in which grapes hang in countless illustrations, not from vines but from the most unlikely trees, would probably not have troubled child readers so much.

It is from this fable of course that we get the expression 'sour grapes' and two illustrators of the twentieth and twenty-first centuries choose the end of the fable as their illustrated moment. Rackham's fox shows wonderful indifference to the grapes above him – eyes closed, head thrown back, mouth turned down at the corners and long throat and chin stretched out. Winter's fox (1919), rather than leaping up, departs disdainfully, while Ward (2004) has her fox slinking away, glancing backwards with disgust. Facial expressions are very clear in these illustrators' work and lend support to the interpretation that the child must make of the fable.

The fable of The Dog and his Reflection also has its fair share of early illustrations which may have left child readers a little impatient or critical. Most, but not all, illustrations show the moment when the dog, crossing over the bridge, looks down and spots his reflection. The unknown illustrator in an early Aesop, translated by Zucco (1479), has his dog alongside the water, totally oblivious of the reflection. This could, of course, increase tension as it is the moment before the great drama arises but it seems less than satisfactory, if you are permitted only one illustration, to frustrate your readers with this tame image.

Other images which might leave readers irritated are those where the dropped meat is easily retrievable (Steinhöwel, 1476) or where the dog is crossing the water but not looking down (del Tuppo, 1485). Illustrators achieve more drama by showing the dog arrested by his reflection (Weir in Townsend, 1867) or, in his greed, distressed at losing his meat (Heighway in Jacobs, 1894).

It is also curious that an illustrator would go to the trouble of showing a turbulent stretch of water in which, of course, no reflection could be seen (Passarotti or Titian in Faerno, 1563/5). Children really do want to see what the dog sees and to feel superior to him. Even Rackham does not give us a clear reflection. Far more satisfying is Cleyn's image in Ogilby's *Aesop* of 1665 who has the calmest stretch of water in which the sharpest reflections of dog, meat and underside of plank bridge are clear for readers to make out. Walter Crane (1887) also has most satisfying reflections in his full colour illustration and it is his dog, with his astounded glare as he sees the reflected piece of meat, that most children will remember.

Most early illustrators use plank bridges for this fable; an indication perhaps of the most common way to cross a river at the time. Steinhöwel, however, does not show a bridge at all and shows his dog wading in the shallow water searching for his and perhaps the other, reflected, piece of meat. Others have stepping stones rather than the bridge of the text (Trery, 1925). Gheeraerts (1567) shows a plank bridge and his influence was such that Oudry (1755) and Bewick (1818) produced similar bridges centuries later and Ward (2004) and Wormell (2005) continue this tradition in the twenty-first century.

The support that illustrators can give to their readers comes in many ways but for several hundred years the idea that you need do more than show the object was not really part of the culture. But even the earliest illustrators manage to have animals looking at each other if they are talking or to have heads tilted up or down if there is a height distance between them. Animals in pain could be drawn with their mouths open and limbs tensed; animals pleading could have their claws retracted and be drawn in submissive poses. With the advent of metal etching and finer printing techniques, more facial expression could be shown. Child readers, we know, pay close attention to facial expression and those illustrators who can indicate fine detail in this respect are supporting deeper understanding of the written text.

One illustration, two illustrations or several

Through four of the five centuries that Aesop has been in print, each fable, when and if it was illustrated, was nearly always accompanied by a single image. (Many volumes of collected tales did not even have one picture per fable.) If only one image was allowed – and usually a small one at that – it was likely that the most significant moment of the narrative would be selected. So if our fable is that of The Wolf and the Crane, the majority of one-image illustrators would choose the moment of the wolf with the crane's long beak – or perhaps his whole head – down his throat. Steinhöwel's illustrator does exactly this – the crane's head has completely disappeared. As we know how much Steinhöwel's prints were copied, it is not surprising that for several centuries this image is the one that prevailed. The variety that arises in the image comes with the work of Barlow (1666) who shows his wolf with one paw held up, perhaps in pain or to show submissiveness, at least whilst the operation is proceeding. Heighway (1894) also depicts an expressive paw, raised and curled, and Rackham's wolf is clearly bracing himself for the removal of the bone. A most striking image of this moment is created by Weir (in Townsend, 1867) where the animals are exquisitely entwined and we can appreciate the crane's bravery and her imminent danger. Griset (1868) breaks the mould by choosing the instant where the wolf, visiting Doctor Crane in his sinister surgery, is explaining his predicament, tears of pain rolling down his cheeks and handkerchief pressed to his mouth. The crane's beak is horribly long and powerful.

A fable such as The Wolf and the Crane can be served by a single image. Some two-part fables can still be illuminated by one image if there is a more dramatic moment in one part than the other. In the fable of The Lion and the Mouse (sometimes, the Rat), illustrators tend to be drawn to the visually arresting image of the lion captured in a hunter's net and the small mouse at her gnawing. Early images, such as in Perret (1578), show a desperate and ferocious lion and a somewhat oversized and cautious rat who keeps a wary eye on the thrashing lion, all set against an elaborate and idyllic rural background, complete with rowing boats, church and millpond. By the time we

Figure 2: Billinghurst's illustration of *The Lion and the Mouse* (1899)

get to Barlow (1667), the rat/mouse has shrunk in size (thus emphasising her heroism) and a kindly lion appears to watch whilst the mouse nibbles. Wormell (2005) waits until the mouse has finished the job; clearly pleased with herself, standing on hind legs with paws outstretched, she looks directly at the wondering lion. Perhaps the most dramatic of all is a Victorian representation by Billinghurst who provides a striking image with the mouse now clearly foregrounded (as so she should be) against a bold white space with the lion patiently waiting in the background.

There are some two-part fables which would appear unbalanced without an illustration to support both parts of the narrative. A single image does not support the reading of these fables very well and thus they really only come into their own from the nineteenth century onwards when illustrators were granted more space on the page. Such fables are The Wind and the Sun (who compete with each other to get a wayfarer to shed his coat) and The Fox and the Crane (in which Fox serves soup to Crane in a flat dish, only, on a return visit, to have the tables turned on him when Crane serves soup in a narrow-necked pitcher). Walter Crane works his magic again with the latter. The written text appears on a Japanese fan which divides the page vertically. To the left we see a smirking fox, lapping up his soup watched by a disconsolate crane. To the right, the crane sips happily from her pitcher whilst the fooled fox can only lick the outside of the jar. (The idea of the fox licking the jar is not Crane's own; it appears in Steinhöwel, in Soloman's illustration (1547) where the pitcher is transparent so we can see what the crane is up to and in de la Fontaine and Oudry's 1755/59 collection, where we see the pair in an elegant 18th century parkland setting, complete with ruined fountain.) Noble (1914) made a speciality of a page divided 1/5th, 4/5ths, with the start of the story in the smaller top section. We see nothing but the feet and beak of the frustrated crane but she is shown triumphant in full in the larger picture. It is a clever device that enables just one plate to be made but in effect to have two sections of the fable illustrated. Bewick, known for his headers and tailpieces, beautifully engraved on the end-grain of box-wood, slips a sly comment into the tailpiece of one of the fables, thereby extending the tale and the moral in a way that we associate much more with recent illustrators of children's books. The fable is of the fisherman who ignores the pleas of the tiny fish that he has caught to return them to the river until they are older. The tailpiece shows his plate of small fish in his pantry with a cat happily helping herself.

For The Wind and the Sun, Crane produces one of his most beautiful designed pages with his (coloured) illustration above the text personifying wind who blows from his bugle, blasting the traveller who only clutches his cloak

Figure 3: Walter Crane's illustration for *The Wind and the Sun* (1887)

closer. The illustration curls down the page and then swells out below the text where the sun, a glowing youth in a circle of fire, has no problem in persuading the man to fling off his cloak.

Child readers would probably prefer this image to that of Robinson (1895) whose dramatic black and white images are balanced so symmetrically that the traveller's fancy hat stays on throughout and it is difficult to tell what he is doing with his cloak. The clarity in Anno's *Aesop* (1989) where his delightful image shows firstly the huddled traveller, almost bent double and then stripped off to his vest; his coat and other garments hung beside him makes the point more clearly.

There are some fables that in recent times have been taken by illustrators and turned into single fable picture books. This is not always satisfactory as a protracted telling does not always suit Aesop's succinct tales but Wildsmith (1963) achieves painterly delight with The Lion and the Rat, as we follow his golden, glowing lion through every page of the book.

In some collections of fables, an illustrator creates a composite picture which cunningly includes characters and elements from a group of fables. A successful example appears in Hayes' collection of tales (1987) illustrated by Ingpen. A woodman with his three axes walks into the picture from the left, past the proud fallen oak tree and alongside the cat (whom the mice have successfully felled), a wolf and a sheep. He moves towards a couple about to slay their goose of golden egg laying fame. Just glimpsed to the right we see the fox after the grapes. The whole is bathed in a golden light and makes a pleasing composition. Other examples, such as those of Rackham and Winter, have composite pictures for their covers, showing a selection of animals, perhaps grouped around a figure representing Aesop or, as in Rackham's case, a group of animals assembled to watch the start of the race between hare and tortoise. Steinhöwel and Caxton also had Aesop surrounded by animals as their frontispieces.

Detail, originality and humour
Steinhöwel and Caxton's unknown illustrators had very little opportunity to include detail in their simple woodcuts. The setting for each fable and the central animals would have to be sketched in with a minimum of detail, shading, cross-hatching, light and shade and, even if there were detail – curls on the dog's coat or bones protruding from the joint of meat – the effort might have been wasted as much would be lost in repeated printing. Nevertheless, the woodcuts in these early days were effective and as we know were hugely

influential on versions of Aesop that followed. But within a hundred years of Caxton, although dogs' tails curl identically, trees grow beside the river in the same place and bridge design remains unchanged, woodcuts give way to etching on metal which allowed fine detail, subtle effects of light and shade, distance and depth of field. Gheeraerts' etchings (1567) are full of rural detail – farmhouses, cows grazing, little figures going about their business, trees and plants everywhere – and all whilst a ferocious lion is caught in a net in the foreground. Gheeraerts in his turn influenced the illustrators in Ogilby and Barlow's Aesop in the mid-seventeenth century and in Bewick's a century later. Some details change; Cleyn, one of Ogilby's illustrators, changed Gheeraerts' backgrounds to something more sophisticated with a turreted castle here and there but on the whole the compositions remained very similar from one century to the next.

Tradition was about to be broken, however, as in the early nineteenth century De la Fontaine produced his verse adaptions of the fables and used Grandville as his illustrator. His artwork introduced new compositional angles, different moments on which to focus, humour and fascinating detail. He also introduced the notion of dressing animals in human clothes in some of his illustrations, the more to drive home the point that fables are really about humans and their behaviour. In his illustrations for two fables that we have already discussed, he has the crow with cheese in her mouth wearing a pair of glasses; the dog who peers mournfully into the water after he has dropped his meat is similarly bespectacled. In this illustration, Grandville is brave enough to select the scene after the meat has gone; the water streaming from the dog's head tells us that his efforts to retrieve it have been in vain. Of the nine figures we can see in the background, perhaps the writer/poet striking his brow for inspiration is the most amusing. Another witty and ingenious illustration from Grandville is that which is placed before the fable of The Fox and the Stork. Stork has returned fox's invitation; the meal is formal with the diners seated at a table. A napkin encircles Fox's throat, a servant duck (clothed) brings another pitcher of soup but Fox turns from the table in despair. If we look closely, we can see the tablecloth is decoratively printed with the first episode of this story; we can just make out Fox supping from the bowl, Stork standing forlornly by.

From Grandville onwards, the conservative, imitative illustration becomes unfashionable. Griset has a dry, even biting, sense of humour and his detail, of numerous bottled specimens in Crane's surgery, of skeletons hanging amid cobwebs from the ceiling and of Crane's immense importance (fantastically frilled shirt) as he peers through his spectacles at the wolf in his agony, has a powerful effect on the reader.

Bennett's Aesop (1857) has an adult, sharp edge, his animals frequently dressed in the height of Victorian fashion to underline the follies and frailties of humankind. Caldecott (1883) produced two illustrations for each fable: one a straightforward animal illustration, the second a 'modern instance'. For example, to interpret the moral 'beware of those who advise what is to their own advantage', he has not only the fox who has lost a tail persuading other foxes of the benefits of being tailless but also a sketch of an old maid telling three young ladies how ridiculous and unnecessary husbands are.

Winter's *Aesop for Children* (1919) also achieves humour through additional anthropomorphic detail. In *Belling the Cat* the mice meet to find a solution to their problem with a cat who is decimating their numbers. A suggestion is made that a bell be put around the cat's neck so that the mice can hear him coming. A wise old mouse asks who will carry out this task. Winter's image is of group of mice, with the elderly mouse distinguished by a red kerchief round his neck, his braces, his slippers half off, his walking stick and his stool all bespeaking his venerable status. The cat is glimpsed half-concealed in the background as she eavesdrops on their plans. Winter's pictures are very cleanly and precisely composed. In another fable, for instance, one can see a drip falling from the fox's watering mouth as he looks up at the crow with the cheese in her beak.

Recent masterpieces of the genre include Smith and Scieszka's (1998) post-modern parody, *Squids Will Be Squids*, with its 'Fresh Morals, Beastly Fables' where homage is paid to Aesop (and Bewick) in the frontispiece and end-papers. Helen Ward, in her sumptuous twenty-first century Aesop, departs completely from any conventional image for the fable of The Fox and the Stork and paints fox wandering amongst a plethora of elaborately decorated pitchers, all of which, we imagine, are emitting a tantalising smell of soup to the fox whose nose tilts longingly up. Stork meanwhile stalks smugly through her fine collection. Ward uses this image for the cover of her book also.

Conclusion

It is hard to imagine a history of children's literature or, indeed, literature generally as Aesop was never intended only for children, had Aesop's fables not been collected so many years ago and had they not been so attractive for artists to illustrate and printers to print. So much that had been produced for children until the mid-nineteenth century had not been very accessible nor much fun, so that to have Aesop must have brought joy to centuries of children. Because the morals which accompany Aesop's stories are generally acceptable to all religious persuasions, the fables never lost their currency and appeal as popular reading material. The fact that versions of Aesop were read in schools (Latin, Greek, French as well as English) and that they could be illustrated, albeit with no great flair, meant that not only the rich could access the texts. It is pleasing to think of generations of schoolchildren poring over the simple woodcuts in their school Aesops. Artistry and imagination are found at their best, however, in editions not for school use, but in the work of some of the illustrators mentioned above and in the work of countless others whom there is no room to mention. They are all part of a long tradition of those who have supported children by lifting words off the page and giving them images to live by. Undoubtedly this fine tradition will continue.

Bibliography

Anno, M (1989) *Anno's Aesop*. London: Reinhardt Books in association with Viking

Barlow, F (texts by Philipott, T and Codrington, R) (1666) *Aesop's Fables with his Life*. London: William Godbid for Francis Barlow

Bennett, C H (1857) *The Fables of Aesop and Others, Translated into Human Nature*. London: W. Kent and Co

Bewick, T (1818) *The Fables of Aesop and Others*. Newcastle: E Walker, for T. Bewick and Son

Billinghurst, P (1899) *A Hundred Fables of Aesop*. London: John Lane, The Bodley Head

Caldecott, R (1883) *Some of Aesop's Fables with Modern Instances*. London: Macmillan and Co

Caxton, W (1484) *Fables of Esope*. London: Caxton

Cleyn, F (1665) in Ogilby, John *Fables of Aesop paraphras'd in Verse*. London: T J Roycroft

Comenius, JA (1658) *Orbis Sensualium Pictus*. Nuremberg: Endteri

Crane, W (1887) *The Baby's Own Aesop, Being the Fables Condensed in Rhyme*. London: George Routledge and Sons

del Tuppo, F (1485) *The Moralized Aesop: Life, Fables*. Naples: del Tuppo

Gheeraerts, M (1567) in de Dene *De warachtighe fabulen der dieren*. Bruges: P de Clercq for Marcus Gheeraerts

Gheeraerts, M (1578) in Heynes, Pierre *Esbatement moral des animaux*. Antwerp: G Smits for P Galle

Gheeraerts, M (1578) in Perret, Steven *Fables des animaux*. Antwerp: C Plantin for E. Perret

Grandville, J and de la Fontaine, J (1838) *Fables*. Paris: Perrotin

Griset, E H (1868) *Aesop's Fables*. London: W Thomas

Hayes, B and Ingpen, R (1987) *Folk Tales and Fables of the World*. Buderim, Australia: David Bateman Ltd

Heighway, R in Jacobs, J (1894) *The Fables of Aesop*. London: Macmillan and Co

Locke, J (1693) *Some Thoughts Concerning Education*. London: A and J Churchill

Noble, E (1914) *Aesop's Fables*. London: Raphael Tuck and Sons Ltd

Osius, H (1574) *Phryx Aesopus Habitu Poetico*. Frankfurt: Kilian Han

Oudry, J B (1755) in de la Fontaine, J *Fables Choisies*. Paris: Desaint et Saillant

Passarotti, B (1563) in Faerno, Gabrielle *Fabulae centum*. Rome: Luchinus

Perret, S (1578) *Fables des animaux*. Antwerp: C Plantin for E Perret

Rackham, A in Jones, V S Vernon (1912) *Aesop's Fables*. London: William Heinemann

Robinson, C (1895) in Jerrold, Walter *Aesop's Fables*. London: J M Dent and Sons

Salomon, B (1547) *Les Fables d'Esope Phrygien en Ryme.* Françoise Lyon: Iean de Tournes and Guillaume Gazeau

Smith, L and Scieszka, J (1998) *Squids Will Be Squids*. New York: Viking

Steinhöwel, H (c.1476) *Vita et Fabulae*. Ulm: Johann Zainer

Trery, P (1925). In M Humphrey *Aesop's Fables*. London: Oxford University Press

Ward, H (2004) *Unwitting Wisdom: An Anthology of Aesop's Animal Fables*. Dorking: Templar Publishing

Weir, H (in Townsend, G F) (1867) *Three Hundred Aesop's Fables*. London: George Routledge and Sons

Wildsmith, B (1963) *The Lion and the Rat*. London; Oxford University Press

Winter, M (1919) *The Aesop for Children*. Chicago: Rand McNally and Co

Wormell, C (2005) *Mice, Morals, and Monkey Business*. Philadelphia, Pennsylvania: Running Press Kids

6

Reading Lessons for 'baby grammarians': Lady Ellenor Fenn and the teaching of English grammar

Karlijn Navest

Introduction

In 1872 Sir Bartle Frere reported in his memoir of his uncle John Hookham Frere that 'There are many now living who can recollect receiving their first reading-lessons in *Cobwebs to catch Flies* (Frere, 1872, xv n2). Frere's contemporary Louisa Twining, indeed, recorded in her autobiography that she remembered 'learning to read the then first book of all children, the *Cobwebs to catch Flies* (Twining, 1893, 16). In her memoirs, written between 1845 and 1854, Elizabeth Grant of Rothiemurchus had likewise noted that she and her younger siblings 'had pleasure in reading to ourselves, for even Jane at three years old could read her *Cobwebs*' (Grant, 1911, 31).

Cobwebs to Catch Flies: or, dialogues in short sentences, adapted to children from the age of three to eight years was first published in 1783. It is for this work that the children's writer, educationist and female grammarian Lady Ellenor Fenn (1744-1813) [neé Frere], who wrote under the pseudonyms 'Mrs Lovechild' and 'Mrs Teachwell', is best known today. Fenn's Cobwebs was published in two volumes, which were immensely popular; they continued to be published in Britain and America until the 1870s (Stoker, 2004, 292; see also Stoker, 2007, 825-828). It was influenced by Anna Letitia Barbauld's popular *Lessons for Children*, which had been published five years previously (Todd, 1984, 122-3). In the preface to the first volume, Fenn showed her indebtedness to Barbauld when she stated that there is no need for her to 'blush to supply prattle for infants, since a lady of superior genius condescended long since, to set the example' (Fenn, 1783a, vii; see also Cajka, 2003, 132).

Just like Barbauld, who had written her Lessons for her adopted nephew Charles, Fenn originally wrote *Cobwebs* for her nephew William, whom she and her husband, John Fenn, had adopted in 1778. Fenn even informs her young audience about the origin of the work when she tells her little readers that she sent William:

> to play in the garden, without me, telling him I should be busy. And what do you think I did? I cut out the prints, wrote some stories to suit them, and pasted the prints into my little book. I covered it nicely; and the next morning, when he had done his lesson well, I took it – 'Here, my dear, said I, is a book for you, in which you can read' – I wish you had seen his joy ... he read in it very well – so I hope *you* little ones will do. (Fenn, 1783a, xxiii-xxiv)

The first volume of Cobwebs was aimed at children aged 3 to 5 and contained stories about animals and toys written in words of one, two, three, four, five and six letters. The second volume offered similar stories written in words of one, two, three and four syllables for children aged 5 to 8. It is this volume which is of interest here because it contains a reference to the teaching of English grammar (Percy, 2006, 120). In the dialogue 'The Useful Play', we meet two girls, who are merely called FIRST GIRL and SECOND GIRL. Second girl asks First girl how to teach her younger brother grammar:

> SECOND GIRL. I wish you would teach me some of your sports; then I could teach *Charles*.
>
> FIRST GIRL. Print words on a card; on the back write the part of speech; let it be a sport for him to try if he can find what each is?-let him have the words, and place them so as to make sense. (Fenn, 1783b, 8)

Fenn must have been interested in teaching children 'by way of sport' (Fenn, 1783b, 12); two years after the publication of *Cobwebs*, her publisher John Marshall started to sell her *Set of Toys* which consisted of a *Spelling, Grammar* and *Figure Box* (Stoker, 2007, 828). There is some evidence that the novelist Fanny Burney taught her son, Alex, the alphabet with the help of Fenn's *Spelling Box*, which consisted among other things of 'little alphabets of roman, italic and black letters for spelling out words' (Immel, 1997, 222). In July 1797, Burney wrote a letter to her sister Susanna in which she told her that she had begun teaching the alphabet to Alex, who was only two and a half at the time. She also added that her little son 'has taken the utmost delight in playing with the Letters, placing, bringing and naming them' (Hemlow *et al*, 1973a, 325).

Alex's practice with the *Spelling Box* evidently paid off because a year later Fanny wrote to Susanna that 'every word he heard, of which he either knew or could guess the orthography, he instantly, in a little concise and steady manner, pronounced all the letters of' (Hemlow *et al*, 1973b, 180). To illustrate this she included the following conversation which she overheard between Alex and her 'old friend' William Weller Pepys (Hemlow *et al*, 1973b, 180):

> Mʳ Pepys – You are a fine Boy, indeed!
> Alex. B,O,Y, Boy. – (every Letter articulated with strong, almost heroic emphasis.)
> Mʳ P. And do you run about here in this pleasant place all day long?
> Alex. D,A,Y, day.
> Mʳ. P. And can you read your Book, you sweet little fellow?
> Alex. R,E,A,D, read. &c-&c-. (Hemlow *et al*, 1973b, 181)

In the *Grammar Box*, which was designed for 'rendering the distinction of the parts of speech easy to a child' (Fenn, 1785, 33), one could find 'Twelve Cards, containing a compendious Set of Grammar Lessons, to be learned by Rote in small Portions; designed for little People to study as they walk, and numbered in order as they should be learned' and 'The Parts of Speech, in little Packets' (Immel, 1997, 224). Shefrin points out that even the children of George III might have had access to Fenn's Boxes in the royal nursery. In 1784 Fenn had sent some of her works to the Royal Governess Lady Charlotte Finch and her *Set of Toys* might have been one of them (2003, 56).

Apart from designing a simpler version of the *Grammar Box*, called *Grammatical Amusements in a Box* [1798?] (Immel, 1997, 227; Alston, 1965, 109), Fenn decided to write a series of grammar books in the 1790s. With these books, Fenn offered mothers assistance in the teaching of English grammar, but she did more. In this chapter I will show that Fenn published two other books, called *A Spelling Book* (1787) and *The Infant's Friend* (1797), which aimed to assist mothers in the teaching of grammar alongside teaching their children to read. Questions that will be addressed are the following: was Fenn the first to combine the teaching of reading and grammar? What does Fenn's practice tell us about the age at which children started to be taught grammar in eighteenth-century Britain? Before I focus on Fenn's reading lessons, I provide some information about the teaching of English grammar in eighteenth-century Britain and about the popularity of Fenn's works.

Fenn and the teaching of English grammar
On 1 February 1770, Hester Thrale, an eighteenth-century literary hostess best known as a friend of Dr Johnson's, recorded in her journal that her eldest daughter

> Hester Maria Thrale was four Years and nine Months old when I lay in of Lucy; and then I first began to teach her Grammar shewing her the difference between a Substantive and an Adjective as I lay in Bed; She has made since then a Progress so considerable, that She this Day 1: Feb: 1770 persed [sic] the first Couplet of Pope's Iliad, beginning of her own accord at the Vocative Case. (Hyde, 1977, 34)

Hester Maria, otherwise known as Queeney, a nickname Dr Johnson had given to her, may have been a precocious child (cf Navest, 2003, 1-2; Navest forthc b), but teaching grammar to such young children was not unusual at the time. According to Michael (1970, 550), John Ash wrote a grammar called *Grammatical Institutes* (1760) for his five-year-old daughter, who 'learnt and repeated the whole in a short Time' (Ash, 1766, Advertisement). According to Tieken-Boon van Ostade (2000, 25-26; 2003, 43), Robert Lowth's authoritative *A Short Introduction to English Grammar* (1762), too, was originally begun as a grammar for his son, Thomas Henry, who was about 4 years old at the time. Evidence for this may be found in example sentences in the grammar such as: ''Thomas's book:' that is, 'Thomasis book;' not 'Thomas his book,' as it is commonly supposed' (Lowth, 1762, 26).

Many ladies, however, viewed the teaching of grammar 'as an arduous undertaking', and were 'fearful of engaging in it' (Fenn, 1798c, v; Percy, 2006, 116-120). One example of such a mother is Georgiana Duchess of Devonshire, who was about to teach her five-year-old daughter 'little G' the rudiments of English grammar, when she wrote the following to her mother in September 1788: 'Tomorrow I shall write you my idea of grammar, and what each part of speech is, that I may see if I am fit to instruct my G. I am asham'd of my own ignorance but I must learn for and with her' (Bessborough, 1955, 134).

In order to help women such as Georgiana, Fenn decided to write a series of grammar books in the 1790s specifically designed for their needs. Of these books, *The Child's Grammar: designed to enable ladies who may not have attended to the subject themselves to instruct their children* (1798a) sold best, and according to Alston (1965, 105) 26 numbered editions of 'the popular little grammar' (its size is only 7.5 by 12.5 cms) were published until 1820. In 1800 *The Child's Grammar* was one of the tiny books issued in John Marshall's *Juvenile, or Child's Library* (Alderson, 1983, 13; Laws, 2002). The Child's Grammar could still be purchased after Fenn's death, as was shown by the bookseller John Harris who in 1816 advertised the grammar as follows: 'This is certainly the best introduction to English grammar ever printed; and, as proof of its excellence, the publisher can assure the public that ten thousands are sold annually' (St John *et al*, 1975, 117). By about 1830, 200,000 copies of *The Child's Grammar* had been sold, and there is an advertisement for the 50th edition in Morell's Essentials published in 1876 (Michael, 1987, 453). Fenn's sequel to *The Child's Grammar, The Mother's Grammar* (1798b) was also a great success. Alston (1965, 104) records 21 numbered editions of the grammar until 1820. Despite the fact that it enabled mothers to teach grammar 'to the female part of their family' and to instruct 'their little sons before they go to school' (Fenn, 1798c, iv), *The Mother's Grammar* was not really a children's grammar but, as the title suggests, a grammar specifically designed for mothers. Thus, in *Parsing Lessons for Elder Pupils* (1798d) Fenn advised mothers who had not had the opportunity of studying grammar themselves 'to read over, carefully, the Mother's Grammar, whilst their Pupils are going through the Child's' (Fenn, 1798d, ix). Fenn's *Mother's Grammar*, according to Cajka, thus gave ladies the 'opportunity to study grammar on their own, saving them from the potential shame and embarrassment of buying, using, or even being discovered studying a book at a child's level of learning' (2003, 169).

Reading lessons for 'baby grammarians'

Fenn's series of grammar books, her *Grammar Box* and the accompanying book to her *Set of Toys, The Art of Teaching in Sport* (1785), were not the only works which assisted mothers in the teaching of grammar. Apart from alphabets, monosyllables and words of two or more syllables, Fenn's *Spelling Book* (1787) contained 'A Course of easy Reading Lessons for young Children; beginning with single Words of three Letters, and advancing gradually to Sentences of six or seven Words' (Fenn, 1787, iii). However, these reading lessons could also be used by mothers for teaching grammar: 'The columns of words arranged in sets of nouns, adjectives, verbs, &c. are further designed to be of use to young grammarians; and to assist youthful mothers in teaching the rudiments of grammar' (Fenn, 1787, x). The first reading lesson in Fenn's *Spelling Book* consists of nouns, beginning with words of three letters such as

Man	boy	**Ann**	Tom	Job	Sam
ape	**bat**	bee	hen	kid	hog

(Fenn, 1787, 109; emphasis added)

In the second reading lesson there are sets of adjectives like:

hot	low	**new**	odd	old	raw
red	sad	six	two	wet	bad

(Fenn, 1787, 109)

Because the words in Fenn's *Spelling Book* were 'arranged under their respective denominations of nouns, adjective and verbs' (Fenn, 1809, 17) ladies could easily test their children's grammatical knowledge. According to Fenn, the only thing a mother had to do was to 'enquire, what is *Ann*? what is *bat*? what is *new*?' (Fenn, 1809, 18) (see the quotation above). In order to provide mothers with an idea how they could combine the reading lessons of nouns and verbs, Fenn included the following dialogue:

> *M.* What do we *do* with a drum?
>
> *C.* We beat it
>
> *M. Beat* then is something which we do; so it is – what?
>
> *C.* Is it a verb, mamma?
>
> *M.* Look in page 114 [where one can find a list of 70 verbs] and inform yourself.
>
> 'Oh yes!' (cries the happy child) 'it is the first word among the verbs.'
>
> (Fenn, 1787, x-xi)

Beat is indeed the first word mentioned in lesson VI which includes a list of 70 verbs. Apart from *drum*, lesson IV lists 65 other nouns which can similarly be linked to the verbs that can be found in lessons VI and IX of the *Spelling Book*. Following the above-mentioned example a mother could ask similar questions such as *What do we do with a book?*, *What do we do with a dice?* Her child will then answer *We* read *it*, *We* throw *it* and he or she will be able to find these verbs on pages 114 and 116 of the *Spelling Book*.

In addition to the above-mentioned lessons on nouns, adjectives and verbs, Fenn also included lessons of more than one word in her *Spelling Book*, such as Lesson XIII and Lesson XIV:

Article.	Adjective.	Noun.
a	neat	doll
a	sweet	plum
a	**ripe**	grape
a	clean	**frock**

(Fenn, 1787, 120)

Noun.	Verb.	Adjective.
mice	are	shy
flies	are	**brisk**
crows	are	black
swans	are	white

(Fenn, 1787, 120)

According to Fenn, the advantage of these lessons is that they

> will enable the teacher, as she sits at her needle, to examine the progress of elder children, and *that* even without the knowledge of grammar herself; it is only to break

the sentences, and ask;'What part of speech is *ripe*? – what is *frock*? – what is *brisk*?' (Fenn, 1787, x).

In her *Spelling Book* Fenn also provided mothers with the definitions of a noun, adjective, verb and pronoun. Although she did not define the article and the preposition, these parts of speech were included in her reading lessons. This is the reason why in Lesson XVIII we encounter sentences such as: 'birds fly through the air', 'fish swim in the water' and 'moles live under the ground' (Fenn, 1787, 124). While describing an adjective Fenn makes a clear distinction between young children and older ones, just as she did in her grammar books (cf Navest, 2008). Rightly conjecturing that '[an] Adjective is not very intelligible to a very young child', Fenn informed mothers that young children had better learn this definition by heart. In the case of older children, Fenn told mothers that they needed to point out to them 'that an adjective has in itself no meaning; for instance, *red, pretty, neat, kind, fond, dutiful*, these have no meaning alone; a *red*, a *pretty*, give you no idea; but add the noun to which one of these adjectives belongs, and the sentence is intelligible; as a red *knot*, a pretty *doll* ...' (Fenn, 1787, 112). Fenn also made such a distinction while describing the verb:

> WHATEVER you *do* is a verb. This is easily exemplified to the little one. For elder children, amusive and instructive sports may be found, by asking,-'what does the dog do?' '*Bark, growl.*' (Fenn, 1787, 113)

The sentence 'Dogs bark' (Fenn, 1787, 117) can be found in lesson XI of Fenn's *Spelling Book*. In this lesson mothers could find inspiration for similar questions. Examples that are given here are:

Noun.	Verb
cats	mew
hens	cluck
owls	hoot
lambs	bleat
bees	hum
ducks	quack

(Fenn, 1787, 117).

In this same lesson Fenn also explained the use of the pronoun. She advised mothers to tell their children that

> Sometimes *instead* of a *noun,* we use a pronoun before a verb; as if I ask, 'What sound does the dog make?' and you answer – '*He* barks.' -'What does the cat do?' – '*She* mews.' What do *Owls*? '*They* hoot.' (Fenn, 1787, 117)

By studying the sentences in lesson XI mothers could ask their young ones similar questions like *What sound does the hen make?* and *What do bees?* and the answer of the children would then be *She clucks* and *They hum*. Finally, it is worth mentioning that Fenn did not include any cuts in her *Spelling Book* because she wanted to avoid, as she puts it, 'drawing little eyes aside' (Fenn, 1787, ix). Instead, she advocated the use of 'cuts of objects, whose names the child had been reading'. According to Fenn, these sets of cuts, could be purchased from John Marshall 'The Child's Printer, in London' (Fenn, 1787, 113).

Despite the fact that *The Infant's Friend – Part I* was a spelling-book, and that the second volume consisted of reading lessons, both books could be used for the teaching of grammar (Fenn, 1798c, x-xi). Apart from the obvious alphabets of roman and italic letters, the first volume of *The Infant's Friend* contains 26 pages with sets of monosyllables. Examples of such sets are:

wage bake cake lake make

dice lice mice nice rice vice

word world work worse worm

house louse mouse rouse ounce

squeeze cheese geese fleece sleeve

(Fenn, 1797a, 19; 20; 26; 31)

According to Fenn, these monosyllabic words which were placed in sets so 'as to make the acquisition as easy as possible by paying attention to the sound in the first word of that set' (Fenn, 1797a, ix) could also be used for the teaching of English grammar because they gave elder children the opportunity of picking out nouns, adjectives and verbs (Fenn, 1797a, vi; ix).

The so-called 'short sentences' (eg *good boys, tall girls, nice cake, a mouse is brisk, babes cry, the dog has claws, the cat loves fish*), in *The Infant's Friend-Part II*, similarly assisted 'young Mothers in their attempts to instil early the rudiments of grammar' (Fenn, 1797b, 5;7; Fenn, 1799a, 63). Whereas the short sentences served as 'easy Parsing Lessons' for young grammarians, mothers could use the reading lessons in this volume as parsing lessons for elder children who were already more advanced in grammar (Fenn, 1798c, xi). As we might expect by now, the majority of these reading lessons are about animals, but there are also lessons that deal with dolls and toys.

The *Spelling Book* and the two volumes of *The Infant's Friend* thus enabled mothers to teach their elder children grammar with the same book with which they were instructing their younger ones to read. In the second volume of the *Infant's Friend*, however, it seems that Fenn is advising mothers to teach young children grammar as soon as possible since this would have its effect by the time they were ready to read long sentences:

> In longer sentences ... [the child] must read slowly and deliberately, observing carefully every stop, and every emphatical word; must slide over insignificant words, such as *so, or, and, if, but,* &c. &c. and reserve the stress of his voice for words of more importance. – In this, a knowledge of Grammar is of great use (Fenn, 1797b, x).

Fenn thus believed that while teaching their children to read it was essential for mothers to remark 'that the *Noun* is the word of consequence; upon *that* the emphasis should be laid. – "What did you see?" – "I saw a *cart.*" – "Was it empty?" – "No; it was full of *lambs.*"'(Fenn, 1797b, iv-v)

As for the question whether Fenn was the first to combine the teaching of reading and grammar, I have so far not come across a spelling or reading-book which looked like those of Fenn. There were, however, spelling-books published before hers that contained an English grammar, such as Thomas Dilworth's *A New Guide to the English Tongue* (1740). Dilworth's spelling-book includes a 'Practical English grammar', written in the form of question and answer, a common approach at the time:

> Q. *What is a Noun* Substantive?
>
> A. A Noun *Substantive* is the Name of any Being or Thing, perceivable either by the Senses, or the Understanding; as a *Horse*, a *Book.* (Dilworth, 1751 [1740], 97)

Dilworth's spelling-book was highly popular and continued to be published until 1822 (Alston, 1967, 87). We know that Fenn was familiar with Dilworth's spelling-book because she referred to it in *The Art of Teaching in Sport* (1785):

> When the little learner is perfectly acquainted with all these sheets [of syllables], then recourse may be had to the copious collection of monosyllables in *Dilworth's* Spelling Book; whence an elder child can dictate. (Fenn, 1785, 26)

But unlike Fenn, Dilworth does not state whether his 'copious collection of monosyllables' (Dilworth, 1785, 26) could be used for teaching grammar as well. In her *Spelling Book* Fenn referred to Sarah Trimmer's *Little Spelling Book for Young Children* (1787), which just like her own work, was 'written with the same benevolent intention of smoothing the path of infancy' (Fenn, 1787, xv). Though Trimmer's spelling-book was aimed at the same audience as that of Fenn's, the work was not designed to combine the teaching of reading and grammar. Interestingly, in her spelling-book Trimmer did refer to Fenn's *Set of Toys* and described the hero of her work as engaged in playing with Fenn's 'nice box of Letters and Pictures (Trimmer, 1791 [1787], vi; 23). This quotation does suggest that when it came to teaching grammar Trimmer regarded Fenn as the authority. That Fenn remained an authority even in the nineteenth century is shown by the following reference to her works in *Short and Easy Rules for Attaining a Knowledge of English Grammar* (1800), one of the nine volumes in the miniature library *The Book-Case of Knowledge or Library for Youth* which was reprinted in 1801, 1803 and 1813 (Alderson, 1983, 19; Alston, 1965, 108):

> Thus much we have introduced for our grammatical department. More copious information may be obtained by consulting the little works of the ingenious and philanthropic LADY FENN; we mean the little grammars and lessons which she has with so much care compiled for the instruction of the rising generation. (Anon, 1800, 33)

Conclusion

In this chapter I have tried to show that, apart from her popular series of grammar books, Fenn's *Spelling Book* and her *Infant's Friend* could be used by mothers for teaching the first rudiments of grammar to their children. Since they do not list all the parts of speech, I believe that these works form a separate category of grammar. They are similar to the small grammar that can be found in Fenn's *Art of Teaching in Sport*. In this grammar, which she described as a grammar 'for babies' (Fenn, 1785, 40), Fenn only gave the definition of five parts of speech (ie noun, adjective, pronoun, verb and article). The reading lessons for 'baby grammarians' (Fenn, 1809, 21) in the *Spelling Book* and *The Infant's Friend* thus prepared children for Fenn's other works on grammar which, unlike her 'baby' grammars, all included ten parts of speech.

In the preface to her *Parsing Lessons for Young Children* (1798c) Fenn noted that 'Men of learning are incapable of stooping sufficiently low to conduct those who are but entering the paths' (Fenn, 1798c, vi). This appears to be a direct reference to Lowth's grammar, which, though originally written for his little son, reads more like a scholarly treatise, and this is also how it was received at the time (Tieken-Boon van Ostade, 2003, 43; forthc; Percy, 1997, 131). In *The Child's Grammar*, which she had offered as an introduction to Lowth's, Fenn added that 'his Lordship's Commentary might render it intelligible to those of his own family; but for general and public Use there is certainly Need of an Introduction to it' (Fenn, 1798a, vi). Although Ash understood much better than Lowth what it took to write a children's grammar (Tieken-Boon van Ostade, 2003, 43), it was not at home but in schools that his grammar was mostly used, as appears from a comment by the grammarian J.G. in his *Easy Introduction to the English Language* (1796). J.G. notes that Ash's grammar 'has been more frequently used in Schools, both in London and the Country, than almost any other' (J.G. 1796, 118; Navest in prep).

Unlike the grammars of Lowth and Ash, Fenn's grammars were specifically designed for mothers who were educating their young children at home. That this was common at the time was made clear by James Fordyce in his *Sermons to Young Women* (1765) where he quotes 'the words of an old writer' who had stated that '[a]ll mankind is the pupil and disciple of female institution; the daughters till they write women, and the sons till the first seven years be past' (Fordyce, 1766[1765], 26). Fenn indeed hoped that by having studied her series of grammar books 'a little Boy may derive great comfort at his entrance upon school from having learned in a chearful manner the rudiments of grammar to which he might conceive disgust, if he had at once the double difficulty of a new language [ie Latin] and a new study' (Fenn, 1799a, 59). In the case of little girls she believed that the teaching of English grammar could provide them with a basis for learning French (Smith, 1996, 212; see also Percy, 1996, 137). Since in Georgian Britain boys went to school when they were between 5 and 9 years of age (Earle, 1989, 238; Martin, 2004, 246), Fenn's grammar books and reading lessons must have been aimed at children aged 3 to 8 ('baby grammarians' indeed (and in these works she saw it as her task 'to conduct young Students, till a Superior shall deign to take them by the hand (Fenn, 1798c, ix).

Note

The research for this chapter was carried out in the context of the NWO research project *The Codifiers and the English Language: Tracing the Norms of Standard English.*

Bibliography

Alderson, B (1983) Miniature libraries for the young. *The Private Library* 6(1), 3-38

Alston, R C (1965) *A Bibliography of the English Language from the Invention of Printing to the Year 1800.* Vol. 1. English grammars written in English. Leeds: E.J. Arnold and Son

Alston, RC (1967) *A Bibliography of the English Language from the Invention of Printing to the Year 1800.* Vol. 4. *Spelling books.* Leeds: E.J. Arnold and Son

Anon (1800) *Short and Easy Rules for Attaining a Knowledge of English Grammar.* London: printed by T. Gillet for John Wallis

Ash, J (1760) *Grammatical Institutes: or grammar, adapted to the genius of the English tongue.* Worcester: R. Lewis

Ash, J (1766) *The Easiest Introduction to Dr. Lowth's English Grammar: designed for the use of children under ten years of age, to lead them into a clear knowledge of the first principles of the English language.* London: printed for E. and C. Dilly

Barbauld, A L (1778-9) *Lessons for Children.* 4 vols. London: printed for J. Johnson

Bessborough, The Earl of (1955) *Georgiana: Extracts from the correspondence of Georgiana Duchess of Devonshire.* London: John Murray

Cajka, K (2003) The forgotten women grammarians of eighteenth-century England. Unpublished PhD thesis, University of Connecticut

Dilworth, T (1740 [1751]) *A New Guide to the English Tongue*. London: printed and sold by Henry Kent

Earle, P (1989) *The Making of the English Middle Class: business, society and family life in London 1660-1730*. London: Methuen

Fenn, J (1782) Memoirs of the life of John Fenn Esqr. M.A. F.A.S. &c. including some short notices of his friends and contemporaries. MS. Norfolk Record Office, SO 50/4/13

Fenn, Lady E (1783a) *Cobwebs to Catch Flies: or, dialogues in short sentences, adapted to children from the age of three to eight years*. Vol. I. London: printed and sold by J. Marshall

Fenn, Lady E (1783b) *Cobwebs to Catch Flies: or, dialogues in short sentences, adapted to children from the age of three to eight years*. Vol. II. London: printed and sold by J. Marshall

Fenn, Lady E (1785) *The Art of Teaching in Sport: designed as a prelude to a set of toys, for enabling ladies to instill the rudiments of spelling, reading, grammar, and arithmetic, under the idea of amusement*. London: printed and sold by J. Marshall

Fenn, Lady E (1787) *A Spelling Book: designed to render the acquisition of the first rudiments of our native language easy and pleasant*. London: printed and sold by J. Marshall

Fenn, Lady E (1797a) *The Infant's Friend – Part I. – A Spelling Book*. London: printed for E. Newbery

Fenn, Lady E (1797b) *The Infant's Friend – Part II. – Reading Lessons*. London: printed for E. Newbery

Fenn, Lady E (1798a) *The Child's Grammar: designed to enable ladies who may not have attended to the subject themselves to instruct their children*. London: printed by and sold by John Marshall

Fenn, Lady E (1798b) *The Mother's Grammar: being a continuation of the child's grammar*. London: printed for E. Newbery

Fenn, Lady E (1798c) *Parsing Lessons for Young Children*. London: printed for E. Newbery

Fenn, Lady E (1798d) *Parsing Lessons for Elder Pupils*. London: printed for E. Newbery

Fenn, Lady E (1799a) *The Friend of Mothers: designed to assist them in their attempts to instil the rudiments of language and arithmetic, at an early age, and in a manner agreeable to their children*. London: printed for E. Newbery

Fenn, Lady E (1809) *The Teacher's Assistant in the Art of Teaching Grammar in Sport: designed to render the subject familiar to children*. London: printed for J. Harris

Fordyce, J (1766 [1765]) *Sermons to Young Women*. Vol 1. London: printed for D. Payne

Frere, Sir H B E (ed) (1872) *The Works of the Right Honourable John Hookham Frere in Verse and Prose*. Vol. 1. London: Pickering

G, J (1796) *An Easy Introduction to the English Language*. Bristol: printed for the author

Grant, E (1911) *Memoirs of a Highland Lady: the autobiography of Elizabeth Grant of Rothiemurchus*. London: John Murray

Hemlow, J *et al* (1973a) *The Journals and Letters of Fanny Burney (Madame d'Arblay)*. Vol. III. Great Bookham 1793-1797. Oxford: Clarendon Press

Hemlow, J *et al* (1973b) *The Journals and Letters of Fanny Burney (Madame d'Arblay)*. Vol. IV. West Humble 1797-1801. Oxford: Clarendon Press

Hyde, M (1977) *The Thrales of Streatham Park*. Cambridge, Mass. and London: Harvard University Press

Immel, A (1997) 'Mistress of Infantine Language': Lady Ellenor Fenn, her *Set of Toys* and the 'Education of Each Moment'. *Children's Literature* 25, 214-228

Laws, E (2002) Miniature libraries from the children's books collection, National Art Library, 20 May-17 November 2002 http://www.vam.ac.uk/vastatic/wid/exhibits/miniaturelibraries/itemsondisplay.html

Lowth, R (1762) *A Short Introduction to English Grammar*. London: printed by J. Hughs for A. Millar, and for R. and J. Dodsley

Martin, J (2004) *Wives and Daughters: women and children in the Georgian country house*. London: Hambledon and London

McCarthy, W (1999) Mother of all discourses: Anna Barbauld's *Lessons for Children*. Princeton University Library Chronicle LX(2), 196-219

Michael, I (1970) *English Grammatical Categories and the Tradition to 1800*. Cambridge: Cambridge University Press

Michael, I (1987) *The Teaching of English, from the Sixteenth Century to 1870*. Cambridge: Cambridge University Press

Navest, K (2003) Epistolary formulas in Queeney Thrale's letters. Unpublished MA thesis, University of Leiden

Navest, K (2008) 'Borrowing a few passages': Lady Ellenor Fenn and her use of sources. In Ingrid Tieken-Boon van Ostade (ed) *Grammars, Grammarians, and Grammar-Writing in Eighteenth-Century England*. Berlin/New York: Mouton de Gruyter

Navest, K (forthc b) Queeney Thrale and the teaching of English grammar. In R Hickey (ed) *Ideology and Change in Late Modern English*. Cambridge: Cambridge University Press

Navest, K (in prep) John Ash and the rise of the children's grammar. PhD thesis, University of Leiden

Percy, C (1996) Paradigms for their Sex? Women's grammars in late eighteenth-century England. *Histoire, épistémologie, langage* 16, 121-141

Percy, C (1997) Paradigms lost: Bishop Lowth and the 'poetic dialect' in his English grammar. *Neophilologus* 81, 129-144

Percy, C (2006) Disciplining women? Grammar, gender, and leisure in the works of Ellenor Fenn (1743-1813). *Historiographia Linguistica* 33, 109-137

Shefrin, J (2003) *Such Constant Affectionate Care: Lady Charlotte Finch, royal governess and the children of George III*. Los Angeles: Cotsen Occasional Press

Smith, R D (1996) Language for everyone: eighteenth-century grammarians, Elstob, Fisher and beyond. In D Cram, A Linn and E Nowak (eds) *History of Linguistics* 1996. Vol. 2: From classical to contemporary linguistics. Amsterdam/Philadelphia: John Benjamins

St John, J, Edgar, O and Dana, T (1975) *The Osborne Collection of Early Children's Books: a catalogue prepared at boys and girls house by Judith St. John*. Vol. II. Toronto: Toronto Public Library

Stoker, D (2004) Fenn, Ellenor (1744-1813). In HCG Matthew and B Harrison (eds) *Oxford Dictionary of National Biography*. Vol. 19. Oxford: Oxford University Press

Stoker, D (2007) Ellenor Fenn as 'Mrs. Teachwell' and 'Mrs. Lovechild': a pioneer late eighteenth-century children's writer, educator, and philanthropist. *Princeton University Library Chronicle* 68(3), 817-850

Tieken-Boon van Ostade, I (2000) Robert Dodsley and the genesis of Lowth's Short Introduction to English Grammar. *Historiographia Linguistica* 27, 21-36

Tieken-Boon van Ostade, I (2003) Tom's grammar: the genesis of Lowth's Short Introduction to English Grammar revisited. In F Austen and C Stray (eds) *The Teaching of English in the Eighteenth and Nineteenth Centuries. Essays for Ian Michael on his 88th birthday. Special issue of Paradigm* 2(7), 36-45

Tieken-Boon van Ostade, I (forthc) Age and the codification of the English language. In A Duszak and U Okulska (eds) *Crossing Age in Language and Culture*.

Todd, J (ed) (1984) *A Dictionary of British and American Women Writers 1600-1800.* London: Methuen

Trimmer, S (1791 [1787]) *The Little Spelling Book for Young Children.* London: printed for Joseph Johnson

Twining, L (1893) *Recollections of Life and Work: being the autobiography of Louisa Twining.* London: E. Arnold

7

The Kildare Place Society:
an influential force in 19th century
Irish education

Valerie Coghlan and Geraldine O'Connor

Mystery surrounds the origin of two pictorial rolls which were found in the archives of The Kildare Place Society. They contain intriguing images and text for teaching young children, but there is no record of how they came to be there although the records of the Society are in general meticulously recorded.

The Society for Promoting the Education of the Poor in Ireland, later popularly known as the Kildare Place Society (KPS) in recognition of the location of its headquarters in Kildare Place in central Dublin (Parkes, 1984), was founded in 1811 by a group of philanthropically inclined professional and business gentlemen. The names of the founder members of the Society reflected many Dublin businesses of the day: Guinness, Bewley, La Touch and others. A number of those present at the early meetings were Quakers, members of the Society of Friends, which may have been a factor in the KPS's determination to offer non-denominational education to the poor. In this, the Society was in accord with a government commission on education in 1806, and it received government support from 1816; indeed, the work of the Society pre-dated the national and state-sponsored primary school system which was introduced in Ireland in 1831.

The KPS, during its relatively short existence, developed an extensive publishing programme. One of the influences on its publications was the London firm of William Darton, the connection perhaps being that the Dartons were also Quakers. Following the establishment of the Society's publishing programme, the Society's archives show that J.J. Monk Mason, a committee member of the KPS, visited Dartons at Holborn Hill in London for information and advice about publishing for schools. It is possible that Monk Mason in addition returned with information about certain fascinating scrolls, known as the Darton rolls, and 'The Rudiment Box' in which it seems they were displayed.

The present KPS archive largely consists of materials stored in the basement of the college that evolved after the demise of the KPS, the Church of Ireland Teacher Training College. When in 1969 the college moved to the Dublin suburb of Rathmines, the material was brought there, and is now part of the archives of the Church of Ireland College of Education, as the Teacher Training College is now called. Although the KPS section of the college archives contains extensive information relating to the training course undertaken by the students who attended the college in Kildare Place, as well as detailed records of correspondence between schools supported by the KPS, and equally minutely recorded accounts of the Society's publications, there is no mention of the rolls, nor of the Rudiment Box. The contrast between the careful recording of so much of the Society's business and the lack of information related to the 'Darton rolls' forms the basis of this essay.

Ireland and education

By the nineteenth century, Ireland had established a long and respectable tradition in education. The secular and exclusive bardic schools of ancient Gaelic Ireland had educated poets, chroniclers and judges through the medium of Irish. Irish monastic schools by the sixth century attracted students from Western Europe and Britain as well as from Ireland. Evidence suggests that by the fourteenth and fifteenth centuries such schools were educating at least some students other than those bound for the religious life. As well as the existence of a strong indigenous education tradition, from Tudor times Ireland experienced state intervention in schooling which had a very definite political purpose. At its root was the desire to foster a loyal Anglicised population in a country which was hostile to the force of English law. An act of 1537, for instance, promoted the teaching of the English language and under Elizabeth 1 attempts were made to set up free diocesan schools to promote the Protestant faith, where the teacher was to be an Englishman, or of English birth. During the reign of the Stuarts and after the Plantation of Ulster in the early 1600s some grammar schools and royal schools were established with the same purpose but these had a very limited influence on the majority of the population. By the eighteenth century many voluntary Protestant religious societies had became involved in education in Ireland. Most placed an emphasis on proselytising and some received grants from public funds (Dowling, 1968, 15, 26, 27).

Establishing the Kildare Place Society

By the early nineteenth century there were a variety of schools in Ireland, most of which were run without state support. It is calculated that in 1824 about 11,000 schools existed with a total of about half a million children and 12,000 teachers within them. Of these, the largest category, with about 9,000 schools, were private and native pay schools known as hedge schools (Coolahan, 1981, 9-10). Hedge schools had their origin in the late seventeenth century when the education of Irish Catholics at home and abroad was proscribed under penal laws. Later, in the nineteenth century, Catholic religious orders began to set up schools. Despite these varied endeavours, by the early nineteenth century schooling for many in Ireland was irregular and some parts of Ireland lacked schools of any kind (Moore, 1904, 59). This lack of free schools for the poor and the proselytising nature of others prompted the foundation of the KPS.

The guiding principle of the KPS was to distinguish between secular and religious instruction in its schools. This, and the Society's successes in providing a highly regarded system of education, paved the way in 1815 for the award of annual government grants. By 1825 this annual grant had reached £25,000, an amount which indicated the degree to which the Society's work was viewed by government as successful (Parkes, 1984, 18). Government aid enabled the Society to fund a model school for teacher training, to grant-aid the construction, outfitting and running of schools, to contribute to teachers' salaries, to publish texts and to organise an inspection system for the schools it supported throughout Ireland. The KPS archives contain letters and reports from these inspectors and record the standard of teaching in their schools. By 1825 the Society supported 1,490 schools containing around 100,000 pupils and had already trained 207 teachers. By 1831, the year in which government grants were withdrawn, the Society was responsible for some 1,621 schools and 137,639 pupils (Moore, 1911, 13). Within these schools *The Bible* was read 'without note or comment' and it was this approach and the lack of alternative state provision of schooling which accounted for the early inter-denominational support received by Kildare Place schools from the general population. Later it became one of the factors which drew on it the disapproval of the Roman Catholic church and which caused the demise of the Society once the national school system was set up in 1831.

Teacher Training

What distinguished the KPS from other education societies in Ireland in the nineteenth century was not only the non-denominational education which it instigated, but also the systematic attention it gave to teacher-training and the publication of educational texts for children. The Society's system of training teachers was largely influenced by the monitorial system developed by Joseph Lancaster who attended the Society's opening meeting on 11 December 1811. Indeed, in response to a request for assistance in setting up a teacher-training scheme from the fledgling organisation, Lancaster persuaded his protégé, John Veevers, to go to Dublin for this purpose in 1813 (Parkes, 1984, 20-21). Under Veever's guidance a system of training was put in place, initially in schools in Dublin's Liberties, then a very poor part of the city. In 1819 a model school consisting of two large schoolrooms, one for boys and one for girls, each holding around 400 pupils, was opened in Kildare Place on land purchased by the KPS with the aid of a government grant. Modest accommodation was also provided for the teachers-in-training, initially all males, who stayed for between four to six weeks before being awarded a certificate of competence to teach.

In 1824 a women's department was opened for the training of schoolmistresses. Much of the professional course they followed was similar to that of the men, but there was also an emphasis on domestic economy, in accord with the Society's aim of promoting practical skills that would encourage good habits in the poor of Ireland (Moore, 1904, 203). Schoolmistresses were expected 'to be capable of instructing in the several kinds of needlework usually taught in female schools' (208). The Society published *Mode of Instructing in Needlework* to indicate the very comprehensive stages of such instruction to be undertaken with pupils, particularly by female monitors within its schools. A needlework specimen book or sampler dated 1831 survives in the archives of the Society and the exquisite work displayed in it demonstrates the serious attention which was given to this subject. Some of those who received training in the Kildare Place model schools were already teaching. Many however were new recruits and taught in new schools founded from 1811 (176-7). Both Protestants and Roman Catholics were called to training and while Bible reading in the evenings was allowed by Veevers, discussion of religion was not (Parkes, 1984, 29).

The Kildare Place Society Publishing Programme

The remarkable publication programme of the KPS and the educational intention of these publications is particularly noteworthy. By 1824 the Society had distributed over one million texts and had printed almost one and a half million more (Hislop, 1997, 109). Many of these books were sold cheaply while others were given free as grants to schools, school libraries and lending libraries. The impetus for this publication drive was two-fold. Firstly, the KPS schools were intended to attract all denominations, and therefore the bible could not be used to teach reading and spelling. There was a lack of doctrinally non-contentious texts as well as affordable books of good quality. Secondly, the Society was aware that texts considered to be 'discreditable' were being read by children for want of any alternative. The final report of the Commissioners of Education in Ireland (1812) had stated as much when it concluded that the inability of the poor to purchase books fit for children left them at the mercy of texts which were likely to corrupt young minds and cause dissension. The report lists racy texts such as *The Pleasant Art of Money Catching, Nocturnal Revels*, and *The Life of Moll Flanders* (Moore, 1904, 215). Many of these texts were used in Irish hedge schools of the day, so altogether the situation made the publication of affordable text books and more general reading books an imperative for the Society.

In 1813 a KPS sub-committee of all denominations was appointed to work on the Society's first publications for schools. These were spelling and reading materials published at first in tablet form. *The Dublin Spelling Book* which resulted from this had a series of progressive spelling lessons, some arithmetic tables as well as reading passages considered to be 'improving extracts'. *The Dublin Reading Book* (1830) which followed had more advanced prose and poetry and was influenced by existing children's texts such as Lindley Murray's reading books. The reading material within the extracts of each publication was carefully scrutinised so that all Christian groups might be satisfied with their content. Both books were stated not to be exclusively for the children of the poorer classes but 'for young persons of every condition' (3). Each book was published first as a series of large wall charts before they became bound books in 1819. Instructions for their use were contained in *The Schoolmaster's Manual*, and *Questions in the Dublin Reading Book with Suitable Answers* published later so that skills of comprehension as well as reading could be developed by the Society's teachers and monitors.

The stated intention of *The Dublin Reading Book* was 'to provide amusement and instruction' and 'to inculcate upon the young reader, a reverence for virtue, as well as the dual sentiments of piety and goodness'. Extracts within it were from writers who were held to be distinguished 'for correct and perspicuous language, and also for the moral tendency of their works' (iv). Stories in it such as 'Dishonesty punished', and 'The advantages of a constant adherence to the truth' show an emphasis on moral education while others such as 'Virtue in Humble Life' and 'No Rank or Possessions can make the Guilty Mind Happy' drew attention to virtuous habits considered to be desirable in various social classes of society, not only the poor. Despite their improving tone, these publications were enormously popular and were produced in quantities of 10,000 to 15,000 per year (Moore, 1904, 222). School texts in areas such as arithmetic and geography were also published accompanied by a series of some thirty maps (225-8).

In 1816 a cheap book department was set up which led to the development of the library readers, or chapbooks, for the society (Hislop, 1997, 100). The secular nature of these texts points to the advantages which the Society found in printing reading material that was popular yet not denominationally controversial. Some texts were editions of popular tales such as *Robinson Crusoe* and travel or natural history books while others were written for the KPS.

Altogether more than eighty library books were published by 1832. By the beginning of 1825 the number published had reached one million in categories such as natural history, voyages and travels as well as some religious and moral texts which were largely illustrations of the scriptures (Moore, 1904, 246; Goldstrom, 1972, 59). Books were published which concerned travel in the Arctic, as well as Europe and Africa. Some, such as *Travels in Africa* (1824) stated to be 'an abridgement of the accounts given by different travellers', had an Irish focus as its fictitious narrator began his tale in Enniscorthy, Co. Wexford. In texts published under the category *Instructions in Arts or Economy*, the advantages to the poor of hard work, sobriety and schooling are emphasised in *Hints to Farmers* and *The School Mistress*. Each year some 60,000 cheap books were produced.

Determined efforts were made to ensure that teachers of the Society used KPS publications; books were sold cheaply or were given free to KPS schools and the Society's training college in Dublin drilled teachers in their use. From 1822 books were also distributed by the Society to individuals or committees willing to establish local lending libraries. These non-school lending libraries numbered 1,100 by 1831. While the number of libraries assisted by the Society is impressive, little is known about how many of the poor actually read the books they contained (Hislop, 1997, 109).

The Darton Rolls
As we have seen, the KPS was often innovative in its approach, and this may be reflected in an interest possibly on a trial basis, in the rolls and the Rudiment Box produced by William Darton. Each roll consists of a strip of calico

wound around wooden rollers at either end. Each has about 25 sheets measuring 47cm by 35cm stuck on to it, and some of these sheets carry the name of William Darton, Holborn Hill, London and are dated in the early 1820s. Both rolls in the KPS archive are broadly similar in content but with a few variations in content. The rolls are hand-coloured and the painting on the Biblical scenes is particularly vivid. It is worth noting that most of the Biblical scenes are in excellent condition – some other parts of the scrolls are quite worn, suggesting that they may have received greater exposure to the light and therefore were used more.

Lawrence Darton, who has written a history of his family company, managed to glean very little information about the rolls or the Rudiment Box, referring to the origins of the rolls as 'something of a mystery'[1]. He recalls in his letter, some time ago being shown 'a wooden box, roughly 18 x 18 inches, with glazed doors front and back through which one could see a series of picture sheets hand-coloured, mounted on a linen roll, rather like an old-fashioned kitchen roller towel. This was a 2-seater model with a different set of prints visible through the back window. The box had on either side a handle rather like an old gramophone handle so that the two sequences of prints could be rotated and viewed separately. The box was, as far as I remember painted grey' (Darton, 2001). This Rudiment Box was in private hands, and a hoped for follow-up meeting with the person who had the box, and the possibility of acquiring it, never materialised.

The letter from Darton goes on to say that the rolls were 'an ingenious way of using up old unsold picture sheets' from the Darton store at a time when they were produced in large quantities. He says that when he was shown the box he 'had little difficulty in assuming that this was something I had only known about from advertisements'. The Rudiment Box, or 'Drawing Room Mine' was advertised in a mid-nineteenth century Darton and Co catalogue for six guineas, and could be obtained in pine or mahogany.

Jill Shefrin, a scholar who is engaged in research into the non-book productions of the Dartons and other contemporaneous companies, also refers to this advertisement, and to another in *Gleanings of Truth* (1842) which offers for sale 'a Rudiment Box in polished mahogany for nine guineas ... In this box is a complete collection of the coloured prints, maps, &c., used in infant schools, and peculiarly adapted to the home education of children of the higher classes' (Shefrin, 2005[2]). She has carried out further investigations into the use of the Rudiment Box in infant schools referred to in her forthcoming book (2009).

Shefrin has also located a Rudiment Box in a private collection in England that also holds a copy of a publication by William Darton and Son, called *Introductory Lectures to the Subjects in the Rudiment-Box at the Liberty Infant School, Cole Alley, Meath Street Dublin* (Shefrin, 2005). There is also a copy of the booklet in the National Library of Ireland. The booklet outlines the purpose and use of the Rudiment Box and the rolls:

> The idea of the Rudiment box was taken from a box called the Excitor, at the Chelsea Infant School; it runs upon rollers, on which are fixed a long piece of calico or linen (ten or twelve yards) on which is posted a succession of pictures and words, and figures, arranged as they are wanted, to convey the system of instruction to the children, beginning with a Scripture series. Each side holds about ten or twelve yards; the opening at each front of the box is sixteen inches by fourteen, and care is taken that the pictures, etc which are provided for it, should each fill the vacant space as they appear, and be placed in view as the lecture belonging to it is read to the children; they will roll backwards and forwards at pleasure, as one roller is always filling when the other is emptying.

The booklet goes on to suggest that the Rudiment Box and rolls are not necessary 'to teach children upon this plan'; instead, the posters may be pasted onto millboard and shown when required, and the booklet provides a brief lesson to accompany each picture.

The 32 page pamphlet, published in 1834, describes the contents of the rolls which were placed in the Rudiment Box, and this corresponds, with only a few differences, to the contents of the two rolls in the KPS archive, which also differ slightly from each other, though both start with biblical scenes. This bears out Lawrence Darton's assertion that the rolls were a means of using up surplus picture sheets produced by William Darton in the 1820s.

Some of the sheets listed in *Introductory Lectures to the Subjects in the Rudiment-Box* are:

- Biblical scenes
- Good Dispositions to be Cultivated and Evil Dispositions to be Avoided
- The Principal Roman Emperors, from Julius Caesar to Justinian
- The British Sovereigns from William the Conqueror to William the Fourth
- Grammar
- The Chain or Combination Table
- Rustic Scenes for Infant Schools – Agriculture
- Costumes of Nations

- Intellectual Sciences
- Geometry for Use of Infant Schools and Nurseries
- A Merchant Ship
- Mariner's Compass

These broadly correspond to the two rolls in the KPS archive. A glance at their content may cause present-day observers to wonder at what children in nineteenth century infant schools were expected to learn. However, an effort to make learning interesting is also noticeable; for example the Grammar sheet contains a rhyme about parts of speech surrounded by a pictorial alphabet, although again one might question the choice of 'Xenophon' to illustrate the letter X. The selection of 'Good Dispositions to be Cultivated and Evil Dispositions to be Avoided' chimes with the didactic intent of the times, and includes 'Obliging', 'Rude', 'Idle', 'Honest', 'Sly' and 'Industrious' among the terms to be sorted under the appropriate heading. A more modern observer might perhaps wonder at the inclusion of 'Passionate' and where it should be placed.

Although the rolls have been found in the archive, there is no sign of the Rudiment Box. From what has been discovered about it, and from what the booklet describes, it seems the box was made of polished wood, or was painted green or grey, and had two hinged doors, each fronted with a glass pane, and the rolls were placed on axles within this and turned by a handle.

The derivation of the Darton Rudiment Box does, however, remain 'something of a mystery', and why two of the rolls which would appear to be from a Rudiment Box ended up in the KPS is also rather strange, given the otherwise extensive documentation of the work of the KPS. It would seem that the Rudiment Box was used, perhaps even pioneered, at the Liberty Infant School in Dublin. There is now no record of this school, and it is not referred to in the KPS archives. That it was likely to have been a school under the management of the Society of Friends does, however, provide a clear link to the KPS, and it is also possible that the KPS had no particular part in bringing the Rudiment Box to Dublin, but that when the school ceased, the rolls were passed to the Kildare Place Training College.

Whatever their origin, the rolls and their Rudiment Box would seem to provide evidence of a desire to engage pupils and to enliven their educational experience. In this day of electronic teaching aids and fast moving images, the Rudiment Box could seem rather tame, but we might imagine the excitement that these 'moving pictures' would have generated in an early to mid-nineteenth century audience, perhaps giving it its alternative name of 'The Excitor'!

Its link with the KPS, however tenuous, does confirm that the Society was recognised as advanced in its programme to educate the poor of Ireland. Although it really only existed for 20 years, the KPS legacy continued and, almost 200 years after its establishment, the effects of many of the educational practices that it introduced to Ireland can still be recognised.

Notes
1 Darton, Lawrence (2001) Letter to Pat Garrett, 19 February
2 Shefrin, Jill (2005) Email to Valerie Coghlan, 14 November

Bibliography
Coolahan, J (1981) *Irish Education: its history and structure.* Dublin: Institute of Public Administration

Darton, Lawrence. Private letter. Lewes: 2001

Dowling, PJ (1968) *The Hedge Schools of Ireland.* Cork: Mercier

Goldstrom, JM (1972) *The Social Content of Education 1808-1870: a study of the working class school reader in England and Ireland.* Shannon: Irish University Press

Hislop, H (1997) Kildare Place Society Chapbooks. *Aspects of Education* 54, 98-117

Introductory Lectures to the Subjects in the Rudiment-Box at the Liberty Infant School, Cole Alley, Meath Street Dublin (1834) London: William Darton and Son (author unknown)

Moore, H K(1904) *An Unwritten Chapter in the History of Education being the history of the Society for the education of the Poor in Ireland, generally known as the KPS 1811-1831.* London: Macmillan

Moore, HK (1911) *The Centenary Book of the Church of Ireland Training College 1811-1911.* Dublin: The Educational Depository Kildare Place

Parkes, SM (1984) *Kildare Place: the History of the Church of Ireland Training College 1811-1969.* Dublin: Church of Ireland College of Education

Shefrin, J (forthc 2009) *The Dartons: Publishers of Educational Aids, Pastimes and Juvenile Ephemera, 1787-1876. A Bibliography and Critical Study. Together with a description of the Darton Archive as held by the Cotsen Children's Library,* Princeton University Library. Princeton: Cotsen Occasional Press

Shefrin, J (forthc 2009) 'Adapted for and Used in Infants' Schools, Nurseries, &c.': Booksellers and the Infant School Market. In M Hilton and J Shefrin (eds) *Educating the Child in Enlightenment Britain: Beliefs, Cultures, Practices.* Aldershot: Ashgate

Archives of the KPS, The Church of Ireland College of Education
These books were all published in Dublin.

The Dublin Spelling Book

The Dublin Reading Book (1830)

Travels in Africa (1824)

The School Mistress or instructions and entertaining conversations between a teacher and her Scholars (1824)

The Schoolmaster's Manual: recommended for the regulation of schools (1825)

Needlework sampler book

8

The Child as Common Reader:
the 'true complexity of reading' and
the progress from hell to paradise

Francesca Orestano

In 1925, in one of her first attempts at defining the nature and aims of a reader who is neither critic nor scholar, but is instead 'uncorrupted by literary prejudices' and deprived of 'all the refinements of subtlety and the dogmatism of learning' (Woolf, 1984, 1), Virginia Woolf focuses on a figure she chooses to define as 'the common reader'. Inspired by Dr Johnson's *Life of Gray*, Woolf decides to address 'the common sense of readers' who are 'hasty, inaccurate, and superficial' and apparently read just for 'affection, laughter, and argument' (*ibid*): thus offering a series of remarks which are ideally suited as an introduction to our investigation.

The child as common reader is indeed naturally uncorrupted by prejudice and dogma and, moreover, endowed with 'an instinct to create' (Woolf, 1984, 1), perhaps as a consequence of literary innocence and the capacity to suspend disbelief which, through the very act of reading, enable the child to become the *cosmoplastes* – the maker of her or his expanding universe. In this respect one may even agree with Rousseau, who stimulates Emile's creativity with the archetypal adventures of Robinson Crusoe – and, conversely, lament Mary Shelley's reading list for her ill-starred creature, a list which encompasses creation and fall by starting with Milton's *Paradise Lost* and ending with Volney's *Les Ruines, ou Méditation sur les Révolutions des Empires*.

With the essays collected as *The Common Reader, Second Series*, Woolf would focus again upon the act of reading, placing at the end of her collection a memorable essay entitled 'How Should One Read a Book?' – emphasis on the question mark. Once more, one is reminded that reading must be untainted by prejudice, that one should 'banish ... all preconceptions': in fact, the only advice Woolf gives to the common reader is 'to take no advice, to follow your own instincts, to use your reason, to come to your own conclusions' (Woolf, 1935, 258). This active, creative, lusty reader might again be a child, insofar as Woolf does not seem to make much of the equipment of learning, whereas she values freedom above habits and notions acquired in adult years. In order that we may keep alive this creative attitude, Woolf suggests that we must never become critics: 'after a lifetime of reading... we must remain readers' (269). In other words, when reading, we must try to stay forever young – forever common – forever children.

There is no doubt that reading is an act conferring power, distinction, and experience upon those who undertake it. Involving hermeneutics as well as a mediated act of perception, or that twofold process which has been often described as having its source and end in the third eye of the reader, reading entails a process – 'the true complexity of reading' (266) – which has been connected, even in these recent years of visual studies, with active creative power: according to Malcolm Bradbury, a selection of great modern writers for a television series would entail in the spectator a visual response much less valuable than that obtained through reading, because 'the viewer ... is a far more passive figure than the reader' (Bradbury, 1989, ix).

Given these terms, one is naturally drawn to search the reasons, no doubt inherent in the child-adult relationship, which prevent these 'common readers' yet uncorrupted by dogmatism and prejudice to enhance their creative powers, to experience at once pleasure and independence. The first part of my essay explores a number of eighteenth century texts which discuss reading lists supposedly fit for the child reader: it highlights those strategies coming from adults, parents, educators who, by means of warnings, cautions, and prohibitions, transform the act of reading of the child, maiming and reducing it, the pleasure of reading being restricted by notions derived from the fields of pedagogy and religious dogma and, above all, from gender assumptions. The first object of this investigation, then, is the nature of the barriers erected between reading and freedom, reading and creativity, reading and power: these fences being not arbitrary, but culturally motivated throughout a wide range of prescriptions and caveats. At times altogether forbidden as unhealthy, reading is enforced at others as a kind of slave labour. In either case, social and ideological pressures transform the act of reading into the problematic experience this paper is going to examine.

The period under consideration is that in which the prevalent educational and pedagogical discourses cut across the expanding territory of children's literature: towards the end of the eighteenth century, the need for educational statements complements the rise of the young customer in a literary market which seems to be already in full sail, as far as children's books are concerned. It is easy to discern that, besides the anxiety they register as they contemplate the exciting new state of affairs, parents and educators tend to underline distinctions directly mirrored by the book market. The list of taboos may vary if the reader is a boy or a girl, but reading is altogether dangerous territory, in some cases described as the easy avenue to hell.

The second part of this chapter explores the changing attitude towards reading expressed by popular Victorian writings: according to many authors working for the Religious Tract Society, reading provides an effective strategy of social and moral rescue, whereby the lost child may progress on her or his way to self-improvement. Class distinctions make for two distinct sets of Victorian readers: there are the Ragged School Children, on the one hand, while on the other there are the Tom Browns and many Little Princesses who are being freely allowed into the garden of reading.

Dangers, vices, temptations and sins connected with reading

In *Thoughts on the Education of Daughters* (1787) Mary Wollstonecraft devotes an entire chapter to 'Reading'. Speaking of young girl readers, Wollstonecraft offers the following prescription: 'a relish for reading ... should be cultivated very early in life' because 'reading is the most rational employment, if people seek food for the understanding' (Wollstonecraft, 1994, 49). Here reading is considered a virtuous activity, good to 'fill the up the time and prevent a young person's being lost in dissipation' (46). But of course, this rational writer and early feminist is speaking of 'judicious books', which 'enlarge the mind and improve the heart'. There are several *caveats*, mainly due to the young age of the reader and her lack of worldly experience: 'Those productions which give a wrong account of human passions, and the various accidents of life, ought not to be read before the judgement is formed, or at least exercised' (50).

For Wollstonecraft, the age and maturity of the reader matter: reading bad books may cause in girls 'affectation', excess of 'sensibility', 'false taste', and may make them 'ridiculous' and prone to prize 'gallantry'. Yet this educator is not keen 'to recommend books of an abstract or grave cast': while on the one hand sentimental novels should not be read by girls, on the other hand Wollstonecraft frankly admits of being 'sick of hearing of the sublimity of Milton, the elegance and harmony of Pope, the original and untaught genius of Shakespear' (50-52).

She tends to solve the problem by recommending some good novel in which the right principles are extolled. As for the Bible, Wollstonecraft issues a severe warning against its use as a book fit for teaching reading skills: 'The Bible should be read with particular respect, and they should not be taught reading by so sacred a book' (53-54). In this respect, she differs from several educators, teachers and parents, who tend to adopt the religious text as the first step on the way to literacy. She concludes her chapter by observing that reading may eventually become a source of pleasure for life, although daughters must be aware that 'no employment of the mind is sufficient excuse for neglecting domestic duties' (56). The pleasure and freedom of the reader are subordinated here to the requirements of female education and the obligation of domestic duties, and a gap obviously opens up between reading for pleasure and the expectations linked to the social and domestic role of women.

Even more clearly, Catharine Macaulay in her *Letters on Education* (1790) warns parents and educators against books that have a negative effect on the minds of children of both sexes. Boys and girls should, in theory, enjoy the same education: 'Confine not the education of your daughters to what is regarded as the ornamental part of it, nor deny the graces from your sons ... Let your children be brought up together (Macaulay, 1994, 50). In spite of this statement, however, the reading list will change with age, and according to sex. In Letter V, Books proper for the Amusing of Children, Macaulay remarks that 'the task of amusing the fancy of children, has in general fallen into the hands of persons contemptible both in their judgement and abilities.' In this remark and in the following statement one can easily discern the argument of the *cause célèbre* set in motion by Rousseau, which will obviously pit supporters of fantasy – such as Samuel Johnson and, later, Coleridge – against a legion of upholders of practical education:

> Ghosts and hobgoblins, giants and dwarfs, sorcerers and witches, with many strange tales and unaccountable acts of human prowess and human atrocity, have afforded such constant delight to children and their attendants that parents, to induce habits of reading, have in general indulged their offspring with lectures so well calculated to gratify a childish imagination. What were the baneful effects, which raising commotions in the minds of young children produced, I shall not in this place notice, but proceed to observe, that as every kind of trash calculated for the circle of a nursery was a saleable commodity, authors without numbers enlisted in this service. (Macaulay, 1994, 52)

100

From these words we get a glimpse of an already flourishing literary market, where a small niche in the Temple of Fame is occupied by authors of saleable commodities for the nursery. According to Macaulay, fairy tales, Thom Thumb, Jack Hickathrift, Jack the Giant Killer 'may be regarded as mere negatives as to their effects on the mind' (53). The dangers envisaged by Macaulay reside in the constant connexion, typical of these stories, of virtue with personal charms; and in the consequent lack of profound morality. Despite the literary laurels tributed to La Fontaine and Gay, she criticises, quoting the authority of Rousseau, the morality of La Fontaine's fables, too complicated and disproportionate to the child's experience; thus she warns parents against Gay's and Aesop's fables, not really fit for the nursery but for grown up young readers. Macaulay obviously approves of Madame de Genlis, whose *Adéle et Theodore* was translated by Maria Edgeworth, and of Berquin's *L'Ami des Enfans*, often read without translation to facilitate French lessons. And the indulgent Fénélon, although bent on the moral improvement of young aristocratic minds, 'has pointed out many ways of enticing the fancy of children to an attention to their books, by decorations on the outside, and ornamenting the inside with pictures' (56). In this respect the author of *Telemachus* aimed to enhance the pleasure of reading by recourse to 'visual baits' – illustrations – upon which parents, wishing their children to become fond of reading, should not place too much trust.

In this educational programme, full of warnings internal and external, addressed to the inner frailty of the child's mind and to the wilderness of the literary market, Macaulay observes that the age between the hour of birth and twelve years of age is, according to Rousseau, 'the most critical interval in human life' (126). What acts of reading should then be performed within this interval? Not many indeed, because 'we should not tamper with the mind till it has acquired all its faculties' (126). Macaulay recommends that the first 'ten or twelve years in human life' should be mainly devoted to 'the strengthening of the corporeal faculties'; and reading should be limited to a little Latin grammar, geography, arithmetic, 'such parts of physics as lie open to the attention of children' (128). These subjects are sufficient to fill up the time of childhood; because the mind should 'exercise its growing faculties without the use of books, which I should seldom introduce but with the view of amusement' (*ibid*).

Amusement connected with reading should only start at the age of ten, with the most celebrated fables. At the age of twelve Plutarch, Addison's *Spectator*, Guthrie's geography may be read; at fourteen Johnson's practical precepts, Rollin's ancient history, Ferguson and Gibbon; at sixteen some moral essays,

Cicero, Epictetus, Fénélon's *Telemachus*, and a little tasting of poetry, Shakespeare, Milton, Pope ... and so on until Letter XV, in which 'Literary Education is Continued' and the subjects of religion, foreign travels and novels are discussed. Here indeed comes the great divide. At the age of 21, a tour of Europe should take the place of reading and introduce the youth – the male youth – to the practical experience of the world. But then comes the backlash, because posting through the capital towns of Europe, the young gentleman 'forgets every part of his learning which is worth remembering ... and having acted the thoughtless fool' he will only learn to become a 'confirmed knave' (140-1). Rather than books, the masculine character needs sports, cricket, riding, fencing; while girls may walk, ride, dance, and play battledore. As a last lesson in her course in practical education, Macaulay recommends that novels should be banned. 'They are apt to deceive' (143). The act of reading, not too warmly extolled in the previous pages, and wisely administered like drops of a powerful medicine which may turn into poison, is here decidedly 'not to be taken'. The reason, one may guess, has to do with the success of the novel: 'The principal objection which lies against these compositions is, that they are all the history of lovers; and love tales are always improper for the ears of youth' (143).

Thus if reading teaches the young that love is an unconquerable passion, an infection of reason, a dangerous consequence of the power of sympathy, then reading has to be banned. Fielding and Cervantes, however, are admissible: but Richardson's *Pamela* and *Clarissa*, despite their claims to morality, are unfit for the perusal of youth. Macaulay maintains that 'To confine literary occupation entirely to novels, and the lighter parts of the belle lettre, is a perversion of reason and common sense, which distinguishes the present age' (148). Hers is a reader who encounters barriers at every age and vetoes in every direction, against fantasy in infancy and impropriety in adolescence, actually experiencing life as a sequence of 'critical intervals' starting from the nursery up to school days, and beyond.

Even more dangerous is the act of reading in the opinion of religious writers such as Hannah More. In *Strictures on Female Education* (1799) even those instructive books which facilitate children in their first act of reading and learning are to be avoided. She devotes a whole chapter to the dangers that may arise from untutored reading, expanding 'On female study, and initiation into knowledge', 'Error of cultivating the imagination to the neglect of the judgement' and 'Books of reasoning recommended' (More, 1995, 167). The already-flourishing children's literature market threatens by its abundance the very act of reading, inasmuch as 'with such books the rising generation is far more copiusly furnished than any preceeding period has been' but these 'multiplied helps which facilitate the entrance into learning ... render our pupils superficial through the very facility of acquirement' (168).

In order to cultivate learning, reading cannot be experienced as a free pleasure, achieved without diligence and hard labour; no short cuts are allowed. Parents, or educators, cannot 'cheat children into learning, or play them into knowledge, according to the smoothness of the modern creed' (168). One cannot but compare these statements with the idea, often expressed by Locke, that one may read for diversion and delight, or even more specifically with Jane Johnson's playful, pretty stories, their vivid illustrations, the alphabet cards and games made to facilitate the acquisition of literacy and an early taste for literature (Arizpe and Styles, 2006). For More, instead, as well as for the majority of practical educators and dogmatic pedagogists who are convinced of the inner wickedness of the child, the tree of knowledge, as a deserved punishment indeed, cannot be climbed without difficulty. More believes that 'education is but an initiation into that life of trial to which we are introduced on our entrance into this world' (More, 1995, 170). So education here rhymes with tribulation. Acts of reading entail hard times of trial, and the child is by no means viewed as an uncorrupted common reader, but rather as a sinful creature, needing to be taught the hard way, with plenty of awful warnings – and such would indeed be, according to Maria Martha Sherwood, the experience of the young members of the Fairchild family.

Parents and educators are warned by More against 'that profusion of little, amusing, sentimental books with which the youthful library overflows' (170); against 'the wordly morality of many a popular little story' (171); against 'frivolous reading' and 'the hot-bed of a circulating library' (173), conducive to the inevitable infection; and even against 'the swarms of *Abridgements*, *Beauties* and *Compendiums* which form too considerable a part of a young lady's library' and are indeed 'the infallible receipt for making a superficial mind' (173-4). Fine passages culled out of texts, herded together by some extract-maker, are the shallow sources of those hackneyed quotations 'of certain accomplished young ladies' (174). Reading for pleasure is dangerously apt to produce an appetite for idleness, indolence and vanity. In these acts of reading there seems to be hell lurking inside, rather than a promise of paradise.

Reading becomes even more complex when girls, in the process of growing up, are to be allowed its freedom and pleasure: physiology enters the act of reading in ways that remind us of the idea of female inferiority – physical, mental, and moral – as addressed by Woolf in *A Room of One's Own*. For More, the softness of girls' bodies is mirrored by their soft minds and soft hearts, and these must not be indulged with 'seducing books' (178); some rational learning, sound philosophy, and practical precepts should take the place of 'English sentiment, French philosophy, Italian love songs, and fantastic German imagery and magic wonders'(179). More is convinced that the act of reading for women must be 'serious study', meant to harden their mind: otherwise the 'indolent repose of light reading' (179) may breed visionary indolence, soften the mind and set fancy at work, so that eventually the mind will be open to error and the heart to seduction.

At almost the opposite pole from the strictures of Hannah More is Maria Edgeworth in *Practical Education* (1801), (in part written with her father, Richard Lovell Edgeworth) where she sets at the centre of her concerns the Rousseauian child, a being halfway between the state of nature and the achievement of literacy. But again, between children and the creative pleasure of reading there are some missing links, some gaps and barriers; not all books are considered desirable at all times and for all readers.

At first Edgeworth discusses in great detail several books which, in her time, were considered ideal reading for children aged four or five, such as Mrs Barbauld's *Lessons for Children* and *Evenings at Home*, and Berquin's *L'Ami des Enfants*: but she believes that even in this morally safe territory there may be episodes which should be avoided by careful parents because they are inconsistent with real experience (why should a cat catch mice and not little birds?) or because they teach vice, falsity, dishonesty, to a being who does not yet have a notion of these negative realities.

At the core of Edgeworth's conception of the child there is indeed a potentially uncorrupted young reader, free from prejudice, but this *tabula rasa* must not be inscribed with any kind of fantasy or fable, or indeed with any kind of reading matter that cannot be empirically tested and tried. Thus the reading list must be restricted:

> The enumeration of the months in the year, the days in the week, of metals, &c. are excellent lessons for a child who is just beginning to learn to read. The classification of animals into quadrupeds, bipeds, &c. is another useful specimen of the manner in which children should be taught to generalise their ideas. (Edgeworth, 1996, 85-6)

One cannot but think of the way Sissy Jupe is taught to describe a horse at the school in Coketown, and of the educational restrictions Gradgrind imposes on his mathematic Tom and on his metallurgical Louisa. In Dickens's *Hard*

Times we catch the long wave of an educational theory; Rousseauian votaries – principally Thomas Day and the Edgeworths – are to be held responsible for its early launch in England.[1] For Edgeworth, careful parents have the duty to investigate their children's readings and never trust their children with books, pages, lines that have not been previously inspected with scrupulous attention. A mother's duty consists of having several books

> marked by her pencil, and volumes which, having undergone the necessary operations by her scissors, would, in their mutilated state, shock the sensibility of a nice librarian. But shall the education of a family be sacrificed to the beauty of a page, or even to the binding of a book? Few books can be safely given to children without the previous use of the pen, the pencil, the scissors. In the books which we have before us, in their corrected state, we see sometimes a few words blotted out, sometimes half a page, sometimes many pages are cut out (Edgeworth, 1996, 88).

Parents should trim – indeed censure, erase, cut, mutilate – acts of reading by their children. This less-than-common reader is made so not only because of over-anxious parents, but because Rousseau's theory casts ideological shadows over the very act of reading, creating on the one hand the nursing conditions for Romantic creativity, while on the other breeding the fallacy of the noble savage. This entices many among Rousseau's English followers into curtailing their children's reading altogether: Dorothy Wordsworth educates young Basil Montagu without letters, and so does Thomas Day with the orphans Lucretia and Sabrina; similar educational experiments were also attempted in the Edgeworth household where, according to the Introduction to *Practical Education*, Richard Edgeworth had applied 'a fair trial of Rousseau's system' when his son Dick was three years old:

> I dressed my son without stockings, his arms bare ... I succeeded in making him remarkably hardy ... He had all the virtues of a child bred in the hut of a savage ... a knowledge of things, for of books he had less knowledge at four or five years old than most children have at that age ... He was bold, free, fearless, generous ... But he was not disposed to obey... (Edgeworth, 1996, vii)

Behind this unbookish education there is the concept of a general book bonfire, out of which only the Bible and Rousseau should be saved; but the experiments of Day and Edgeworth failed to give happiness to Dick, Lucretia, or Sabrina. Maria Edgeworth tries with remarkable good sense to discuss the merits of several literary works for children, and she finds that Day's *Sandford and Merton* is still largely reliable, according to her pedagogical standards. For Edgeworth, there are no sentimental stories to be recommended for girls, no adventure stories suitable for boys, and no historical narratives advisable for either on account of the prejudices and commonplaces they spread. Only histories related to real life are advisable for children, and such are for Edgeworth the stories about bees, caterpillars, silkworms, butterflies. Selborne's *Naturalist Calendar* was indeed a hit.

As for the act of reading itself, in *Practical Education* she devotes many pages to recommendations which make her book an interesting pedagogical tool. Reading aloud must be banned, as a fatiguing habit, conducive to gaps in attention, and the child should not be encouraged to persevere when reading becomes tedious, but rather invited to interrupt the act of reading when the book is tiring, boring or incomprehensible. Shakespeare must be read and enjoyed only at the right age.

Indeed, the abridgement of Shakespeare makes for a long and interesting story, starting in 1807 with Charles and Mary Lamb's *Tales from Shakespeare*, conceived for William Godwin's Juvenile Library: the addressee is mainly a girl rather than a boy, the young sister who's not allowed to enter father's library. I won't dwell on this rich chapter, but just remark that the Rousseauian phase is likely to affect the child's acts of reading more or less until the end of the century when, because of Darwin and Freud, savage instincts are likely to suggest unpleasant connections. Then Edgar Rice Burroughs would create in 1912 the last avatar of the noble savage, namely *Tarzan of the Apes*, that is to say Lord Greystoke, a young aristocratic hero nursed and brought up by a great ape in the jungle, who eventually learns to read in total solitude. This act of self-taught reading, however, does not infuse Tarzan with the knowledge of human ways, fears, fancies and opinions. Versions of Darwinian theory take their toll here, mutilating literacy by implying the dangers of an apeish upbringing, even when the reader's aristocratic breed ought in theory to bridge the evolutionary gap compressed within his life.

Steps up the ladder: reading to gain paradise

On the other side of the question, philosophically speaking, the so-called golden age of children's literature implies the full recognition of the pleasure of reading. In Carroll's classic story, an affluent and well-taught child such as Alice can already state that she does not enjoy books without dialogues or illustrations and, moreover, make fun of schools and bookish notions. Dickens, who in ironic pieces such as Frauds on the Fairies is among the staunch supporters of the blessings of unadulterated reading (Dickens, 1997, 566-572), thematises in *Hard Times* (1854) a dangerous system of education cleansed from the 'destructive nonsense' of Fairies, Dwarfs, Hunchbacks, Genies, and providing the child with 'leaden little books' which are meant to teach 'how the good grown-up baby invariably got to the Savings-bank, and the bad grown-up baby invariably got transported'(Dickens, 1982, 89-90).

Things have changed now. And not only as far as Shakespeare is concerned; the well-to-do Victorian child has routine access to books, and receives them as Christmas presents, cowering among the leaves of 'The Christmas Tree'.[2] If poor, he or she is energically stimulated to learn to read as a way to salvation. I shall directly focus upon *Steps up the Ladder, or, the Will and the Way. A True Story*, by an unknown author, printed by the Religious Tract Society between 1860 and 1865, in order to stress the emphasis that this booklet and thousands of similar stories placed on the act of reading. As it happens for most protagonists of city-waif novels, otherwise named 'street arab stories,' the story of Tim Roberts starts on a cold and stormy winter night, when he seeks refuge against the storm, and accidentally enters a school for Ragged Children.

After pioneering attempts in Portsmouth and Edinburgh, the Ragged School Union was started in London in 1844 by John Ashley Cooper, Lord Shaftesbury. In the following decade, over 200 free schools were established all over Britain. By the 1880s, over 300,000 destitute children receive education from the Ragged Schools. Their spread decreases with the Foster Education Act of 1870. These basic facts are meant to emphasise that *Steps up the Ladder,* for all its anonymity and uncertain date of publication, is a story that covers a collective social experience spanning several decades – the dreadful living conditions of many children – as well as the reading public awareness of it (Mearns, 1970; Gauldie, 1974; Hollingshed, 1986; Hardy, 1993). The Evangelical Tract Society with its rich publishing list gives visibility to the Ragged Schools and to their active presence on that blackest part of the map of London, as drawn by Charles Booth between 1892 and 1903 with *The Life and Labour of the People of London*. Among the writers actively operating for the Religious Tract Society, one should mention Mary Charlesworth, the author of the frequently-quoted *Ministering Children: A Tale Dedicated to Childhood*, published in 1854 and so successful that she soon writes a sequel (1866). Hesba Stretton's (Sarah Smith) *Jessica's First Prayer* (1867) sells over one and a half million copies, *Jessica's Mother* being the sequel. Strettons' chosen protagonist is the city waif, the destitute child: her many stories devoted to this theme include *Pilgrim Street* (1867), *Little Meg's Children* (1868), *Alone in London* (1869), *In Prison and Out* (1880).

The theme of ignorance is touched upon in *Jessica's First Prayer* when the minister, who has followed Jessica to her squalid den, inquires whether she would like to learn to read:

'No,' answered Jessica; 'mother says she'll never let me learn to read, or go to church; she says it would make me good for nothing. But please, sir, she doesn't know anything about your church, it's such a long way off, and she hasn't found me out yet. She always gets very drunk of a Sunday' (Stretton, nd 84).

Like Jessica, Tim Roberts, the young protagonist of *Steps up the Ladder*, also lives in a single room, with his father, a confirmed drunkard, regularly in and out of prison; with a mother who does not care about her family, which 'existed, year after year, in their wretched garret, without God, without Christ, without hope in the world'(12). The unknown author of this booklet is aware of placing this narrative within a well-known, perhaps over-popular genre: 'The miserable abodes of the poor in our great towns have been too often described to need a place in these pages (18). Like many city waifs, Tim is accustomed to beg and even steal, to sleep in holes and corners; but after his first visit to the Ragged School his redemption starts and he returns, night after night, for learning and religion: 'To learn to read, and not to read the bible, was to get the shell and throw away the kernel' (32). Gradually he gets a job, decent clothes, a regular place where he can board and lodge, and a Bible. Tim visits his parents, but his words of encouragement do not shake their deep-seated mistrust in books, learning, and religion. In Tim's new lodgings, the son of his employer teaches him to read the Bible, and Tim decides to take the book with him on his Sabbath visit to his parents, notwithstanding the 'scoffs and jeers from his mother and a surly rebuke from his father' (75). His reading performances become a regular feature of Sunday afternoons. His father and mother listen, silently.

> The news of Tim's scholarship, however, took wind through the house. It was one of those ill conducted dwellings, occupied by a number of families who lived, crammed together, more like beasts than human beings. Some of these persons, led by curiosity, were accustomed to gather round the door, to hear Tim read... Tim was not sorry to see them ... He read on in spite of their whispers and their stifled laughs. (82)

As might be expected, the conversion of his listeners comes with their decision to learn to read: 'I'll tell you what we'll do boys; we'll learn to read!' cries one among his listeners. 'What's the good of hear, hear, hear, and not know a letter for ourselves? I'm not above learning!' (89).

The booklets of the Evangelical Tract Society emphatically stress the joint value of reading and religion. In this context, one cannot overestimate their cultural role, although some voices cried against those sensational stories of ragged London depravity. But this depravity is the concept that one must

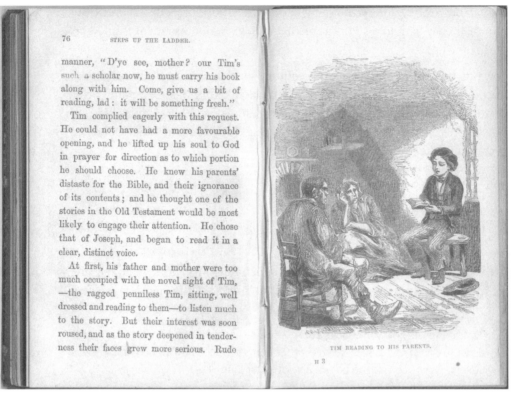

manner, "D'ye see, mother? our Tim's such a scholar now, he must carry his book along with him. Come, give us a bit of reading, lad : it will be something fresh."

Tim complied eagerly with this request. He could not have had a more favourable opening, and he lifted up his soul to God in prayer for direction as to which portion he should choose. He knew his parents' distaste for the Bible, and their ignorance of its contents ; and he thought one of the stories in the Old Testament would be most likely to engage their attention. He chose that of Joseph, and began to read it in a clear, distinct voice.

At first, his father and mother were too much occupied with the novel sight of Tim, —the ragged penniless Tim, sitting, well dressed and reading to them—to listen much to the story. But their interest was soon roused, and as the story deepened in tenderness their faces grew more serious. Rude

TIM READING TO HIS PARENTS.

H 3

Figure 4: Tim reading to his parents from *Steps Up the Ladder*, anon *circa* 1860

follow in its historical displacement and cultural transformation, from the potential danger of vice and sin lurking within the pages of a book, denounced by writers in the 1790s, into the social awareness of the real condition of the poor, which includes the danger of depravity among many other evils. Hence the book and the blessing of reading are invoked and sought as antidotes to the social drama which has its peak between the 1840s and 1870s. Instead of an avenue to hell, reading literally becomes a ladder to paradise, bearing the promise of better social circumstances for many illiterate city waifs.

To describe, at the opposite end of the spectrum, the acts of reading performed by wealthy children, would bring us back to Alice and to the chapters where school and lessons are made fun of. When the Mock Turtle mentions her courses in the different branches of Arithmetic, 'Ambition, Distraction, Uglification and Derision' (Carroll, 2001, 102), Dickens's statement in *Hard Times*, 'By means of addition, subtraction, multiplication and division, settle everything somehow and never wonder' (Dickens, 1982, 89), signals not only the gap between children belonging to the two nations of Victorian times, but also the newly-acquired status as readers that girls, not dissimilar from Alice, are achieving.

Towards the end of the nineteenth century, girls practise reading with more freedom than in the past, and the turn of the century has many little princesses who can even teach their dolls to read; indeed who can gobble up books. One of these is Sarah Crewe, who eagerly devours all kinds of books, according to her father:

> She is always sitting with her little nose burrowing into books. She doesn't read them, Miss Minchin; she gobbles them up as if she were a little wolf instead of a little girl. She is always starving for new books to gobble, and she wants grown-up books – great, big, fat ones – French and German as well as English – history and biography and poets, and all sorts of things. (Hodgson Burnett, 1905, 9-10)

In these years Sarah is not the only girl experiencing starvation and hungering for reading. Leslie Stephen's comment about Virginia's attitude in this respect is revealing:

> 'Gracious child, how you gobble,' Leslie would say as he got up from his seat to take down the sixth or seventh volume of Gibbon, or Spedding's *Bacon* or Cowper's Letters. 'Ginia is devouring books, almost faster than I like.'

It was about this time, however, that the system of issuing books came to an end and Virginia was granted the freedom of her father's library (Bell, 1996, 51).

In the case of Shakespeare, one may remark that acts of reading are strictly connected with gender; but in this survey philosophy and religion, flanked by editorial strategies meant to improve social conditions, also play a significant role. Reading apparently may rank with *caveats*, mutilation, starvation, sin, or conversely with innocence, freedom and rescue from evil, a reward and act of creation. To round it all up, Virginia Woolf optimistically places at the end of her 'How Should One Read a Book?' a funny story about readers, which has to be quoted:

> When the Day of Judgement dawns ... the Almighty will turn to Peter, and will say, not without a certain envy when he sees us coming with our books under our arms, 'Look, these need no reward. We have nothing to give them here. They have loved reading.' (Woolf, 1935, 270)

According to Woolf, reading is paradise. One should read this as an early lesson.

Notes

1 Thomas Day's educator, Mr Barlow, will be described by Dickens as 'the instructive monomaniac' and a 'great bore': see 'Mr Barlow', first in *All the Year Round* (1868), then in *The Uncommercial Traveller* (1875) London: Dent, 1969, 332-338. F.Orestano, in F.Orestano, C. Pagetti, eds, *Il gioco dei cerchi concentrici: saggi sulla letteratura inglese da Shakespeare al Novecento*. Milano, Unicopli, 2003, 75-88.

2 C. Dickens, The Christmas Tree (*Household Words*, 21 Dec 1850), now in *Selected Journalism 1850-1870*, ed. D. Pascoe, 3-16. Among the branches of the tree, laden with toys, 'how thick the books begin to hang': primers, alphabet books, Grimm's stories, Robin Hood, Mother Bunch's wonders, *The Arabian Nights, Robinson Crusoe, The Adventures of Philip Quarll* (1727), Day's *Sandford and Merton* (1783-89): already a canonic list of children's books.

Bibliography

Anon (circa 1860-1865?) *Steps up the Ladder, or, the Will and the Way. A True Story*. London: The Religious Tract Society

Arizpe, E and Styles, M (2006) *Reading Lessons from the Eighteenth Century*. Lichfield: Pied Piper

Bell, Q (1996) *Virginia Woolf, A Biography*. London: Pimlico

Booth, C (ed) (1892-1903) *The Life and Labour of the People in London*. London: Macmillan

Bradbury, M (1989) *The Modern World. Ten Great Writers*. London: Penguin

Carroll, L (2001) *The Annotated Alice,The Definitive Edition*. (M Gardner, ed) Harmondsworth: Penguin

Day, T (1863) *History of Sandford and Merton. Intended for the Use of Children (1783-1786-1789)*. Paris: Baudry's European Library

Dickens, C (1969) Mr Barlow. In *The Uncommercial Traveller* (1875). London: Dent

Dickens, C (1982) *Hard Times, for These Times* (1854). (D Craig, ed) Harmondsworth: Penguin

Dickens, C (1997) Frauds on the Fairies. In D Pascoe (ed) *Selected Journalism 1850-1870*. Harmondsworth: Penguin

Dickens, C (1997) The Christmas Tree. In D Pascoe (ed) *Selected Journalism 1850-1870*. Harmondsworth: Penguin.

Edgeworth, M and RL (1996) *Practical Education (1801)*. Oxford and Poole: Woodstock Books

Gauldie, E (1974) *Cruel Habitations. A History of Working-Class Housing. 1780-1818*. London: Allen and Unwin

Hardy, A (1993) *The Epidemic Streets*. Oxford: Oxford University Press

Hodgson Burnett, F (2002) *A Little Princess* (1905), ed U.C. Knoepflmacher, Harmondsworth: Penguin

Hollingshead, J (1986) *Ragged London in 1861*. London: Everyman

Jameson, A (1905) *Miranda's Library. Shakespeare's Heroines*. London: Dent

Lang, J (nd) *Stories from Shakespeare*. London: Thomas Nelson

Macaulay, C (1994) *Letters on Education* (1790). Oxford: Woodstock Books

Mearns, A (1970) *The Bitter Cry of the Outcast London* (1885). Leicester: Leicester University Press

More, H (1995) *Strictures on Female Education* (1799). Oxford: Woodstock Books

Nesbit, E (1910) *Children's Stories from Shakespeare*. London: Raphael Tuck

Orestano, F (2003) 'He taught Laughing and Grief': la figura del maestro nella letteratura per l'infanzia. In F, Orestano and C Pagetti (eds) *Il gioco dei cerchi concentrici: saggi sulla letteratura inglese da Shakespeare al Novecento*. Milano: Unicopli

Stretton, H (nd) *Jessica's First Prayer. With Twenty Illustrations by Gordon Browne.* London: The Religious Tract Society

Woolf, V (1935) *The Common Reader. Second Series.* London: The Hogarth Press

Woolf, V (1984, 1925) *The Common Reader. First Series.* A Mc Neillie (ed). New York: Harcourt

Wollstonecraft, M (1787/1994) *Thoughts on the Education of Daughters.* Oxford: Woodstock Books

9

Hiding Places of Power: The child as a site of resistance in William Wordsworth's poetry

David Whitley

Wⁱˡˡⁱᵃᵐ Wordsworth's poetry contains some of the most profound and searching images of childhood in the whole of modern literature. The range and implications of the territory Wordsworth opened up in his thinking about childhood are more far-reaching than can be found in the work of any of his contemporary writers and indeed continue to raise challenging questions for us now. Yet while many of these questions have been explored implicitly – in exciting, new ways – in relation to literary history and theories of Romanticism, the connections to our contemporary understanding of childhood remain less developed. This chapter will therefore consider how Wordsworth's poetry may shape changes in the way we perceive childhood.

Repositioning childhood

It is now common to see the subjects of Wordsworth's poetry – the beggars, leech gatherers, mad women, discharged soldiers and so on – as being drawn distinctively from the margins of his society. Yet it is worth noting that Wordsworth's rereading of childhood, as it were, is also an act of bringing childhood experience in from the margins so that its centrality in shaping consciousness can be provocatively asserted and explored. Wordsworth's famous aphorism, 'the child is father to the man', not only establishes a new prospective basis for developmental psychology; it also confounds many of the premises on which his culture was built, destabilising hierarchies of knowledge with its radical revaluation of the primitive. Although the tone of Wordsworth's poems often seems soberly authorititive, at critical points the writing can appear strangely

113

– even disorientatingly – open. Hence, even in Wordsworth's shorter poems, the child is configured within an uneasy cultural space where implicit tensions are left unresolved. The little girl in 'We Are Seven', who steadfastly refuses to be persuaded by increasingly insistent adult rationalist definitions that her siblings are 'dead,' is granted an authority in the poem that subtly undermines attempts to read her stance dismissively as charmingly naïve. And in 'Nutting' – perhaps more alarmingly – the boy's testosterone-fuelled assault on a tree to harvest nuts is construed figuratively as an act of rape. Rather than being judged or moralised, however, the act is offered in a form that, though powerfully suggestive, resists easy categorisation.

The repositioning of childhood in modes that resist earlier, more straight-forward kinds of categorisation is made possible by writing that centres itself – paradoxically perhaps – on the margins. Even in an autobiographical mode, it has been claimed, Wordsworth 'was best able to write about those times in his own childhood when he considered himself to be marginal' (Bewell, 1989, 46). Indeed the very category of childhood itself – so central to Wordsworth's poetic project and fundamental sense of being – had only recently emerged from the margins of cultural production. Its power – both as a concept and an experiential domain – was therefore untested.

In order to see more clearly what Wordsworth made of this untested domain, consider the following passage from the 1805 version of *The Prelude*. The lines I want to examine particularly closely occur towards the end of Book 5 in both the 1805 and 1850 versions of the poem, though the 1805 version will be used exclusively here. In the passage in question, Wordsworth celebrates the process of children's acquisition of knowledge, from both books and Nature, in quite distinctive terms. The passage begins by expressing a wish that Nature may long continue to:

> Behold a race of young ones like to those
> With whom I herded – easily, indeed,
> We might have fed upon a fatter soil
> Of Arts and Letters, but be that forgiven -
> A race of real children, not too wise,
> Too learned, or too good, but wanton, fresh,
> And bandied up and down by love and hate;
> Fierce, moody, patient, venturous, modest, shy,
> Mad at their sports like withered leaves in winds;
> Though doing wrong and suffering, and full oft
> Bending beneath our life's mysterious weight
> Of pain and fear, yet still in happiness

> Not yielding to the happiest upon earth.
> Simplicity in habit, truth in speech,
> Be these the daily strengtheners of their minds!
> May books and Nature be their early joy,
> And knowledge, rightly honoured with that name –
> Knowledge not purchased with the loss of power!
> (1805 V 431-449)

The passage is justly famous for its advocacy of the image of 'real children'. Wordsworth distinguishes his 'real children' equally from the rationalist educators' conception of children as miniature adults in training and from the new evangelical Christian view of childhood as a precarious realm that must be rescued from the twin forces of social evil and original sin. Wordsworth's children, by contrast, do not pursue goals of moral and intellectual excellence with utter diligence. Rather, they wear their guilt more lightly, are subject to a full range of mixed emotions and live – fully – as children rather than miniature adults.

Childhood and power

Striking and influential though this central image of childhood is, there are other aspects of this passage equally worthy of attention. Why is the closing assertion of children's 'power' phrased in this particular way, for instance? The expression here seems particularly designed to be provocative of thought. Exactly what kind of power do children possess that might be lost through acquiring knowledge? And what kind of exchange is being suggested in which the price of knowledge is diminution of human potential? Alan Richardson highlights how odd, as well as remarkable, Wordsworth's well known formulation on childhood and power at this point in the poem really is, when he argues that:

> childhood, particularly infancy, has traditionally been represented as a condition of relative impotence, while education has been usually viewed as adding to, rather than diminishing, the child's stock of power. It is more than a little paradoxical for Wordsworth to portray socialisation, and education in particular, as a threat to the child's power, rather than as a prime source of cultural and self-mastery leading the child towards adult autonomy. (1994, 34)

Some commentators have sought to resolve this inherent paradox by seeing Wordsworth's concept of power here as delineating, rather unproblematically, the realm of the imagination. Wordsworth clearly did perceive the faculty of imagination as being under threat within contemporary schools of thought, particularly rationalist understandings of education. Equating power simply with the imagination, conceived in this way as individuals' full psychological potential, fails to ask, however, whether there are not other, broader determinants. Power is usually invoked as a quality that people hold in relation to each other or, in a more Foucauldian manner, as inhering within discourses that structure and lend authority to social practices. If we begin to examine Wordsworth's assertion from perspectives such as these, there are good reasons for being wary of resolving the issue too neatly.

To start with, the passage in question develops out of a narrative instance of unusual complexity. It is from this context that the more generalised assertion of what constitutes childhood and power seems to emerge. The two incidents that frame the reflections in this passage are examples of those enigmatically intense recollections (or 'spots of time') so central to *The Prelude*. Immediately preceding the passage in the 1805 version is a reminiscence of the Winander boy, who learns to imitate the hoots of the local owl population with such enthusiasm and precision that he sets up a kind of mock dialogue with them. Subsequently the incident of the 'drowned man', witnessed being pulled 'bolt upright' with a grappling hook from the serenely beautiful waters of Esthwaite Lake, provides an aftermath.

Both incidents are worked up in the poetry in ways that enact a mysterious rupture with normative modes of being. The temporary cessation of the owls' responses produces a strange experience of profound silence within the boy, a loss or momentary emptying of selfhood, while the sudden emergence of the corpse from the serene lake evokes a more obvious sense of rupture from the normal. The latter incident is also treated as exemplary of the way in which childhood reading may enable such troubling incidents to be assimilated in deeper, more beneficent forms. Earlier the assertion has been made that stories such as Jack the Giant Killer and Robin Hood have the virtue 'at least' of enabling children to forget themselves, in an age when fashionable educational practices promote an overly conscious – and controlled – cultivation of the self.

Wordsworth adds the rider that popular tales may have a more profound function in preparing the child to be receptive to an inherent grandeur within ordinary – or even potentially ghastly – experiences. The emotion that possesses the child on witnessing the body being pulled from the lake is not one of vulgar or sensationalist fear since, the poet asserts, his 'inner eye had seen such sights before' in imagined forms while reading fairy tales and romances. Hence the ghastly image of mortality, framed by the lake's beauty, is assimilated in a 'spirit hallowing' and is imbued with a mysterious power.

Coleridge had formulated a similar notion in a letter of 1797 where he asserted how 'from my early reading of Faery Tales, and Genii &c &c – my mind has been habituated to the vast ...' (1956, 354). Clearly the power associated with 'real children' for Wordsworth accrues from such breaks or ruptures in the patterns of their normative experience of the natural world. The formative effect of such ruptures is greatly enhanced and facilitated by the imaginative reading available in forms of popular culture. Reading thus plays a key role in allowing this mysterious power to inhere deeply within childhood.

The power of literature

If the narrative context suggests one reason for being wary of explaining the issue of children's association with power too simply, then further dimensions are suggested by the way children are construed in relation to their reading. It is clear from the passage we have been considering that Wordsworth conceives of childhood as properly engaged in a largely unregulated or, as Milton put it in the *Areopagitica*, promiscuous diet of reading. The children might have 'fed upon a fatter soil of Arts and Letters' but instead, as other passages in Book 5 attest, they have been involved passionately with a whole range of sub-literary genres (as well as Arts and Letters) including fairy tales, legends and chapbooks. Indeed children's potential to imbibe knowledge 'without loss of power' appears to depend, to a significant extent, on their access to such competing narrative discourses.

The range and quantity of literature available to children had, of course, increased dramatically in the latter half of the eighteenth century. In the wake of this increase, perhaps inevitably, came intense debates about the the quality of reading matter that was now accessible to young readers. The niche market for a new children's literature that Newbery had opened up so successfully in the mid-eighteenth century had, for many middle class observers, become an alarmingly unruly beast by the time the century closed. Newbery's social roots, like Defoe's before him, had been among lower middle-class tradespeople. His idea that stories for children might sell better if they were entertaining and fun effectively enabled him to open up a literature for children as a mass market in mid century, making a sizeable fortune for himself, but also opening the floodgates for a new kind of children's literature for the future (Townsend, 1994). With Newbery, children outside the aristocracy and the very rich finally arrived as consumers of culture on a significant scale.

The terms on which Newbery was able to create a new market for children's books did not go uncontested, however. Newbery's child heroes and heroines tended to be invested with something of the rumbustious spirit of characters in Henry Fielding's adult fiction, with whom they were coterminous. But where Fielding's heroes' enthusiastic immersion in life – mixing with characters from a wide range of class backgrounds – tended to be anchored in the discovery of the central protagonist's true aristocratic roots towards the end of the novel, Newbery pitched his appeal towards the lower classes unashamedly and without qualification. The liveliness, lack of deference and (often) narrative drive towards social advancement of the child characters in Newbery's stories therefore came to be perceived as more of a threat to upper middle class reformers, who increasingly sought to control both the form and content of the emerging literature for children.

The reformers found an avid readership amongst middle class families who, as Mary Jackson puts it, 'disliked the trade fiction's encouragement of imagination and whimsy at the expense of reason and, even more, its too realistic tales of children, often of the lower middle class, who were depicted as having a degree of independence that many considered dangerous to the gently nurtured child' (1989, 130). Anna Barbauld's *Hymns in Prose for Children*, published between 1778 and 1781, can be seen as one of the most successful attempts to offer a more refined alternative to the coarsening, politically suspect, effects of trade literature.

In the years which followed, and particularly in the wake of the French Revolution, the newly constituted literature for children would become an even more heated battleground within which ideas and images of childhood were increasingly caught up in the ideological, social and philosophical debates that exercised the adult community. Amongst the next generation, Hannah More and Sarah Trimmer were the most prolific in publishing texts for working class children designed, in Trimmer's words, 'to counteract the pernicious Tendency of Immoral Books ... (and to make) good apprentices, and conscientious, faithful servants' (*ibid*, 174).

By the late 1790s, then, when Wordsworth began to plan and write the first versions of *The Prelude*, children had clearly begun to move in from the cultural margins; indeed they had acquired central significance for all parties in the impassioned blows which were being struck to determine the kind of culture and society that would hold into the future. The point I want to bring into focus here is that, both because children had begun to accrue significance as consumers and because childhood figured so strongly within political arguments, the question of how children should be represented – the construction of childhood within culture – acquired a quite unprecedented importance. It is in this context that William Wordsworth's exploration of the meaning of childhood in *The Prelude* needs to be read.

One consequence of this is that we need to see the sense of rupture on which Wordsworth's most intense images of childhood are founded as not only psychological. It is interesting, for instance, in the passage we have been examining in detail, that Wordsworth's formulation of a particular kind of knowledge should be couched in the language of the market: 'Knowledge not purchased with the loss of power'. This idiomatic use of 'purchase' is sufficiently well worn for its literal meaning to be overlooked, but so many of the most interesting resonances in *The Prelude* come through obliquely that it is worth considering the particular force of the phrasing here. For it is precisely the kind of knowledge that children can 'purchase' from chapbooks, cheap versions of fairy tales, legends and political propaganda that so exercised Hannah More and her followers in the 1790s. Moreover, the somewhat anarchic, undeferential modes of behaviour characterising the popular fiction that More attempted to supplant with her *Cheap Repository Tracts* seem remarkably similar to many of the qualities celebrated in Wordsworth's 'real children'.

Even if we grant that the passage functions as one of the many building blocks in the poem serving to structure and define a crucial concept of the 'imagination', it is clearly inflected in a quite specific political context. The defence of the imagination, in other words, derives energy and force through its association with certain kinds of resistance and nascent rebelliousness countenanced in popular literature for children. The phrasing of Wordsworth's conjunction of childhood and power has additional resonance in the context of anxieties generated by the recent emergence of children's literature as a mass market.

Some recent writing has tended to stress the ambivalence of the first generation of Romantics' commitment to progressive values in relation to children and education. Alan Richardson has argued that Wordsworth's opposition to the coercive elements implicit within the rationalist educators' vision of childhood was seriously undermined by Wordsworth's own advocacy of the Madras system of education (1994, 91-103). The Madras system, as its name implies, had strong imperialist links and, it is argued, offered a model of institutional social control which appealed precisely because it allayed fears of rebellion and insurgency that might otherwise be fomented in working class children.

Even if we take Wordsworth's endorsement of such educational schemes as an attempt to counter the power of an increasingly literate and militant working class, however, the language within which Wordsworth configures childhood in his poetry retains a potentially radical force. Despite successive revisions of the text, designed to shift the centre of its social and political philosophy towards a Burkean ideal of organic, incremental change within a fundamentally hierarchical community, *The Prelude*'s images relating childhood to power remain entrenched within a set of values which are fundamentally oppositional.

The child as subject

One reason for this may be that Wordsworth's social thinking remained more rooted in eighteenth century enlightenment perspectives than is often perceived (Bewell, 1989). The distinctive form in which Wordsworth's concept of the child is linked to more radical strands of enlightenment thought can be seen more clearly if we compare his concept with the images of childhood deployed by Thomas De Quincey in his essays.

Consider, for instance, the following passage from De Quincey's essay 'Alexander Pope', better known through its subsidiary title 'The Literature of Knowledge and the Literature of Power'. As this sub-title makes clear, De Quincey is here dealing in the same intoxicating abstractions as Wordsworth: knowledge and power.

De Quincey's essay draws on the example of children in a way that reveals subtle differences from Wordsworth's thinking, however. Defining power (rather idiosyncratically) as 'a deep sympathy with truth' (an attribute which he takes to be rarer than the occurrence of truth itself), De Quincey goes on to assert, rather surprisingly, that literature and children share a similar social function; both act so as to help realise this potential for 'deep sympathy with truth'. 'What is the effect, upon society, of children?' he asks.

> By the pity, by the tenderness and by the peculiar modes of admiration which connect themselves with the helplessness, with the innocence, and with the simplicity of children, not only are the primal affections strengthened and continually renewed, but the qualities which are dearest in the sight of heaven – the frailty, for instance, which appeals to forbearance, the innocence which symbolises the heavenly, and the simplicity which is most alien from the worldly – are kept in perpetual remembrance and their ideals are continually refreshed. A purpose of the same nature is answered by the higher literature,viz the literature of power. (1973, 269)

De Quincey puts literature and children together then, in one of those instinctive, imaginative conjunctions characteristic of Romantic writers working at the limits of conventional understanding. Literature and children are similar in the effect they have on society because each has the capacity to move individuals towards a realisation of the ideals which they hold most dearly and most deeply. The power of both literature and children then, for De Quincey, resides in their effect on people's deepest feelings. Literature is akin to the 'frailty' and 'innocence' of children in radically affecting the emotions. Indeed, the word 'radical' is especially appropriate here, not only because it touches the roots of deepest feeling but also because, in the examples which De Quincey goes on to offer, these deep emotions relate to fundamental social ideals such as justice. 'Tragedy, romance, fairy tale or epopee,' De Quincey expounds,

> all alike restore to man's mind the ideals of justice, of hope, of truth ... which else (left to the support of daily life in its realities) would languish for want of sufficient illustration ... It is certain that, were it not for the Literature of Power, these ideals would often remain amongst us as mere arid notional forms, whereas, by the creative forces of man put forth in literature, they gain a vernal life of restoration, and germinate into vital activities. (*ibid*)

It is not, I would argue, accidental that De Quincey includes the children's literary form of the fairy tale alongside tragedy and romance as his chosen exemplary genres. The fairy tale had recently been championed by several Romantic writers as a valuable form of children's narrative against the dicta of rationalist and evangelical educationalists, who saw fairy tales as fanciful and potentially subversive (Tucker, 1997, 104-116). More broadly though, we are reminded that, in the period when both Wordsworth and De Quincey had come to maturity, children's literature, as much as adult literature, had become a battleground for competing ideas, ideologies and values. One reason for choosing the word 'power' over more value neutral alternatives is that it suggests active agency. The experience of a period in which the persuasive effects of literature were linked to explicitly ideological purposes in effecting social change is formative, I would argue, in developing a theory of the 'Literature of Power'.

This connection is not straightforward, though. De Quincey's made use of the distinction between the Literature of Knowledge and the Literature of Power throughout his career as a writer. His most extended reflections on the terms occur in 'Oliver Goldsmith' (1823), 'Letters to a Young Man Whose Education Has Been Neglected' (1823) and 'Alexander Pope' (1848). In the earlier writings the Literature of Power tends to be configured predominantly in terms of its psychological effects, while the emphasis in the later writing shifts more towards the realm of the ethical (Schneider, 1995, 13-14). Both emphases avoid any direct consideration of power in a political context (a deconstruc-tive approach might argue that this is a structured absence, indeed) but the image of a social context, a community of readers for whom literature has the special function of securing active allegiance to fundamental values, is pre-sent throughout. Interestingly, the concept of a Literature of Power is also linked, repeatedly, to the theme of violence in an ultimately unresolved way. Just as the French Revolution haunted the imaginations of Romantic writers as a double-faced image of potential liberation and destructive force, so De Quincey's concept of the social efficacy of power within literature is twinned, obsessively, with the theme of violence.

In centring his concept of a 'Literature of Power' within the realm of sympathy and the emotions, then, De Quincey is not divorcing it from its functions as social agency. Indeed he is drawing on late eighteenth-century traditions of thought underlying the culture of sensibility, which perceived in the capacity to make men and women feel more deeply a potential for critical engagement with the organisation of contemporary society and an impulse towards social change. The range of ideals which De Quincey invokes in defining the effect of literature (and children's power) may be congruent with his own high Tory values. He speaks of the 'qualities which are dearest in the sight of heaven – the frailty, for instance, which appeals to forbearance ... innocence ... and the simplicity which is most alien from the worldly' (1973, 269). This is hardly the language of political militancy. But in moving on to focus so insistently on the specific ideal of 'justice', and in invoking 'power' in the first place, he is releas-ing a genie that will not easily be pushed back into the bottle of traditional conservative values. The association of power with literature is dangerous in this period; it is this which gives such strange energy to his writing.

It has sometimes been claimed that De Quincey's use of the term power in relation to literature is virtually synonymous with Wordsworth's concept of imagination. '(T)he word 'imagination' as Wordsworth and Coleridge used it is very similar to De Quincey's power', writes Devlin (1983, 78), speculating further that 'the authority of the two poets gave to the word a currency which De Quincey's could not manage'. Yet there is a marked difference in range of meaning between the two words. Wordsworth (1974a, 81) himself acknow-ledged that 'IMAGINATION – is a word which has been forced to extend its services far beyond the point to which philosophy could have confined them', and this is nowhere more marked than in its application in relation to society. Wordsworth (1974b, 126) once wrote that he had given 'twelve hours thought to the conditions and prospects of society, to every one for poetry'. When, in book 11 of the 1805 *Prelude* he describes his sense of failure as:

> the hiding places of my power
> Seem open, I approach, and then they close;
> I see by glimpses now ...
> (XI, 328-330)

his personal sense of loss is connected to broader issues. These lines are placed between two of the most striking and famous 'spots of time' in *The Prelude*: the feelings evoked when as a child he is confronted by the scene surrounding a gibbet on which a murderer has been hanged and the episode leading up to the death of Wordsworth's father. The link between these intense recollections and the thoughts they inspire is supplied by a keen sense of the 'power ... left behind' by 'these remembrances', a power which now seems only partly, and illusorily, available to the poet. 'So feeling comes in aid of feeling, and diversity of strength attends us, if but once we have been strong'.

But 'strength' and 'power' applied to what purpose? If in childhood the onset of powerful feeling is so often associated with guilt and fear, then strength in adulthood, this passage implies, must surely be used in relation to some larger project? In Wordsworth's case the immediate focus for that project is clearly the poem, but the poem itself bears witness to a correspondence between growth and renewal within the individual poet and his society. As Turner (1986, 171-2) has remarked, Wordsworth's periodic and deepening loss of faith in himself is related to loss of faith in the project of political liberation: *The Prelude* can be read as representing the 'meditative process by which Wordsworth recovered that faith through recovery of the child within.' That process, however, as Wordsworth records it, is necessarily incomplete, subject to reversals, unstable.

De Quincey claimed that the distinctions he developed between the Literature of Knowledge and Literature of Power were the result of 'many years conversation with Mr Wordsworth' and the slightly quirky definition of power which he offers in his essay on Pope is undoubtedly closely linked to the ideas which Wordsworth had been evolving over a long period of time. If this is so, then perhaps it sheds a clearer light on the kind of power children are envisaged as possessing when young, which may be diminished through education. For it is children's troubled but also vital openness to feeling which is at the centre of Wordsworth's project in *The Prelude*, an openness which he takes great pains to express in forms which are not reducible to neat categories or formulations. That he should insist that this capacity is – in itself – a power, suggests continuity with the potentially radical ideas of the interconnectedness of deep feeling and social critique that were part of both De

Quincey's and Wordsworth's intellectual inheritance. But whereas De Quincey makes children figure as objects (indeed, by analogy, texts) inspiring deep feeling in adults who respond to them, Wordsworth configures children as themselves subjects, often in complex and challenging new ways.

This is, I want to argue, a crucial shift whose implications may be compared to those key moments at which other marginalised groups can be perceived as defining themselves as speaking subjects within cultural discourses. That it was a shift which was provocative, even deeply disturbing, in terms of contemporary cultural and political concerns is attested by Hannah More's startling denunciation of cultural change in *Coelebs in Search of a Wife* (1808). More's character Mrs Stanley is dismayed by what she perceives to be happening within the culture of childhood. 'I know not,' she states, 'whether the increased insubordination of children is owing to the new school of philosophy and politics, but it seems to me to make part of the system'. And she concludes roundly, that 'There certainly prevails a spirit of independence, a revolutionary spirit, a separation from the parent state. It is the children's world' (1995, 215). The phrasing of Mrs Stanley's speech seems to register a break from the past in which the power attributed to children is crucial. The telling final phrase suggests – with horror – that children may now be perceived as subjects with full agency, shaping the form in which a new and dangerous order is emerging.

Wordsworth was thus not alone in perceiving children to have a power which required a searching new response. To a greater degree than with De Quincey and More, however, Wordsworth's response to that power was complex, involving both conservative and radical movements of thought, and many phases of revision. One of the major legacies of his thought resides in the way he consistently allows images of childhood in his poems to retain difficult and troubling elements, yet enables readers to perceive this as a necessary stimulus to growth, a force leading to greater depth of feeling and understanding. In this respect he differs sharply from More's character, who recoils fearfully from the power associated with children's new position.

By contrast, Wordsworth makes his images of childhood resistant to the easy projections and formulations, the kinds of categories within which adults might readily desire to see children. In doing so he develops an imaginative space within which childhood can seem to acquire a subject position, not easily assimilated within the dominant culture, and quite different from De Quincey's parallel notion, within which an idea of childhood is attributed power but actually remains objectified within adult thought and feeling.

Hence the question of the kind of power children both have and aspire to is put in a more probing and far-reaching form within Wordsworth's poetry than in the writing of any other of his contemporaries, retaining a challenging edge for readers to this day.

Bibliography

Bewell, A (1989) *Wordsworth and the Enlightenment*. New Haven and London: Yale University Press

Coleridge, S (1956) *Collected Letters of Samuel Taylor Coleridge* vol. 1. (E Griggs, ed) Oxford: Oxford University Press

De Quincey, T (1973) Alexander Pope. In J Jordan (ed) *De Quincey as Critic*. London: Routledge and Kegan Paul

Devlin, D (1983) *De Quincey, Wordsworth and the Art of Prose*. London: Macmillan

Jackson, M (1989) *Engines of Instruction, Mischief and Magic: Children's literature in England from its beginnings to 1839*. Lincoln: University of Nebraska Press

Richardson, A (1994) *Literature, Education and Romanticism: Reading as social practice 1780 – 1832*. Cambridge: Cambridge University Press

Schneider, M (1995) *Original Ambivalence*. New York: Peter Lang

Townsend, J (1994) *Trade and Plumb-Cake for Ever, Huzza! The life and work of John Newbery 1713 -1767 publisher and bookseller*. Cambridge: Colt Books Ltd

Tucker, N (1997) Fairy Tales and their Early Opponents: In defence of Mrs Trimmer. In M Hilton, M Styles and V Watson (eds) *Opening the Nursery Door: reading, writing and childhood 1600-1900*. London: Routledge

Turner, J (1986) *Wordsworth Play and Politics: a study of Wordsworth's poetry*. London: Macmillan

Wordsworth, W (1974a) *Essay, Supplementary to the Preface. The Prose Works of William Wordsworth*, vol 3. (W Owen and J Snyder, eds). Oxford: Clarendon Press

Wordsworth, W (1974b) *The Prose Works of William Wordsworth vol 1*. (W Owen and J Snyder, eds). Oxford: Clarendon Press

Wordsworth, W (1805) *The Prelude*. All quotations from J Wordsworth, M Abrams and S Gill (eds) (1979) *William Wordsworth: The Prelude 1799, 1805, 1850*. New York: Norton

10

Cultivating the Imagination: Coleridge and his circle on a literature for children

Janet Bottoms

From the time John Locke first voiced the idea that a child might be 'cozen'd' into learning to read with the help of 'some easy pleasant Book suited to his Capacity' (Locke, 1968, 257), publications aimed specifically at children multiplied, and in the last two decades of the eighteenth century increased at a rate that was recognised as unprecedented, even 'alarming' (Trimmer, 1803, 407). In spite of this, in 1801 we find the Edgeworths (Edgeworth, 1996, 121) complaining that 'our greatest difficulty has been to find a sufficient number of books fit for children to read', and in the following year William Godwin described his pseudonymous selection of *Bible Stories* as 'the production of a parent, who could not find, among the numerous works which for the last twenty years have been published for the use of children, one which he could with complete satisfaction put into the hands of his own' (Godwin, 1993, 313).

Neither the Edgeworths nor Godwin would have been satisfied by the others' idea of 'fit' reading matter for children, however. Political events, revolution in France, and the consequent suppression of radical speech and thought in England, were raising urgent questions about education among parents of widely differing persuasions.

As late as 1818 Coleridge noted that 'few questions are oftener or more anxiously asked by parents, than-what are the best books for children?' It was a question, as he said, that for 'all *practical* purposes' focused on fairy tales and 'imaginary travels' (Coleridge, 1987, 2, 188), but this was only a coded way of approaching a more important issue. Every one agreed with Locke that a child's book should not 'fill his Head with perfectly useless trumpery, or lay the principles of Vice and Folly' (Locke, 259), but there was major disagreement about what constituted 'useless trumpery' or, indeed, Vice. To both the rationalists, such as the Edgeworths, and to the conservative high-church-woman Sarah Trimmer, it was obvious that this included those 'wonderful tales' in which the child's fancy had hitherto been allowed to 'roam, un-bridled' instead of 'checked and confined to her proper walk' (*Monthly Literary Recreations*, 18).

For Wordsworth, however, it was 'books about Good Boys and Girls, and bad Boys and Girls' that constituted 'trumpery' (Wordsworth, 1937, 104), while Godwin condemned them as 'artificial, repulsive and insipid', and 'destitute of the firmness and vigour of a healthful mind'. 'The meanest narratives formerly written for the use of children', declared Godwin, in the Preface to *Bible Stories*, 'had at least the merit of going straight forward, and of stating in every sentence some fact to keep alive attention; or some picture to engage the imagination', whereas the 'modern improvers' encumbered their stories with 'abstract and general propositions', while leaving 'out of their system that most essential branch of human nature the imagination' (313).

Defining imagination

This was an issue that went to the very heart of the argument, and to the purpose of literacy, of the act of reading itself. What encouragement should be given to, or what regulation imposed on the imagination? What, in fact, *was* imagination – how dangerous, or how valuable? It is a question, I suggest, that had not been raised in relation to children's reading before this period, though the answer given to it would affect the subsequent development of both their reading and the books available to them.

Its first appearance is perhaps in *Emile*, Rousseau's description of his ideal education, and Rousseau notoriously wished to 'get rid of books'. Even more, he wished to get rid of imagination – or at the least to direct it into strictly con-trolled channels. 'The world of reality', Rousseau wrote, 'has its bounds, the world of imagination is boundless; as we cannot enlarge the one, let us res-trict the other; for all the sufferings which really make us miserable arise from the difference between the real and the imaginary' (Rousseau, 1974, 45).

The argument was taken up by the Edgeworths in their highly influential *Practical Education*. Even *Robinson Crusoe*, the one book approved by Rous-seau, seemed to them dangerous for 'boys of an enterprising temper, unless they are intended for a seafaring life, or for the army'; and 'the degree in which the imagination should be cultivated must be determined by the views which parents may have for their children, by their situations in society, and by the professions for which they are destined' (Edgeworth, 1801, 114, 111).

From her perspective, Sarah Trimmer was equally suspicious. In a long review of Godwin's Preface in her *Guardian of Education* she drew caustic attention to his every use of the word, and was scandalised by his claim that imagination was 'the ground-plot upon which the edifice of a sound morality must be erected'. This was the language of 'modern philosophy', contradicting the word of God that 'the imagination of the heart of man is evil from his youth'. 'We are persuaded', wrote Trimmer, 'that this will be fully exemplified in those who have been accustomed in their earliest days to be led by it' (Trimmer, 1802, 248). Coleridge's claim that imagination contains 'the seeds of all moral and scientific improvement' was, however, a clear challenge to both the scientific rationalists and the moralists. For him it was, in fact, 'the distinguishing characteristic of man as a progressive being', and requiring therefore to be 'carefully guided and strengthened' (1987, 2, 193).

What Coleridge had to say about the imagination goes far beyond the question of children's reading, but he did include this in developing his larger theory, and it is not insignificant that it was a period when he was not only himself a parent of young children, but was in regular contact with others. William Wordsworth, Robert Southey and William Godwin all had young families with whom they lived in close domestic contact; and, whatever Coleridge's own practical failings as a parent, it is clear from a strong similarity of language between what each man wrote about children's books that they must have discussed the question on many occasions.

For each of them, fairy tales, myths and legends were of key importance to a child's emotional, cognitive and moral growth. Coleridge lectured on the subject; Godwin listed the *Tales of Mother Goose, Beauty and the Beast*, and some of the traditional chivalric romances along with the *Arabian Nights* and *Robinson Crusoe*, 'if weeded of its methodism', among those books which might be depended on to 'excite the imagination' as well as 'generating an active mind and a warm heart' (Godwin, 1876, 118-20); while Wordsworth advocated leaving a child 'at liberty to luxuriate in such feelings and images as will feed her mind in silent pleasure'.

> This nourishment is contained in faery tales, romances, the best biographies and histories, and such parts of natural history relating to the power and appearances of the earth and elements, and the habits and structures of animals, as belong to it not as an art of science, but as a magazine of form and feeling. This kind of knowledge

> is purely good, a direct antidote to every evil to be apprehended, and food absolutely
> necessary to preserve the mind of a child like yours from morbid appetites. (Words-
> worth, 1937, 104)

The words 'antidote' and 'food' are significant. Rather than instructing, teaching or illustrating – the vocabulary typical of the rationalists and moralists-
Coleridge and his circle saw their preferred reading as feeding and nourishing
the child.

> Dumb yearnings, hidden appetites are ours,
> And they must have their food. (Wordsworth, 1970, 81)

Such literature was the 'antidote' to what they saw as intellectual precocity
and moral self-consciousness forced onto children by conservative moralists
and rationalists alike. Coleridge went further:

> We should address ourselves to those faculties in a child's mind, which are first
> awakened by nature, and consequently first admit of cultivation, that is to say, the
> memory and the imagination ... The comparing power, the judgment, is not at that
> age active, and ought not to be forcibly excited, as is too frequently and mistakenly
> done in the modern systems of education, which can only lead to selfish views,
> debtor and creditor principles of virtue, and an inflated sense of merit.

'Works of imagination', on the other hand, carried 'the mind out of self', and
showed 'the possible of the good and the great in the human character'(1987,
2, 192-3). As Wordsworth famously declared in Book V of *The Prelude*:

> The child, whose love is here, at least doth reap
> One precious gain, that he forgets himself. (77)

The play impulse

There was more to the Romantic defence of such stories than escapism.
Implicit in it was the idea of a vital freedom-freedom from both physical constraints and the imposition of either a quelling rationality or a restrictive
morality. This relates to a larger argument which Coleridge may have drawn
from the German poet Friedrich Schiller who, in his 'On the Aesthetic Education of Man', had pointed to the constant tension in man between human
aspirations and desires (Nature) and the constraints and limitations imposed
on him by Reason or Necessity. Necessity was what rationalists like the Edgeworths taught in their stories. Individual desires and instincts must submit to
a rational acceptance of the laws governing things 'as they are' which, in the
child's case, included the established social and familial hierarchies.

For the Romantics, however, this was an argument of despair, enforcing moral
as well as physical passivity. 'It will therefore always argue a still defective edu-

cation', said Schiller, 'if the moral character can assert itself only through the sacrifice of what is natural'; and he proposed instead to harmonise Reason and Nature through what he called 'the *play impulse*' [emphasis original], which sets man free 'both physically and morally'. This freedom, of course, could be truly possessed only 'in the unsubstantial kingdom of the imagination', and 'only in so far as it is *candid* (expressly renouncing all claim to reality), and only in so far as it is *self-dependent* [or autonomous]'. 'As soon as it is deceitful and simulates reality', said Schiller, 'it is nothing but a base tool for material ends' (Schiller, 1994, 32, 74, 128). Imagination also has its own reality, however. It is, declared Coleridge, essentially creative, a 'repetition in the finite mind of the eternal act of creation'; and when we are caught up in its realm, whether in play, in reading, or in watching a great drama, 'during the temporary oblivion of the worthless 'thing we are,' and of the peculiar state in which each man *happens* to be' the mind may be transported to 'a sense of its possible greatness', and 'the germs of that greatness' implanted in it (Coleridge, 1983, 1, 304; 2, 46n).

For the Romantics, therefore, it was in the aesthetic realm that mankind found the freedom in which to grow morally. They recognised it in the child's natural and instinctive play, and they believed it to be cultivated or strengthened by the kind of stories that open new realms of possibility. From an early age, Godwin noted, children would act over in 'fond imitation' the fables they were told, and which, in their 'unpractised imagination', they would take literally rather than allegorically (Godwin, 1797, 33).

Coleridge remembered running 'up and down the church-yard' re-enacting the stories he read (1966, 347), and Godwin recalled the 'long reveries' in which, at a slightly older age, he would invent 'whole books' as he walked, 'books of fictitious adventures in the mode of Richardson' or of 'imaginary institutions in education and government, where all was to be faultless' (Godwin, 1992, 37). In his *Life of Geoffrey Chaucer* he described the 'hippogyphs and dragons' and 'miraculous' adventures that fed 'the youthful fancy' of the poet. 'This', said Godwin, 'was the visionary scenery by which his genius was awakened; these were the acts and personages on which his boyish thoughts were at liberty to ruminate for ever' (Godwin, 1804, 62).

Again, the word 'visionary' is significant. For the Edgeworths, stories were a useful means to prevent 'precepts of morality from tiring the ear and the mind', but must be employed with care in order not to spoil the appetite for 'useful knowledge' (Edgeworth, 1796, viii, xi).

The presentation of 'useful knowledge' in such lightly fictionalised forms as Priscilla Wakefield's *Juvenile Anecdotes, founded on Facts*, or *The Beauties and Wonders of Nature and Art in a Series of Instructive Conversations*, was currently fashionable; but this was what Wordsworth called natural history, an 'art of science' rather than 'a magazine of form and feeling', and what Godwin would have excluded from a child's early reading on the grounds that 'such miserable minutenesses of detail ... freeze up the soul, and give a premature taste for clearness and exactness, which is of the most pernicious consequence'. 'Add to which', said Godwin, 'these things may be learned at any age, while the imagination, the faculty for which I declare, if cultivated at all, must be begun in youth' (Godwin, 1876, 18-20).

Coleridge uses very similar language in a letter of 1797, declaring, 'I have known some who have been *rationally* educated, as it is styled. They were marked by a microscopic acuteness; but when they looked at great things, all became a blank'. Seeing 'nothing but parts', the Universe was to them 'but a mass of *little things*'. They lacked a sense of the 'vast', or what we might now call a holistic approach. 'Should children be permitted to read Romances, & Relations of Giants & Magicians, & Genii?' asked Coleridge. 'I know all that has been said against it; but I have formed my faith in the affirmative. – I know no other way of giving the mind a love of 'the Great', & 'the Whole'' (Coleridge, 1966, 354-55).

Imagination in an age of reason

For Coleridge and his circle, it was through imagination that the child learned to place itself in relation to the world around it. However much man may delight in the beauties of nature, said Godwin, he does not enjoy them 'in their most perfect degree of pleasure, till his imagination becomes a little visionary', and Greek mythology, which 'replenished all nature with invisible beings', was 'admirably calculated to awaken the imagination' in this respect (Godwin, 1806, x, 7, 100-01). It was through imagination, also, that the child was able to 'put himself ... into the place of his neighbour, to feel his feelings, and to wish his wishes'. Without it, though he might 'learn by rote a catalogue of rules', and repeat his lesson 'with the exactness of a parrot' and 'the docility of a monkey', he could neither love 'nor be fitted to excite the love of others' (Godwin, 1993, 314). Godwin's claims stand in direct opposition to both Edgeworth's 'practical education', aimed at inducing 'useful and agreeable habits, well regulated sympathy and benevolent affections' (Edgeworth, 1796, viii), and Sarah Trimmer's insistence that everything should be 'subservient to moral instruction' (Trimmer, 1803, 184).

132

Coleridge, however, went further. For him the imagination was, above all, empowering. The figures peopling the Arabian Nights and fairy tales were 'produced by imagining an excessive magnitude, or an excessive smallness combined with great power', and exhibited 'through the working of the imagination, the idea of power in the will' (Coleridge, 1987, 2, 191). These were the 'wild tales' which Lamb said 'made the child a man, while all the time he suspected himself to be no bigger than a child' (Lamb, 1976, 81), and from which Coleridge claimed to have 'first learnt the powers of my nature and to reverence that nature' (1987, 1, 278).

For Edgeworth the qualities of 'generosity and honour, courage and senti-ment' which 'seize and enchant the imagination in romance' must be 'joined with justice, prudence, economy, patience, and many humble virtues, to make a character really estimable' (Edgeworth, 1966, 3, 145), and this de-manded a more systematic education in virtuous principle, based on a rational understanding of cause and effect. 'Enthusiasm', said Godwin, which was 'given by providence as the feature of youth', seemed of little account 'in books at present in use for children on these subjects' (Godwin, 1809, iii-iv).

The weight of educational publishing was heavily on the side of the rational-ists and the moralists. Between Coleridge and his friends, the debate was conducted largely through letters and private conversations, though it was also pursued in his lectures and, most notably, in the books Godwin wrote or commissioned for his Juvenile Library. When this folded, the debate seems largely to have faded away; although fairy tales continued to be published in an unobtrusive way, they were outweighed by the moral stories of writers such as the evangelical Mrs Sherwood.

In 1823, Edgar Taylor noted in his translation of the brothers Grimm, under the title *German Popular Stories*, that 'the popular tales of England have been too much neglected' in this 'age of reason, not of imagination'. Taylor was careful to describe these as 'dreams of fairy innocence', a term which Coleridge would never have applied to them, and justified them on the grounds of their interest for 'the antiquarian'. He also suggested, however, that they might offer 'plea-surable enjoyment', so long as they did not 'interfere with the important department of moral education' (Taylor, 1971, iv-v).

A few years later, George Cruikshank tried to recruit the stories themselves for 'moral education' by inserting didactic speeches within them, a move that Charles Dickens denounced in his famous essay, 'Frauds on the Fairies'. Dickens recognised instinctively what he himself owed to the imaginative fictions read or heard in his childhood, but he found it difficult to justify his belief in their vital importance except, as Harry Stone says, as 'a sort of bene-ficent amulet', 'a favourite way of apprehending reality' (Stone, 1968, 59). He described them as 'harmless' and a 'precious escape' from the real world in 'an utilitarian age' (Dickens, 1998,168), which was a long way from the claims made by Coleridge. Though Taylor ventured to suggest that the imagination was 'surely as susceptible of improvement by exercise, as our judgement or our memory' (v) he offered no further argument in support of the importance of cultivating the imagination in childhood.

Bibliography

Coleridge, S T (1966) Letter to Thomas Poole, 1797. In E Griggs (ed) *Collected Letters*, I, 1785-1800. Oxford: Clarendon Press

Coleridge, S T (1983) *Biographia Literaria*. (J Engell and W Bate, eds) 2 vols. London: Routledge and Kegan Paul

Coleridge, S T (1987) *Lectures 1808-1819 On Literature* (R A Foakes, ed) 2 vols. London: Routledge and Kegan Paul

Dickens, C (1998) Frauds on the fairies. In M Slater (ed) *Dickens' Journalism, 3, 'Gone Astray' and Other Papers from Household Words 1851-59*, 166-174. London: J M Dent

Edgeworth, M (1796) *The Parent's Assistant: or Stories for Children*. London: J.Johnson

Edgeworth, M and R L (1801/1996) *Practical Education*. Poole and New York: Woodstock Books

Godwin, W (1797) Of an early taste for reading, *The Enquirer: Reflections on Education, Manners, and Literature*. London: Robinson

Godwin, W (1804) *Life of Geoffrey Chaucer*, 2nd ed, vol 1. London: Phillips

Godwin, W [pseud Baldwin] (1806) *The Pantheon*. London: T. Hodgkins

Godwin, W [pseud E Baldwin] (1809) *History of Rome*. London: M. J. Godwin

Godwin, W (1876) Letter to W Cole,1802. In C Kegan Paul (ed) *William Godwin, His Friends and Contemporaries*. London: Henry S. King

Godwin, W (1992) Autobiography. In M Philp (ed) *Collected Novels and Memoirs of William Godwin*, vol 1. London: William Pickering

Godwin, W (1993) Preface to *Bible Stories* (1802). In P Clemit (ed) *Educational and Literary Writings*. London: William Pickering

Lamb, C (1976) Letter to Coleridge, 1802. In E Marrs (ed) *The Letters of Charles and Mary Lamb*, vol 2. Ithaca and London: Cornell University Press

Locke, J (1693/1968) *Some Thoughts Concerning Education*. (J A Axtell, ed). Cambridge: Cambridge University Press

Monthly Literary Recreations (1806) An essay on the self-sufficiency of youthful theorists, 18-19

Rousseau, J J (1974) *Emile*. (B Foxley, tr). London: J. M. Dent

Schiller, F (1994) *On the Aesthetic Education of Man*. (R Snell, tr). Bristol: Thoemmes Press

Stone, H (1968) Introduction. In H Stone (ed) *The Uncollected Writings of Charles Dickens: House-hold Words 1850-1859*, vol 1, 3-68. Bloomington, Indiana: Indiana University Press

Taylor, E (1971) Preface. In J and W Grimm, *German Popular Stories*, iii-xii. Menston, Yorkshire: The Scolar Press

Trimmer, S (1802-1806) *The Guardian of Education*, vols 1-5

Wordsworth, W (1937) Letter to an unknown correspondent, ca1806. In E De Selincourt (ed) *The Letters of William and Dorothy Wordsworth: The Middle Years*, vol 1. Oxford: Clarendon Press

Wordsworth, W (1970) *The Prelude: the 1805 text*. Oxford and New York: Oxford University Press

11

The Olympians: Neglect and imagination in late Victorian and Edwardian literature

Peter Cook

This chapter explores relationships between adults and children in Kenneth Grahame's *The Golden Age* and *Dream Days*, Edith Nesbit's *Treasure Seekers* series, and the stories of Saki. The three writers share themes and ideas which shed light on the way childhood was perceived in their era.

Olympian adults and imaginative children: Kenneth Grahame

Kenneth Grahame's (1859-1932) writing career began long before *The Wind in the Willows* appeared in 1908. In the Nineties he contributed to the notorious *Yellow Book*, and published two books of stories which evoke childhood: *The Golden Age* in 1895, and *Dream Days*, 1899. They are not much read now but were hugely successful in their day, selling out many editions up to the Second World War, and inspiring illustrations from Maxfield Parrish (1900) and E.H. Shepard (1928); as his illustrations for *The Golden Age* are among Shepard's best work, I have chosen to quote from his edition. And as neither book is well known now, I have quoted freely to evoke their atmosphere.

The Golden Age and *Dream Days* recount the adventures of a family of five children. But the Boy who narrates (we never learn his name) is no longer a child: he is an adult 'looking back to those days of old, ere the gate shut to behind me' (Grahame, 1928, np), to that *Golden Age* of childhood. At first sight, however, the children's predicament seems anything but golden. Their parents are dead, and they are brought up by aunts and uncles, the 'Olympians'. The irony behind the name is quickly established:

> They treated us ... with kindness enough as to the needs of the flesh, but after that with indifference (... the result of a certain stupidity), and therewith the common-place conviction that your child is merely animal. (np)

The children's lives are ruled by Aunt Eliza, whose world holds no place for young people, and Uncle Thomas, for whom they are 'a butt for senseless adult jokes'. The children are denied the pleasures of childhood, for reasons never explained to them; 'there was a circus coming to the neighbourhood, to which we had all been strictly forbidden to go'. This treatment fosters deep resentment in the Boy:

> ... there grew up in me, as in the parallel case of Caliban upon Setebos, a vague sense of a ruling power, wilful, and freakish. (Grahame, 1928, 18, 55-6, 1)

After these stories, we can no longer read the trial scene in *The Wind in the Willows* as harmless rollicking fun (Grahame, 1908, 139-141). The children's schooling is conducted upon harsh lines, 'hammered into one with rulers and with canes'. Small wonder that this provokes 'a general dogged determination to shirk and to evade' (Grahame, 1899, 254, 4).

One episode encapsulates the relationship between Olympians and children. Aunt Eliza is going to pay a call at a neighbouring 'big house', and bids the Boy accompany her: 'I was ordered also, in the same breath as the pony carriage':

> The lady who received us was effusive to Aunt Eliza and hollowly gracious to me. In ten seconds they had their heads together and were hard at it talking *clothes*. I was left high and dry on a straight-backed chair. (Grahame, 1899, 128)

Aunt and host ignore the child, who wanders off and finds in the library a wonderful book. The illustrations fire his imagination, and he weaves stories around the people and places depicted, losing all track of time. His aunt and host eventually discover him:

> Bitter it is to stumble out of an opalescent dream into the cold daylight ... but cruel-lest and bitterest of all to know, in addition to your loss, that the fingers of an angry aunt have you tight by the scruff of the neck. My beautiful book was gone too – ravished from my grasp by the dressy lady, who joined in the outburst of denuncia-tion as heartily as if she had been a relative. (Grahame, 1899, 141)

The blend of humour and frustration is perfectly judged. This scene touches the essence of the Boy's relationship with the Olympians: he is compelled to do things he doesn't want to do, then neglected. In response he retreats into a rich world of imagination, only to be rudely recalled by the next encounter with adults.

It is this matter of imagination which distinguishes the lives of the Olympians from the children's, and which lies at the heart of the divisions between them. The children's abiding sense of injustice rests chiefly on their perception that 'the sordid unimaginative ones ... rule the roost' (Grahame, 1899, 10). One of the worst acts, in the children's eyes, by the governess, Miss Smedley, is to tell little Charlotte that fairies don't exist. The Boy sums it up: 'grown-up people are fairly correct on matters of fact; it is in the higher gift of imagination that they are so sadly to seek'. The Olympians would have 'laughed' or 'sneered' at the children's imaginings, and returned to their own 'listless, impotent' pursuits (*ibid*, 84, 42, 4, 61). Most of the time they ignore the youngsters. And it is precisely this neglect that gives the children the freedom to inhabit the world of their imagination.

But it is clear from the outset that for the Boy, this world goes deeper than for his siblings. Where they are content with make-believe, the Boy seeks a more profound level of imagining. Nowhere is this more evident than in the very first story, *A Holiday*. Grahame evokes a spring morning with poetry and gusto:

> The masterful wind was up and out, shouting and chasing, the lord of the morning. Poplars swayed and tossed with a roaring swish; dead leaves sprang aloft, and whirled into space; and all the clear-swept heaven seemed to thrill with sound like a great harp. It was one of the first awakenings of the year. The earth stretched herself, smiling in her sleep; and everything leapt and pulsed to the stir of the giant's movement. (Grahame, 1928, 7)

It is also the birthday of one of the children, and all have the day off, 'free of lessons, free of discipline and correction'. But as soon as he can, the Boy slips away from their game:

> It was not that I was unsociable ... but the passion and call of the divine morning were high in my blood. Earth to earth! That was the frank note, the joyous summons of the day ... when boon Nature, reticent no more, was singing that full-throated song of hers that thrills and claims control of every fibre. (Grahame, 1928, 7, 11)

We cannot but think here of Mole at the beginning of *The Wind in the Willows*, summoned from his house-cleaning by the call of spring. (Grahame, 1908, [1]-2). But the echo of John Keats' 'full-throated ease' from the *Ode to a Nightingale* is also unmistakable, while the 'masterful wind' and 'dead leaves' of the opening sentences recall Shelley's *Ode to the West Wind* (Garrod, 1970, 207; Hutchinson, 1968, 577). And later in the story Grahame quotes Coleridge's 'Life-in-Death' from *The Rime of the Ancient Mariner* (Coleridge, 1967, 194). Reference to such famous poems would not have gone unnoticed at a time when poetry was still widely enjoyed by the common reader, to use

Doctor Johnson's phrase. Grahame clearly wants us to feel the links, to sense his roots in the high Romantic sensibility. And the proprietary spirit behind this key evocation is William Wordsworth: 'the divine morning' when Nature summons the receptive child, recalls the opening lines of *The Prelude* and the *Immortality Ode* (de Selincourt, 1969, 1; Hutchinson, 1971, 460). The Boy's lyrical response to Nature resurfaces a few years later in the character of the Water Rat, in Grahame's most famous book.

But Nature's 'full-throated song' is no Song of Innocence: a hawk swoops from the sky and kills a chaffinch:

> ... there rose, thin and shrill, a piteous voice of squealing. By the time I got there a whisk of feathers on the turf – like scattered playbills – was all that remained to tell of the tragedy just enacted. Yet Nature smiled and sang on, pitiless, gay, impartial. (Grahame, 1928, 15)

This new note comes as a shock and, rather than evoking the Romantic poets, looks forward to the early poetry of Ted Hughes. The younger boys, allies of Nature, share her indifference to conventional morality, and go further, showing an active 'contempt for self-constituted authority'. In church on Sundays the boys consider the merits of the local girls: 'The rest of the week afforded no leisure for such trifling; but in church – well, there was really nothing else to do!' (Grahame, 1928, 35, 54).

Strong words for 1895; Grahame was after all a contributor to *The Yellow Book*. The boys' outlook is at all events a flat rebuttal of the Olympians' church-going piety. The children have stronger, warmer ties with servants than with their relatives. Martha the cook has a soft spot for young Harold; she it is who carries him to bed when he is tipsy, and it is to her ample bosom that he runs for comfort. 'She's my idea of a real lady', the Boy confides (Grahame, 1928, 91, 114). Like most middle-class people of his time, he cannot conceive of life without servants. But his affection for Martha transcends class distinctions. She is a surrogate mother to the children. Aunt Eliza and Uncle Tom, along with most other middle-class adults that the children encounter, show no sympathy towards them.

There are exceptions, however, and these are revealing. In the story called *A Harvesting* the Boy is wandering along, preoccupied with his imaginings, when he walks straight into a clergyman. Conditioned by experience to expect a smack on the head for this, he is astounded when the man apologises: 'I noted at once a far-away look in his eyes, as if they were used to another plane of vision, and could not instantly focus things terrestrial'. This is a kindred spirit:

> 'I perceive,' he said pleasantly, 'that we have something in common. I, an old man, dream dreams; you, a young one, see visions. Your lot is the happier.' (Grahame, 1928, 75)

They repair to the Rector's book-lined study, 'a room which struck me at once as the ideal I had dreamed but failed to find' (76). This scholarly stranger treats him with respect and courtesy, as an equal. Walking home in the dark afterwards, the Boy feels more different and isolated than ever, but also strengthened by the experience:

> The dew was falling, the dusk closing ... Lonely spaces everywhere, above and around. Only Hesperus hung in the sky, solitary, pure, ineffably far-drawn and remote; yet infinitely heartening, somehow, in his valorous isolation. (81)

It is a defining moment in his childhood.

In another story: *The Roman Road*, the Boy chances upon an artist painting by the roadside; he is a man of few words, but no less likeable to the Boy: 'He answered your questions briefly and to the point, and never tried to be funny. I felt I could be confidential with him' (113). So the Boy tells him of his ideal city, and the Artist treats his confidences, the secrets of his imaginings, with the utmost respect. Once again the Boy feels the deep pleasure and reassurance of meeting an adult who treats him 'like an equal' and recognises his gift of imagination. And, once again, this makes parting all the more painful:

> I went downheartedly from the man who understood me, back to the house where I never could do anything right. How was it that everything seemed natural and sensible to him, which these uncles, vicars, and other grown-up men took for the merest tomfoolery? (118)

The scholar and the artist: both have a rich interior life, know how precious it is, and recognise it in the Boy. They understand childhood, because they have never lost contact with it. They cannot fully share the Boy's 'visions' (to use the Rector's word), as these are the exclusive gift of youth; but they can 'dream dreams', and this makes them kindred spirits.

And how brief is that lawless, visionary time of youth! Already Edward and Selina, the older children, have 'scant sympathy for make-believe' (159). Only Harold, Charlotte, and the Boy himself are free from the taint of adulthood. For them the day-to-day reality of childhood is grim. But it is a Golden Age indeed in the sense that, in the long hours of leisure that the Olympians' neglect affords them, their imagination has free rein, untrammelled by habit, convention, or self-consciousness. This experience is for the narrator and, one feels, for the author too, the most precious that life has to offer. It is a conviction shared by many writers, which has its origins in Wordsworth's great poems of childhood: the early books of *The Prelude*, the *Immortality Ode*, and *Tintern Abbey*.

What readers found so compelling in these stories is, I believe, precisely this sense that children have their own psychological, emotional and physiological make-up, and are not 'merely animal', to be beaten and hectored into conformity with the adult world. In Grahame's time such convictions were far from universal. In this sense these stories make a valuable contribution to the history of our understanding of childhood. And as literature, as I hope my quotes have shown, they need no special pleading.

Why, then, are they not better known? The problem may be that *The Golden Age* and *Dream Days* are difficult to categorise. Grahame is world famous as the author of one of the greatest works in all literature for children: these books are not written for children, but they are about children. They are neither wholly children's literature, nor wholly adult literature; they fall between the two, and are overlooked as a result.

Loyalty and Neglect: Edith Nesbit

In their own time *The Golden Age* and *Dream Days* were equally popular. But it is clear in retrospect that the first book has the wit, the incisiveness and genuine poetry of ideas the author felt compelled to express; the sequel is not on the same level of inspiration. The same can certainly be said of Edith Nesbit's *Treasure Seekers* stories. Nesbit (1858-1924) had been writing magazine fiction for over fifteen years when *The Story of the Treasure Seekers* was published in 1899. It was an immediate success, and Nesbit followed it with two sequels: *The Wouldbegoods* in 1901, and *New Treasure Seekers* in 1904. The first two were illustrated by Cecil Leslie. But, as with Grahame's *The Golden Age*, the situation out of which *The Story of the Treasure Seekers* arises is closed in the final chapter, so in the sequels Nesbit has difficulty reviving the dynamic tensions of the first book. Nevertheless, all three enjoy perennial popularity.

Like Grahame's stories, the *Treasure Seekers* series describes the adventures of a family of children, the Bastables. But unlike Grahame's narrator, Oswald is still a child when recounting these stories. Rather than looking back on childhood with an adult's hindsight, Nesbit evokes contemporary life at the turn of the century as experienced by children themselves.

Oswald's mother has recently died, and their father's colleague took advantage of the bereavement:

> Father was very ill after Mother died; and while he was ill his business-partner went
> to Spain – and there was never much money afterwards. I don't know why. (Nesbit,
> 1977, 17)

Oswald may not understand what's happened, and younger readers or listeners may not, but we do. This sets the narrative tone for the *Treasure Seekers* books: we have a child talking to other children. The texts can be read by children who are proficient readers, but they can also be read to younger children by adults. And Nesbit aims quite consciously to keep both adults and children amused and involved.

At first glance the children's relationships with adults seem quite unlike those of Grahame's protagonists. Oswald and his siblings are fiercely loyal to their widowed father: 'my father is the bravest man in the world', he tells us. The children resolve to restore 'the fortunes of the ancient House of Bastable' (Nesbit, 1977, 16), just as heroes and heroines do in the books they read. During their first attempt to find treasure, by digging for it in the garden, a neighbour comes to their aid:

> 'I never knew more than one coin buried in any one garden ... Hullo – what's that?'
> He pointed to something shining in the hole ... It was a half-crown. We looked at
> each other, speechless with surprise and delight, like in books. (17, 31-2)

This is the tenor of the children's adventures in this first book: they try different ways of making money, and end up being given money by adults.

'Noel is a poet', Oswald tells us simply; lucky Noel, to live at a time when being a poet was still an aspiration that children could openly relate to! Noel and Oswald go up to London and offer Noel's poems to a newspaper:

> When the editor had read the first poem – it was the one about the beetle – he got
> up and stood with his back to us. It was not manners; but Noel thinks he did it 'to
> conceal his emotions,' as they do in books. (19, 57-8)

And how right Noel was! The editor offers a guinea for the poems, to the boys' amazement and delight. Up to this point, the children's experience of adults has been wholly positive. But at the end of this episode, some weeks later, they discover the Editor's article:

> It was not at all amusing. It said a lot about Noel and me, describing us all wrong,
> and saying how we had tea with the Editor; and all Noel's poems were in the story
> thing. I think myself the Editor seemed to make game of them, but Noel was quite
> pleased to see them printed – so that's all right. (61)

These are the first seeds of doubt sown in Oswald's mind. Adult readers readily recognise Olympian traits in the neighbour and the editor: their tendency to patronise the children and laugh at their endeavours. But for the children the discovery is gradual, and painful. In *The Wouldbegoods* they meet the aunt of two friends, whom Oswald describes as 'like Miss Murdstone in *David Copperfield*. I should like to tell her so' (Nesbit, 1981, 13). He tries to put such experiences out of his mind, but in his heart he is realising that the adult world is not all that the children would like it to be. After another bruising encounter with an unsympathetic adult Oswald confides:

> ... when I went back into the dining-room I saw how different it was from when Mother was here, and we are different, and Father is different, and nothing is like it was. I am glad I am not made to think about it every day. (Nesbit, 1977, 130)

This is as close as Oswald gets to expressing his feelings.

Despite the children's loyalty to their father, he is a rather peripheral figure in their lives. He goes to 'his beastly office every day' (Nesbit, 1977, 23), and the children are left to their own devices. Even after the family fortunes are restored, in the final story of *The Treasure Seekers*, their father has no more time for his children than before. In *The Wouldbegoods* they are soon packed off to the country: 'we knew our being sent there was really only to get us out of the way' (Nesbit, 1981, 26). Essentially, then, the Bastable children are neglected, every bit as much as Grahame's youngsters, and feel that they and their games of make-believe are 'a nuisance to grown-up people' (31). Like Grahame's Olympians, their father regards children as immature, imperfect adults who should aspire to emulate adult behaviour. He leaves his children to their own devices, but then when they get into trouble he vents his disapproval 'in the voice we all hate' (1977, 171). Oswald knows 'but too well that grown-up people like to keep things far different from what we would, and you catch it if you try to do otherwise'. 'Catching it' means, for these children, 'the Malacca cane and ... solitary confinement' (1981, 31, 37, 26). Despite their good humour and good intentions, then, Nesbit's adults are in all important respects Olympians.

In response to adult mockery and neglect, Grahame's children reject the adult world and ally themselves to 'lawless' Nature. But the Bastable children's response is different. They try to conform to the values of the adult world, but in almost every story find that these are at odds with their own. Oswald muses:

> I don't know how it is, but having to consult about a thing with grown-up people, even the bravest and the best, seems to make the thing not worth doing afterwards. (1977, 139)

Brother Dicky puts it more bluntly: 'there must be *some* interesting things that are not wrong' (1981, 34). The dilemma is never resolved; the children cannot reconcile the demands of adults with the delights of their own world of adventure and make-believe.

Nesbit evokes that world with a sure touch. Noel, like Grahame's Boy, aspires to be a poet; but Nesbit's narrator emphatically does not. Oswald's kindred spirit is not a scholar or artist, but a military man: 'there are but too few grown-up people so far-seeing and thoughtful as this brave and distinguished officer' (1981, 50). And when he finds himself evoking the birds singing 'among the leafless trees of our sunny garden in beautiful Blackheath', he stops short and apologises: 'The author is sorry to see he is getting poetical. It shall not happen again!' (1987, 106). How different the stories would be if the bookish Noel were telling them! Thus we never find in the *Treasure Seekers* stories that profound imaginative life that Grahame's Boy experiences. Nor could Oswald, as a twelve-year-old, be expected to express the complexities of Grahame's now-adult narrator. What Nesbit gives us instead is a narrative that evokes the immediacy and transparency of children's self-expression, and their attempts to deal with their experience of a world that grows ever more complex as they get older. As a contribution to our understanding of the child psyche, and as literature, these stories have every bit as much to offer as Grahame's.

Saki and the Power of Imagination

Grahame's Olympians are loftily indifferent. Mr Bastable is well-meaning. But in Saki's world, adults in charge of children are neither. Saki (Hector Hugh Munro, 1870-1916) was not in any sense a children's writer, but there is among his work a handful of stories in which children take centre stage; these few tales are as deeply felt as any he wrote, and betray a profound sympathy with the attitudes and actions of the children portrayed. *The Lumber Room* (1914) tells the story of Nicholas, a young boy who caused havoc at breakfast by claiming that there was a frog in his food:

> Older and wiser and better people had told him that there could not possibly be a frog in his bread-and-milk ... [but] he had put it there himself, so he felt entitled to know something about it. (Saki, 1980, 371-2)

He is brought up by his cousins' aunt, 'a woman of few ideas, with immense powers of concentration' (373), and self-appointed representative of those 'older, wiser and better people': her Olympian credentials are impeccable.

Nicholas easily outwits her and explores a forbidden lumber room. His eye is caught by 'a piece of framed tapestry ... to Nicholas it was a living, breathing story':

> A man, dressed in the hunting costume of some remote period, had just transfixed a stag with an arrow ... but did the huntsman see, what Nicholas saw, that four galloping wolves were coming in his direction through the wood? ... The man had only two arrows left in his quiver. (374)

Like Grahame's Boy in the library, Nicholas becomes absorbed in a rich interior world; the tapestry inspires his imagination to create stories around the figures depicted. Also like the Boy, he is returned to the material world by the voice of an infuriated, Olympian aunt. Reality is bleak that evening, the aunt maintaining a 'frozen muteness' at tea; but imagination sustains the child:

> As for Nicholas, he, too, was silent, in the absorption of one who has much to think about; it was just possible, he considered, that the huntsman would escape with his hounds while the wolves feasted on the stricken stag. (376, 377)

Nicholas's lonely, upper middle class childhood was one that Saki knew intimately. But in *Morlvera* (1919), he takes us into the very different world, with which he was clearly less familiar, of the London poor. The setting, though, is thoroughly upper class: the Olympic Toy Emporium in the West End. The name might be an unconscious echo of Grahame, in that the shop's toys are more attractive to Olympian adults than to children: 'they were the sort of toys that a tired shop-assistant displays and explains at Christmas-time to exclamatory parents and bored, silent children' (491). In the window is a large doll with a striking face, 'cold, hostile, inquisitorial':

> One might have imagined histories about her by the hour, histories in which un-worthy ambition, the desire for money, and an entire absence of all decent feeling would play a conspicuous part. (492)

Saki here is doing with the doll what Nicholas does with his tapestry: using it as a springboard for flights of imagination. And two working-class children, Emmeline and Bert, see the doll in the window and begin to do the same:

> Emmeline ... gave her a horrible reputation, based chiefly on a second-hand know-ledge of gilded depravity derived from the conversation of those who were skilled in the art of novelette reading; Bert filled in a few damaging details from his own limited imagination. (492)

They name the doll Morlvera, after 'an adventuress who figured prominently in a cinema drama' (492-3). A car stops outside the shop door, and a wealthy mother and son enter the shop. The mother forces her son Victor to buy the doll for a cousin he detests. As they leave he takes his revenge:

> The car had to be backed a few yards in the process of turning. Very stealthily, very gently, very mercilessly Victor sent MorIvera flying over his shoulder, so that she fell into the road just behind the retrogressing wheel. With a soft, pleasant-sounding scrunch the car went over the prostrate form, then it moved forward again with another scrunch. (494-5)

As in *The Lumber Room*, a child wages war on the Olympians, and wins. Emmeline and Bert gleefully witness the destruction of the doll they named and animated. Later on, Emmeline's imagination fits Victor into their story:

> 'I've been finking. Do you know oo 'e was? 'E was 'er little boy wot she sent away to live wiv poor folks. 'E come back and done that.' (495)

Some of Saki's comments on these children are patronising; but he does pay them the compliment of seeing in them the same powers of imagination, to him the most precious of gifts, as the middle-class Nicholas possesses. In both stories the children use their imagination as a recompense for the short-comings of the 'stale' material world. In *Sredni Vashtar* (1911), the power of imagination is taken much further, and with cataclysmic results. Conradin is a ten-year-old boy whose life is beset by 'illnesses and coddling restrictions and drawn-out dullness' (136). Far more detrimental to his wellbeing, though, is his grown-up cousin and guardian, Mrs De Ropp, who is 'dimly aware that thwarting him 'for his good' was a duty which she did not find particularly irk-some'. We recognise immediately the recurrent tensions between Olympian and child:

> In his eyes she represented those three-fifths of the world that are necessary and disagreeable and real; the other two-fifths, in perpetual antagonism to the forego-ing, were summed up in himself and his imagination. (136)

But in none of the fictions discussed so far is the chasm between adult and child so absolute as here: 'from the realm of his imagination she was locked out – an unclean thing' (137).

Conradin's haven is a neglected tool-shed where he keeps his two pets: the first is 'a ragged-plumaged Houdan hen, on which the boy lavished an affec-tion that had scarcely another outlet'. But the second animal arouses different emotions:

> Further back in the gloom stood a large hutch ... the abode of a large polecat-ferret ... Conradin was dreadfully afraid of the lithe, sharp-fanged beast, but it was his most treasured possession. (137)

He calls the ferret Sredni Vashtar and cultivates rituals around it; both the exotic, Oriental name, so akin to the author's own pen-name, and the rituals, represent a rebuttal of Mrs De Ropp's Christianity. With all three authors we have discussed, children's instincts are at variance with Olympian morality: the Bastables discover that everything 'interesting' is 'wrong', while Grahame's Boy and Harold find 'nothing to do' in church; but Conradin takes this much further, developing his fear of Sredni Vashtar, and loathing of his guardian, into an alternative religion.

When Mrs de Ropp finds the Houdan hen and takes it away, Conradin goes to the tool-shed in the evening, and introduces 'an innovation in the worship of the hutch-god':

> 'Do one thing for me, Sredni Vashtar.'
> The thing was not specified. As Sredni Vashtar was a god he must be supposed to know. (138-9)

The child repeats his 'bitter litany' in front of the hutch every evening. Mrs De Ropp sees that he still visits the tool-shed, investigates further, and discovers the hutch in its far corner: 'What are you keeping in that locked hutch?' she asked. 'I believe it's guinea-pigs. I'll have them all cleared away.' Conradin watches from the window as she enters the tool-shed, and 'breathe[s] his prayer for the last time':

> Sredni Vashtar went forth,
> His thoughts were red thoughts and his teeth were white.
> His enemies called for peace, but he brought them death.
> Sredni Vashtar the Beautiful. (139)

In the shed Mrs De Ropp opens the cage, and is killed by the 'lithe, sharp-fanged beast'. Conradin is watching the shed door desperately, and 'presently his eyes were rewarded':

> ... out through that doorway came a long, low, yellow-and-brown beast, with ... dark wet stains around the fur of jaws and throat. Conradin dropped on his knees. The great polecat-ferret made its way down to a small brook at the foot of the garden, drank for a moment, then crossed a little plank bridge and was lost to sight in the bushes. Such was the passing of Sredni Vashtar. (139)

At the end Saki leaves us to draw our own conclusions. Did the Olympian Mrs De Ropp, whom the author repeatedly stresses is short-sighted, put her head into the cage and provoke a natural retaliation? Or did Conradin's powers of imagination and incantation play their part? The reader is free to ponder. But there is no doubt where the author's sympathies lie.

For each of these three writers, the world of imagination is central to their portrayal of childhood. It is a source of pleasure, and offers consolation for the Olympians' neglect and lack of understanding. But where for Nesbit it is a game of make-believe, for children to enjoy and adults to smile at, for Grahame it is a sacred place each of us can enjoy as a child, but which is lost as we grow up; and for Saki it has the power to strike at and subvert a hostile adult world.

Bibliography

Coleridge, E H (ed) (1967) *Coleridge: Poetical Works*. London: Oxford University Press

Garrod, H W (ed) (1970) *Keats: Poetical Works*. London: Oxford University Press

Grahame, K (1899) *Dream Days*. London: The Bodley Head

Grahame, K (1908) *The Wind in the Willows*. London: The Bodley Head

Grahame, K (1928) *The Golden Age by Kenneth Grahame. With Illustrations and Decorations by Ernest H. Shepard*. London: The Bodley Head

Hutchinson, T (ed) (1968) *Shelley: Poetical Works*. London: Oxford University Press

Hutchinson, T (ed) (1971) *Wordsworth: Poetical Works*. London: Oxford University Press

Nesbit, E (1977) *The Story of the Treasure Seekers*. Harmondsworth: Puffin Books

Nesbit, E (1981) *The Wouldbegoods, being the Further Adventures of the Treasure Seekers*. Harmondsworth: Puffin Books

Nesbit, E (1987) *New Treasure Seekers*. Harmondsworth: Puffin Books

Saki (H H Munro) 1980 *The Complete Works.* London: The Bodley Head

Selincourt, E (ed) (1969) *Wordsworth: The Prelude.* London: Oxford University Press

12

Arthur de Caldicott and the New Literacy

Vivienne Smith

Introduction

Kevin Crossley-Holland published the first volume in his Arthur trilogy, *The Seeing Stone*, in 2000. The book was enthusiastically received, was shortlisted for the Whitbread children's book of the year and was winner of the Smarties Prize Bronze Award. *Arthur at the Crossing Places* followed in 2001 and *Arthur King of the Middle March* in 2003 but, by then, the children's UK marketing world had changed. The glitz of Harry Potter and the virtuosity and breadth of Pullman's *His Dark Materials* trilogy meant that these quiet and rather understated books could slip through the publicity net almost unnoticed. Apart from reviews in the quality press there was very little fuss. I think there should have been.

In this chapter, I hope to begin to give these books the attention they deserve. I want to argue that not only are they masterly examples of contemporary writing for children, but that they have important lessons to teach and insights to offer the children who read them. Most particularly, I want to look at the way literacy is handled in these books and to consider whether any of the experiences of literacy change that the fictional Arthur encounters in the books are relevant to the experiences of young readers and writers today.

The books tell the story of Arthur de Caldicott who at the beginning of the trilogy is a 13 year old boy, living with his family in a small manor in the Welsh marches in the year 1199. Arthur is growing up. He is at that stage in his life between boyhood and adulthood, between dependence and independence. He sees his childhood wane with the old century and the possibilities of his adult life wax with the new.

The first book shows Arthur with his family at home. It charts his life in the manor – his duties, his relationships with his family and the villagers, his hopes, his triumphs, his disappointments and his worries. The second sees him move to Holt Castle, further to the west, where he becomes squire to Lord Stephen, meets the girl to whom he is to become betrothed and prepares to join the fourth crusade. The last sees him, now 16 and knighted, with the crusaders, delayed and frustrated in Venice and embroiled in the Byzantine politics that would lead to the sacking of Christian Zara (which Arthur sees and abhors) and eventually, brings him home to Holt and Caldicott, and finally to his own manor of Catmole.

In a number of ways, as the title of the second volume suggests, the books show Arthur in places and times of flux. Most obviously, the century is changing: the books take place in those indeterminate times when the certainties of one century give way to the realities of the new. Geographically too, there is indeterminacy: Arthur grows up in a land which is, or has been, both English and Welsh. There is a constant threat to both Caldicott and Holt from Welsh insurgence. In Venice, too, there is uncertainty. He camps with the other crusaders on the island of St Nicholas; like all of Venice, this is a place between land and sea, and at this time, a place between continents and ideologies: here the Christian West and the Muslim East mingle. Physically and emotionally too, as I have already suggested, Arthur is growing, crossing from boyhood to manhood.

In two other important ways, we see Arthur live his life through a crossing place. The first is represented by his seeing stone, the piece of magical obsidian, a gift from Merlin. 'From this moment, here on Tumber Hill, until the day you die, you will never own anything as precious as this,' says Merlin (2000, 54). Through it, Arthur is able to cross into another time and, in scenes that reflect his own concerns, watch his namesake, Arthur of Britain, come to his kingdom, set up his court and face the difficulties of kingship. The way Arthur learns to read his seeing stone is one of the major themes of the novel, though it is not the subject of this paper. Second, and what does concern us here, is the way that we see Arthur at a crossing place of literacy practices. Crossley-Holland has placed him at a time of enormous and far-reaching literacy change – and Arthur de Caldicott is on the cusp of that change.

Literacy in Early Medieval England

The years around 1200 were darkish times for some sorts of literacy in England. Long past was the cultural flowering of the Anglo-Saxon period, which produced religious and secular texts as rich and various as the

Lindisfarne Gospels, Bede's *Ecclesiastical History* and the poem *Beowulf*. Far into the future, and far beyond the predictive imagination of anyone living, were the literary masterpieces of Chaucer and the Gawain poet. Two hundred or so years before, England had been secure in its Latin literacy and its vernacular oral tradition; in another two hundred or so, it would be secure again in increasingly literate varieties of Middle English; but now, in about 1200, it was not secure. Norman French rather than English or Latin had become the language of court, the place of the vernacular in writing had not yet been firmly established and, as Clanchy (1993) makes clear, the purposes to which literacy was put were changing fast. Less obviously was literacy the preserve of monks and academics; more surely was it the tool of lawyers.

At the same time, it seems, another change was happening: increasing numbers of the children of the wealthy were being taught to read. What they did with that reading is less sure. Except for those destined for a career in the church or the law, for whom there were religious and legal documents, there seem to have been few texts for them to read, and not much reason to write, for society around them remained predominantly oral. It is as if these young people were being given a tool, but it was a tool that neither they, nor those people who presented it to them, knew yet how to use.

It is into this indeterminate, half-literate world that Crossley-Holland places his fictional Arthur.

Arthur: the apprentice literate

In the trilogy, Arthur de Caldicott, at the insistence of his father, Sir John, is sent every day to Oliver, the priest, in order to learn to read and write. It is because Oliver is a priest that he is literate and therefore able to teach, and so priestly things are the matter of Arthur's study. Together the two of them read the scriptures. Arthur is instructed to read them aloud, to write them out, discuss them and internalise them. This, as far as Oliver is concerned, is the point of the exercise: one reads and writes in order to know and understand the word of God better and, therefore, to know what is right. Arthur is happy with this: he is an apt pupil who enjoys his work. He is quick and motivated. He rarely forgets a name or a detail and, although Oliver's explanations are often long and tedious, Arthur knows he can usually be persuaded to argue:

> One reason why I quite like my lessons with Oliver is I am allowed to argue with him, and find out new things. It is like climbing Tumber Hill inside my own head: the further I go, the more I see; and the more I see, the more I want to see. (2000, 39)

And later:

> I do like Oliver. I like arguing with him, and although I often disagree with what he says, he always makes me think. (2001, 277)

This ability to argue, to think for himself, becomes an integral part of Arthur's literacy.

Furthermore, Arthur is interested in literacy per se. He likes language. He plays with words and enjoys their flexibility. His delight in identifying and listing *jack* words, for example, (2000, 33) demonstrates this, as does his poem, *Nain in armour* (51) where he borrows the technical terms he has learned for individual pieces of armour to describe his sleeping grandmother. He cares about the sound and weight of words too, and so takes particular care to find the right words for little Luke's grave-stone (181; 200). The technical aspects of literacy interest him. He wants to know about books and their making. 'How many books are there ... in the world?' he asks Oliver (39). He is keen, especially at first, to visit the scriptorium at Wenlock Abbey to see how books are actually made. When the visit finally takes place, he is fascinated by the process, the preparing of the vellum and the mixing of the ink. 'I love making ink,' announces Arthur to the monks, 'It is a kind of magic. Ink is the words' blood' (2001, 281).

But despite his interest and obvious facility for it, literacy poses three difficulties for Arthur. The first is intellectual. He simply doesn't want to do the sort of writing that is expected of him. Oliver urges him to practice for one hour each day, so that he might develop a good writing hand. But what is there to write? For Oliver there is no difficulty: Arthur should copy out the day's reading. Copying and scribing, after all, were most commonly what writing was for in the early Middle Ages. But Arthur is not satisfied with this:

> I don't want to write about Abner and Ner and Ishbosheth and Joel and Asahel, especially not in Latin. I want to write my own life here in the Marches, between England and Wales. My own thoughts, which keep changing shape like clouds. I am thirteen and I want to write my own joys and fears and sorrows. (2000, 12)

The second problem is physical. Arthur is left-handed. At a time when the left (Latin: *sinister*) was associated with evil, unnaturalness and illegitimacy, this was a serious difficulty. Writing at this time was a public act, and for Arthur to use his left hand in public would have been shocking. He is no more allowed to write with his left hand than he is to use his sword left-handed. The problem transcends the physical, and becomes psychological. The writing he is expected to do denies an essential part of his make up – his left-handedness: it positions him as someone he ought to be, rather than the person he actually is.

The third problem, and the one which exercises Arthur most, is societal. He lives in a society that is not convinced that literacy is important. His grandmother, Nain, for example, maintains that literacy is unnecessary. Her husband, a war lord, could not read and had no use for it. 'Think what will happen if you begin to depend on writing,' she says. 'Your memory will weaken. If something is worth knowing ... it's worth remembering' (2000, 40). Writing, she implies, is for the feeble-minded.

More particularly, Arthur is worried about why he is continuing to learn with Oliver. Why, he wonders, is Sir John so keen for him to be literate and have a 'good hand'? He already reads and writes better than Sir John himself and his older brother Serle, and it seems that the literacy they have is enough for the purposes of the knight and landowner Sir John and his heir, Serle. Why should Arthur need more? His fear is that Sir John has other ideas for his future. He knows that the manor of Caldicott is small and will not support two households. Might Sir John solve the problem of his second son's inheritance by sending him to be a priest, a monk or a schoolman? Is this what his literacy training is for? Arthur sincerely hopes not. His dearest wish is to be a knight himself and to marry his cousin Grace. To be seen as a promising scholar might further compromise his chances.

For Arthur, as is the case for some teenage boys today, excelling in literacy carries with it image problems. The active, manly life he hopes for does not accord with how society, both as it is presented in the trilogy, and how it appears through historical sources, seems to have regarded literates. There are, for example, no strong literate role models in the trilogy for Arthur. Lord Stephen cannot read and write at all, and Sir John does so only with difficulty. All the adult literates he meets in the Marches are in service either to the Church or to an overlord. The single exception to this is Marie de Meulan, whom Arthur meets at Wenlock, and she, of course, is a woman. Of Arthur's contemporaries, the girls are more literate and metalinguistically aware than the boys. It is Grace who invents the test of word-play to compensate Arthur for his poor yard skills in the contest with his cousin and brother, and she who composes and receives lyrics when they are disappointed in their betrothal. Winnie, to whom Arthur becomes betrothed, sends him teasing love letters. There is no suggestion of any literate practice between the boys, except in Arthur's tutoring of young Bertie when they are on campaign.

Had Arthur been real, his reading of how society regarded literates would have been reinforced by the representations of literate behaviour available to him. At a time when art work as well as literacy was in the hands of the

Church, these images, like most texts, would have been religious. For example, images of the Annunciation were common throughout the Middle Ages in stonework, on murals and in psalteries. Often they show Mary with a book. The book is significant. Mary is not wiling away her leisure hours with a novel: she is studying the scriptures. Her study is a factor in her submissiveness to the will of God, and this is the point of these images. Submission to the written word, made corporeal in the life of a cleric, is exactly what Arthur most wished to avoid.

A further worry to a boy like Arthur might have been the fact that images of girls reading seem to have been relatively common. At both Corby Glen in Lincolnshire and Chalfont St Giles in Buckinghamshire, wall paintings survive from the early thirteenth century. They show what appears to be St Anne teaching the young Mary to read. Even in this less religiously significant image, the implication is that reading was passive and chiefly for girls. Where images of men and reading do occur, these too are religious. In Bibles and psalteries, for example, the four evangelists commonly appear holding their gospels and, of course, the symbol of St Luke is the book. What might all this suggest to an active boy like Arthur? My guess is that it would suggest that reading was for girls and for the religious. It was not an attainment much to be valued by a romantic young knight.

Arthur: the innovator

It is through overcoming these three difficulties that Arthur shapes his own literacy, and turns what was presented to him as a clerical accomplishment into a tool suited to the needs of an adolescent boy.

First, he must deal with the left-handedness, and the solution to this is both simple and far-reaching: he learns to write with both hands. Arthur's right hand, then, becomes the official face of his literacy; he uses it in lessons with Oliver and on those occasions when his writing is on display. His left hand he uses when he writes for himself. What follows is a significant change in literacy practice, for Arthur's writing can no longer be the public activity of the medieval scriptorium. It must now be secret. No-one must see him use the forbidden left hand, so he must find somewhere to write where he will not be disturbed – his room under the eaves at Caldicott, for example.

This isolation has important consequences. First, the control he takes over transcription concentrates his attention on the private nature of his literacy and his own thinking. If he can write *how* he likes in private, why can he not write *what* he likes as well? In private, writing can be writing by him and for him, and he can be in control of composition as well as transcription. With this control comes freedom. As Arthur realises that he can do with his writing as he likes, he is freed from the necessity of producing the kind of public text that Oliver expects of him. In terms of Britton's (1975) modes of writing, Arthur's enforced privacy enables him to make the move away from the typically transactional texts of the middle ages into what is essentially the expressive mode. He learns to use writing to make sense of his thoughts and his feelings. He writes a personal, reflective diary.

It is through this diary, throughout the three volumes of the trilogy, that Arthur comes to terms with the person he is and the person he is becoming. At Caldicott and at Holt, he presents himself as a teenage lad, perhaps a little more sensitive than most, and intelligent, but with the worries, hopes and mischief of many young boys. It is in the third volume that Arthur grows up and where his journal is especially instrumental in this process. Life in the crusader camp is not easy. Arthur comes face to face with the brutality of warfare, the corruption of leadership, the unfairness of fate, the religious and racial prejudice of his age and the violence and intolerance of his own father. It is as he writes and reflects on these matters that he comes to his last crossing place: the place where idealism gives way to grim reality. The crusade is not the high-minded adventure of his dreams and Arthur needs to reset his thinking. His journal gives him the space to accommodate reality.

It is in this third volume, too, that Arthur, almost unconsciously, sets to rest the matter of image. He has little time now to worry about poor yard skills. As he describes his time on campaign in Venice and Zara, his bravery, chivalry and masculinity are proven beyond doubt. There is nothing effeminate about the boy who helps undermine the walls of Zara and who fights to save the wounded Bertie. Arthur learns the sordid business of medieval warfare alongside foot soldiers and armourers as well as knights. He writes of his experiences and his reaction to them: how he is sickened by the crusaders' murder of a young boy during the siege of Zara; how his friendliness towards a group of Saracens leads to rape and bloodshed. It is his writing that helps Arthur make sense of all this; that enables him to put the horror of it into the perspective of his own developing morality, and see it as it is.

The crusade causes Arthur's writing to change. It turns his thinking outwards. No longer is his central concern himself and his relationships. Now the bigger matters that were always part of his thinking come to the fore: justice, prejudice, morality: Arthur explores each one convincingly, with a sensitivity and a sympathy for humanity beyond the reach of most young people, real or fictional. Now his writing is private because his ideas are mature and serious, and because he has little time: not because he is afraid of being found out. Through his writing, and the reflective thinking that it has made possible, Arthur develops the confidence to be an unusual young man in his world: one who is literate and one for whom, as the Saracen fortune teller notes, heart-line and head-line are one (2003, 303).

The text Arthur produces is a text that would have been quite exceptional in the twelfth century, had it been real. To the best of my knowledge, no text from the time survives that demonstrates personal, reflective writing of this kind. Crossley-Holland has positioned Arthur as a literary innovator. But he is too good a medievalist to make Arthur anachronistic. What makes Arthur's new literacy plausible is its situatedness in the genuine textual practices of the middle ages.

Arthur: transformer of text

One of the strengths of Arthur's text is that it is rooted in the oral and verna-cular tradition of the time in which the novels are set. This is most clear in the set pieces Arthur produces in response to his worries, disappointments and emotional upsets. His reply to Grace, 'a song without a voice' (2001, 200-201), for example, is clearly a re-working of the song 'I gave my love a cherry': Arthur tells us so himself. Less obvious is the inspiration of his list of sorrows, fears and joys (2000, 48). However, a number of poems listing the variously numbered joys and sorrows of Mary exist in manuscripts from the fifteenth century (eg *Mary, for thine joys five*), and one of these survives today as a Christmas carol. It seems reasonable to assume that this counting of joys was a medieval game for centuries before written versions were made. A boy of Arthur's time might well have taken on the idea and applied it to himself. Thirdly, Arthur takes on the cadence and patterning of poetic language. As Arthur and his party prepare to set sail to Zara, Arthur remembers part of an 'old poem' that Oliver used to recite:

> Then those warriors stowed gleaming war-gear
> deep within the galley: they launched
> the well-built boat and began their journey. (2003, 138)

This is *Beowulf* (lines 210-215), preserved and passed down in the fictional cultural memory of the inhabitants of Caldicott. Arthur takes on the allitera-tion, cadence and rhythm for himself. This is what he writes as he sails home with the injured Lord Stephen:

> On deck, the saltspray stings my eyes, and my sight blurs; the roaring wind deafens me and the ocean reach chills me. (315)

In the middle of a prose passage, Arthur has produced a couplet of Old English verse. Here is the alliteration, the rhythm, the caesura and the *feel* of *The Wanderer*; but this is not pastiche. This is Arthur transforming his oral tradition into his own literacy: a literacy that expresses his emotions and serves his needs.

It is fitness to purpose that is central to Arthur's transformation of text. He re-writes the riddle song because the enigma at its heart best fits the confusion he feels about his relationship with Grace. He adopts the bleak elegiac tone of *The Wanderer*, because it matches the dejection he feels in leaving the crusade and his beloved horse, and his worry for Lord Stephen's health. Arthur takes the existing forms of his culture and transforms them to meet his needs. This is one reason why the trilogy is so significant. Its rootedness in cultural possibility makes Arthur's text convincing to the knowledgeable reader, and its innovacy demonstrates how literacy develops.

Arthur in the third Millennium

Why does any of this matter? Why should a novel set in the past about a character who looks to an even more distant past have particular relevance to young readers in the twenty-first century? I think there are two reasons; both concern Arthur's literacy, and both are particularly important to teachers.

First, like Arthur, boys who read and write today sometimes have a problem with image. In the popular imagination, and even in children's literature, it is difficult to find strong, active role models for literate boys. Too often, boys for whom reading and writing are important are minor characters in books. I think of Albert Sandwich, in *Carrie's War* (Bawden, 1973), who is an outsider and bit of a swot, and Noel, the poet of *The Treasure Seekers* (Nesbit 1899), whose poems are included to amuse the adult readership. Neither boy is likely to inspire the young reader to emulate him. Recently, Haddon (2003) has presented us with one of the most literate teenage protagonists for years in Christopher Boone. But Christopher is a dysfunctional adolescent with Asperger's Syndrome.

The problem with literate boys in children's literature is clear. It matters be-cause, as Hollindale (1997) tells us, books are one of the places where children go to learn what childhood is, and what it is possible for children to be. Especially in a time when we are concerned about boys' literacy and under-achievement, we need books that show that it is possible to be a normal literate boy: that boys can and do read and write, and that they do so without compromising their masculinity or becoming misfits. Arthur, who is mischievous, independent, brave, loyal and active, shows this in spades. He is, as Sir John tells him, a boy 'fit to be a king' (2000, 300). Arthur has the potential to make literacy cool.

Furthermore, and rather more subtly, Arthur is important because he can teach us about dealing with changes in literacy practice. For we, at the turn of the twenty-first century are in another time of literacy change. The last twenty years have seen enormous changes in both public and private literacy. The production and reception of newspapers and of electronic media have been transformed. The word processor has overtaken the typewriter; the fountain pen, and even the ballpoint, for many writers have become almost obsolete. We email instead of writing letters, we use spell checks, predictive text, instant messaging and photo-messaging. We communicate via websites, blogs and chatrooms. The pace of change is so fast that many adults fear they are being left behind.

As it was for fictional Arthur, so it is for many of the real youth of today. As Carrington (2004) shows, it is they who, on their mobile phones and at games consoles, outside the influence of adults and teachers, are in the vanguard of this literacy change. It is they who grasp the new technology eagerly and bend it to their social and interpersonal needs.

The problem, if there is one, rests with the older generations. Like Nain and Oliver, it is adults, sometimes those in authority, who resist the change and resort to moral panic (Carrington, 2005). It is the traditional literates who complain that the spell check has rendered it unnecessary for children to learn to spell properly, that the organisational properties of websites which favour radial rather than linear reading have made it difficult for children to learn to follow and construct sustained logical arguments (Greenfield, 2006). Literate adults worry that the literacy which sustains the way their world is ordered is passing. They suspect that whatever will come in its place will be fast, facile and deficient.

Perhaps they are right to worry. Who can tell? But there is a lesson here from the fictional Arthur. The new literacy he forged out of his cultural resources and his personal need was rich, meaningful and moral. It shaped his thinking, established his independence and moulded his understanding of and sympathy for humanity in ways that were not easily accessible to his more conventionally literate peers. It might be that the new literacies currently being developed by the young people in our classrooms will be just as strong and just as rich as Arthur's. Like his, their literacies will be based on need and existing cultural resources. For them to make the most of those resources, we need to give them space and encouragement and confidence, so that the literacies they eventually shape can blossom as Arthur's did. And, if what does develop is a literacy so different from ours that we find it hard to recognise, then we need to hold faith: we need to look to see what good is there already and celebrate it, and we need to continue to hope and believe that its richness will increase.

Bibliography

Anon (circa 8th Century/1978) *Beowulf*. (M Swanton, ed). Manchester: Manchester University Press

Anon (10th Century/1966) *The Wanderer.* (R F Leslie, ed). Manchester; Manchester University Press

Anon (*circa* 12th Century/1972) *The Owl and the Nightingale.* (G Stanley, ed). Manchester: Manchester University Press

Anon (13th Century/1993) *Ancrene Wisse Guide for Anchoresses.* (H White, tr). London: Penguin

Anon (15th Century) *Mary, for thine joys fyve. Index* no. 2099. MSS: BL Royal 8.F.6, fol. 21a; Lincoln Cathedral 91 (Thornton), fol. 177b

Bawden, N (1973) *Carrie's War.* London: Hamish Hamilton

Bede (8th Century/1955) *A History of the English Church and People.* (L Sherley-Price, tr). London: Penguin

Britton, J (1975) *The Development of Writing Abilities* (11-18). London: Schools Council Publications /Macmillan

Carrington V (2004) Texts and literacies of the Shri Jinrui. *British Journal of Sociology of Education* 25 (2) 215-228

Carrington, V (2005) Txting: the end of civilisation (again). *Cambridge Journal of Education* 35 (2) 161-175

Clanchy, M T (1993) *From Memory to Written Record: England 1066-1307.* Oxford: Blackwell

Crossley-Holland, K (2000) *The Seeing Stone.* Orion: London

Crossley-Holland, K (2001) *Arthur at the Crossing Places.* Orion: London

Crossley-Holland, K (2003) *Arthur King of the Middle March.* Orion: London

Greenfield, S (2006) We are at risk of losing our imagination. *The Guardian* April 25 2006

Haddon, M (2003) T*he Curious Incident of the Dog in the Night-Time.* Oxford: David Fickling

Hollindale, P (1997) *Signs of Childness in Children's Books.* Stroud: Thimble Press

http://www.paintedchurch.org/

Nesbit, E (1899) *The Story of the Treasure Seekers.* London: Andre Deutsch

13

What do fairy tales teach? Updating and challenging the didactic canon

Laura Tosi

Over the last few decades, critics have started to challenge the assumption that the best fairy tales of the canon are universal, timeless and eternally true, providing the basis for a critique of dominant cultural patterns. Perceiving fairy tales simply as historically determined documents, mere vehicles for past ideological configurations, may elicit some unusually bitter reactions in those of us who have built an intense personal relationship with the genre. After all, fairy tales happen to be the first examples of narrative form we are faced with in life; a fairy-tale canon can probably be more personal and emotionally charged than any other kind of literature. It may seem natural to think that most popular tales are uncontaminated and eternal, that when we read or listen to them we feel part of a universal community with common values and norms, with which we share a reassuring myth of happiness and order and where some behaviours will be predictably and effectively rewarded or punished (see Zipes, 1994, 5). But fairy tales are not innocent, harmless, and unhistorical, as is testified by studies of their transformations throughout the centuries, until a certain body of texts happen to be selected and preserved because they are believed to express the most typical rendering of a tale-type, in accordance with the values appreciated by a society.

If we take *Beauty and the Beast* as an example, the version we invariably find reprinted and translated is the one by Mme Leprince de Beaumont, first published in French in 1756, of which the English translation came out in 1761. A typical beast bridegroom story, which recalls Apuleius's story of Cupid and Psyche, as well as Straparola's *Re Porco* (1550) and Basile's *Il Serpente* (1634), this version has won over its French precedents because of 1) its conciseness (Mme de Villeneuve's version of 1740, which introduced the plot as we know it today, was very long and included digressions in form of dreams and elaborate descriptions) and 2) a clear didactic message directed to a young audience (see Zipes, 1983). Her version also superseded Mme D'Aulnoy's stories of monster bridegrooms *Le Mouton* (1697) and *Le Serpentin Vert* (1697), which had contributed to dictating the standards of female *civilitè* (sincerity of feeling, decorum etc) in the French salons by placing her female characters, especially a fairy or a group of fairies, in a position of power. As Jack Zipes has put it, 'What began as a fairy-tale discourse on manners with examples set for adults and children developed into a fairy-tale sermon primarily for children' (Zipes, 1983, 41). Obviously the change of ideal reader/listener was critical; at the turn of the eighteenth century the literary fairy tale was starting to widen its audience. No longer a genre primarily directed to adult audiences, it underwent a process of sanitation (in Villeneuve's version, for example, the Beast bluntly asks Beauty to go to bed with him, while in De Beaumont's tale he politely asks for her hand in marriage) and simplification, as it had to be now ready to teach children, in clear language, a code of unambiguous behaviours which supported current cultural values. In the Beauty and the Beast tale, Belle displays self-denial, obedience, humility – virtues that might have been desirable in a bourgeois wife, especially if marriage was conceived as a form of male domination.

The passage from folktale to literary fairy tale, from the irreverent, sexually and excrementally aware popular culture to the more refined middle-class children's nursery, placed increased emphasis on moral instruction and warning children about the perils of disobedience and curiosity (see Carter, 1990). In Maria Tatar's words (1992, 11), 'Once fairy tales entered the realm of children's literature, they took on a protective didactic coloring that has been virtually impossible to remove'. Therefore the vocation of the bourgeois fairy tale appears to have been primarily to initiate and socialise the child into a cultural inheritance of values, experiences and prohibitions. By providing exemplary stories of punished violations and rewarded suffering, emphasising at the same time the importance of securing luck or beauty, the Western fairy-tale tradition of Perrault and the Grimms, translated into English, share with eighteenth century and early nineteenth century English stories for children an active interest in a degree of moral intimidation. It is precisely this cautionary side that unites forms of literature which are normally believed to have very little in common (one only needs to think of the English resistance to fairy tales in the eighteenth century, born out of a combination of Puritan disapproval and a rationalist distrust of the imagination).

The authors who contributed to the extraordinary flowering of the fairy tale in Victorian England (see Zipes, 1991), partly stimulated by continental translations, both welcomed and challenged the bias in favour of a strong moral framework. While, for example, Margaret Gatty's *The Fairy Godmothers* (1851) agree that the most desirable christening gift for a girl is the love of employment, Dickens and Wilde were using fairy tales as an imaginative form of protest against the growing alienation of an increasingly industrialised society which badly needed reform. In Ruskin's *King of the Golden River* (1841), inspired by the Grimms' *The Water of Life*, amassing a fortune through the exploitation of servants, as well as lack of compassion, are punished with the transformation of the green, fruitful valley into 'one mass of ruin and desolation' (Ruskin, 1991 23). Similarly, Wilde's protest against social injustice and private property as the source of poverty and privilege replaced the traditionally bourgeois values of prudence and acquisitive behaviour with an emphasis on the supremacy of aesthetics and the investigation of the relationship between physical and spiritual beauty (the implications of which had already been explored in *The Picture of Dorian Gray*).

The potential of the fairy tale to communicate new ideas about what children should be made more sensitive to, in an increasingly technological world, was exploited in many directions. In Nesbit's *Fortunatus Rex and Co*, for example, we find a king turned into speculative builder, who makes a fortune by spoiling the countryside: 'it is curious that nearly all the great fortunes are made by turning beautiful things into ugly ones' (Nesbit, 1901, 205). The happy ending will result in restoring the landscape to its original state: 'So Fortunatus Rex and Co. devoted themselves to pulling down and carting off the yellow streets they had built. And now the country there is almost as green and pretty as it was before (221).

In *The Last of the Dragons* (1925) the fierce, mythical creature which symbolises evil is degraded from predator to prey and the pattern of 'prince rescues princess', passively handed down from generation to generation (as the king says, 'I rescued your mother from a dragon, and you don't want to set yourself up above her I should hope' [Nesbit, 1975,10]), clashes with typically contemporary environmental concerns. In a changing world which is increasingly seen with Victorian/Edwardian nostalgia, the preservation of the dragon is a way to cling to the magical atmosphere of the English romance epic. The typically urban reality of private transport is accommodated into the romance-like atmosphere of the tale as is the use of the domestic dragon (named Fido) as an aeroplane. As to its gender politics, Nesbit's story ends conventionally with marriage – the assertiveness of the heroine does not extend to defying patriarchal authority over arranged marriages. Nesbit, however, despite her personal ambivalence towards gender issues (see Fromm, 1984), was one of the authors who challenged stereotypical female roles in her fairy tales.

As is proved by a continual critical interest in the field, and a number of fairy tale collections like Auerbach and Knoepflmacher's *Forbidden Journeys* (1982), the Victorian and Edwardian periods were rich in innovative writing by women, a Golden Age of children's literature which included literary fairy tales and fantasies. As Lazaros Honig has remarked:

> While the feminist movement of the late 19th century was fighting bloody battles, the mode of fantasy was fostering a quiet rebellion fuelled only by pen and ink – one that held out great hope for the future equality of the sexes because it worked in a magical way in the minds and hearts of future generations. (1988, 2)

Tales like Mary de Morgan's *The Toy Princess* (1877), the story of a plain-speaking and unsophisticated princess who is rejected by her Court in favour of a more docile toy replica, are harshly critical of the empty formulas and the artificiality of social conventions in the education of girls. The female accomplishment that is most highly praised in the toy is the fact that it can only speak four phrases: 'If you please'; 'No thank you'; 'Certainly' and 'Just so'. In this fairy tale in particular, acting in passive obedience to one's parents and elders and conforming to their idea of a ladylike behaviour, is represented in strongly negative terms. Independence of mind and the capacity to feel are perceived as infinitely better qualities than formality and good manners.

The Fairy Taboret is strikingly different from the fairy in Perrault's *Les Fées*, who punishes the girl who fails the test of civility with the gift of having snakes and toads drop from her mouth every time she speaks. On the contrary, Taboret constantly encourages and praises a woman's right to speak up. When the king and the court finally vote to choose the toy princess instead of the real one, she calls them 'a pack of sillies and idiots' (De Morgan, 1991, 174) and flies away with her ward.

As for the revaluation of female curiosity, one obvious example would be the Alice books, whose subversive potential has been perceived by some critics as paving the way to portrayals of unconventional domesticity – one only needs to think of the satire of the 'Angel in the House' myth in the kitchen scene of *Alice in Wonderland* (1865) to realise that things were changing dramatically in the representation of women. According to Auerbach and Knoepflmacher (1982, 6) Carroll's books 'had licensed female dreaming and liberated aggressive subtexts for women writers'.

If it is true that translations contributed to the creation of a national fairy-tale tradition, it is also true that the ideological meanings of the Perrault-Grimm tradition (see Zipes, 2001) were immediately questioned and subverted. The literary fairy tale, by incorporating oral traditions into highly literary discourses, is by nature a hybrid, 'elastic' [see Hearne, 1988] and highly intertextual genre that relies on retelling – and rewriting – for its very existence. Although in the second half of the nineteenth century the pedagogy of fear tended to be less obtrusive in fairy tales (though still lurking in a number of texts such as Lane Clifford's tale *The New Mother* (1882), which punishes curiosity in harsh terms), they cannot repress an irresistible impulse towards the cautionary: they still want to teach, albeit a different message.

The twentieth century has appreciated the fact that the fairy tale genre has been able in all the stages of its development to accommodate alternative versions which have challenged and subverted standard formal conventions as well as ideological conformations. As retellings constantly question the value of canonicity, a tendency to update and subvert the conservatism of fairy tales as the repository of a humanistic tradition has become more and more evident in recent times.

As we have seen, there has always been a tendency to challenge the moral view of traditional fairy tales: many contemporary retellings have tried to redress the moral balance by means of a change in the narrating voice and point of view. For example, in Granowsky's *Giants Have Feelings, Too*, the wife of a benevolent and peaceful giant exposes the ambiguous morality of a tale, 'Jack and the Beanstalk', which rewards greed and stealing: 'He had no right to take what was ours or to hurt my husband. Giants have feelings, you know' (Granowsky, 1996, 25).

In the last decades, feminist critics and writers have collaborated in the critical exposures of some classic fairy tales as narratives voicing patriarchal values, both by providing critical readings which investigate the social construction of gender, and by rewriting traditional fairy tales in order to produce non-sexist adult and children's versions. The feminist project to subvert and feminise the fairy-tale canon has problematised the fairy tale's relation to gender construction in its attempt to assess to what extent female responses to fairy tales have changed in the light of social changes (see Haase, 2004).

It is interesting to notice that precisely those tales which in the last few decades have been decreed unsuitable for children, like 'Bluebeard', have been appropriated by authors for adults (such as Angela Carter, Margaret Atwood or even directors like Jane Campion) who have plunged into their disturbing potential in order to bring, as Keiser (1994, 32) has written of Carter's *The Bloody Chamber*, 'the sadomasochistic subtext of the original into the foreground'. In versions of Bluebeard addressed to an adult audience, Perrault's warning against curiosity has changed into caution about the motives for getting married ('Curiosity in spite of its great charms/Often brings with it serious regrets. ... For once satisfied, curiosity offers nothing/And ever does it cost more dearly' [Perrault, 1999, 77]).

Whereas Carter has shown that the fascination for a sexually experienced, mysterious man in possession of a good fortune can make a young woman blind to his faults and enter into a hasty marriage, Atwood's third sister, who knows about Bluebeard's past crimes but 'also wanted to cure him. She thought she had the healing touch' (Atwood, 1995, 111), is a classic example of where a rescuer's role, the desire for husband reforming, can take a woman.

So, in the same way that other faults have superseded the typically female sin of curiosity in contemporary fairy tales, identifying the dangers hidden in modern society appears more cogent than expecting the modern child addressee to be afraid of the big bad wolf. An example of a cautionary tale inspired by Little Red Riding Hood is Gillian Cross's *Wolf,* where the 13-year-old Cassy is involved in a theatrical school project which researches the historical and mythical associations with the predatory wolf along the ages as well as the threat of extinction posed by humans. In the story, it is Cassy's father, an IRA terrorist nicknamed Mick the Wolf, who is not afraid to kill and is even ready to use and harm his own mother (Cassy's grandmother, the only dependable adult in her dysfunctional family) and daughter to achieve his political ends. The wolf as the incarnation of evil, is 'the wolf where no wolf should be. Behind the door, invading the house, inside the skin of a familiar, trusted person ... with his fangs at her grandmother's neck' (Cross, 1990, 10).

Similarly, Wendy Wheeler's *Little Red*, addressed to an adult readership, explores the bestial instincts of the hairy narrator, who, after giving his fiancée's young daughter a red cap as a gift, devises a seduction scheme for when mother and daughter will move to his place and start a family life together: 'This is the reward for my role soon to come, husband and father. It's what I deserve ... I am all appetite' (Wheeler, 1995, 146). Wheeler's story takes Perrault's subtext of sexual initiation to extremes: the modern Little Red Riding Hood must beware of an explicitly paedophiliac wolf. Both rewritings, in their different ways, are cautionary tales that question the nature of evil in innovative ways, by inviting the reader to identify the risks little girls may have to face in their lives today.

Feminists have always been interested in the didactic potential of fairy tales (see Joosen, 2005). Some retellings actively question stereotyped notions of femininity (and sometimes masculinity) in the hope of acculturating women into new, rewarding social roles. The question is: can you teach feminist ideology through fairy tales? By writing stories of resourceful heroines who achieve self-fulfilment by other means than waiting passively for a prince to save them, do readers (especially female) receive them 'as an echo of their own struggles to become human beings' (Stone, 1985, 144)? Much controversy surrounds this central issue, and a lot has been written on the subject of female subjugation and voicelessness in the bourgeois fairy-tale canon, to be contrasted with the presentation of active heroines in collections of folktales as well as original tales for younger audiences.

An interesting example of the juxtaposition between the Cinderella paradigm and a plot pattern which subverts this paradigm, in the same story, is Ellen Jackson's *Cinder Edna*. This tale is more subtly constructed than other Cinderella-based stories in that it provides no less than *two* Cinderella characters, Cinder Ella and Cinder Edna, whose very different personalities and choices produce two separate Cinder plots and endings. Given a similar background and starting point for the story, Cinder Edna's determination, energy and optimism make her a perfect foil for Ella's more characteristic passivity and self-pity:

> Once upon a time there were two girls who lived next door to each other. You may have heard of the first one. Her name was Cinderella. Poor Cinderella was forced to work from morning till night, cooking and scrubbing pots and pans and picking up after her cruel stepmother and wicked stepsisters. When her work was done, she sat among the cinders to keep warm, thinking about all her troubles.

> Cinder Edna, the other girl, was also forced to work for her wicked stepmother and stepsisters. But she sang and whistled while she worked. Moreover, she had learned a thing or two from doing all that housework – such as how to make tuna casserole sixteen different ways and how to get spots off everything from rugs to ladybugs. (Jackson, 1998 np)

Edna, the antiheroine, 'wasn't much to look at. But she was strong and spunky and knew some good jokes'. The device of juxtaposing the canonical story with the politically correct version also has the effect of highlighting differences in time and class. While the Cinderella story unfolds in a timeless and aristocratic context, with Ella wearing the impractical clothes and the notoriously uncomfortable glass slippers conjured up by her fairy godmother and living an uneventful court life, Edna's plot is set in a realistic context in which ball gowns are bought with savings, buses stop running at midnight and refreshments at the castle are enthusiastically approached.

A new creative configuration of Cinderella, with counter-cultural patterns which dispense with the supernatural is therefore fused into the familiar configuration. Readers can reflect, for example, on the different degrees of freedom and independence of the two heroines or draw parallels between the two princes, the handsome narcissistic heir to the throne who will marry Ella versus his environmentally aware and fun-loving brother who falls in love with Edna. At the end of the story the reader is called on to judge which marriage is more likely to be successful in the long run:

> So the girl who had once been known as Cinderella ended up in a big palace. During the day she went to endless ceremonies and listened to dozens of speeches ... at night she sat by the fire with nothing to look at but her husband's perfect profile ... And the girl who had been known as Cinder Edna ended up in a small cottage with solar heating. During the day she studied waste disposal engineering and cared for orphaned kittens. And at night she and her husband laughed and joked, tried new recipes together and played duets on the accordion and concertina. Guess who lived happily ever after (Jackson, 1998 np).

The coexistence of the canonical and the modernised version in Jackson's text is a very interesting attempt to produce an ironic distancing from the conventional morality of the original tale. In a way *Cinder Edna* is a cautionary tale, which implicitly asks the reader to distrust beauty and love at first sight as conducive to happiness.

The poetics of postmodernism and poststructuralism has placed even greater emphasis on parody, intertextuality, ironic discontinuity with the past, fragmentation, and self-referentiality. As boundaries between the centre and margins are crossed and deconstructed, the unity of meaning of a text is constantly challenged by the production of multiple perspectives.

A classic example of a metafictional fairy tale for adults (in novel form) is Donald Barthelme's *Snow White* (1967), set in what resembles a commune, where the character representing Snow White is involved in a series of sexual relationships with seven young men, who stand for the dwarfs. In a context of diegetic fragmentation, Snow White realises that she is cast in the role of the princess waiting for the prince, and that she cannot escape from her literary prison. At some point the disjointed narrative is interrupted by a questionnaire which reflects, metafictionally, on fairy-tale values and disrupts every form of linearity and rationality by asking increasingly surreal questions:

1. Do you like the story so far? Yes ( ) No ( )

2. Does Snow White resemble the Snow White you remember? Yes ( ) No ( )

3. Have you understood, in reading to this point, that Paul is the prince-figure? Yes ( ) No ( )

...

5. In the further development of the story, would you like more emotion ( ) or less emotion

( )?

...

8. Would you like a war? Yes ( ) No ( )

...

14. Do you stand up when you read? ( ) Lie down? ( ) Sit? ( )

(Barthelme, 1967, 82-3)

Similar foregrounding and boundary-breaking techniques, which can be found in books addressed to an implied adult audience, are employed in metafictional fairy tales for children, which activate the implied reader's intertextual competency (ie the implied child reader's familiarity with more traditional fairy tales) and his/her active collaboration in the production of meaning. Jon Scieszka's tales, for example, dispense with the narrator's characteristically didactic tone. In *The Stinky Cheese Man and Other Fairly Stupid Tales*, the various narratives are constantly interrupted by arguments between the narrator and the characters and the reader is ordered to skip the introduction because 'it just goes on and on and doesn't really say anything' (Scieszka, 1992). As a self-questioning text, *The Stinky Cheese Man* turns traditional fairy tales, with clear morals to be drawn, into comic clusters of clichés that cannot be taken seriously. However, Scieszka's exposure of the arbitrariness of bookmaking draws attention to the rules, conventions and inner logic of fairy-tale composition. As Patricia Waugh remarks, 'one method of showing the function of literary conventions, of revealing their provisional nature, is to show what happens when they *malfunction*. Parody and inversion are two strategies which operate in this way as frame-breakers' (1984, 31).

If the fairy tale, like a particularly ingenious toy, is broken to see how it works, it follows that the young reader can be made to grasp some of the most elementary rules of fairy-tale construction and even suggest his/her own version of the story.

This is all the more evident in Allan Ahlberg's *Ten in a Bed* where Dinah's bed becomes the textual space where fairy-tale characters play out their social/fictional roles and are confronted by the girl character as a competent reader and narrator of their stories. In the context of a world which is organised according to a predictable routine (every chapter marks the beginning of a new day at school and home in Dinah's life), every evening a fairy-tale character unceremoniously occupies Dinah's bed (some appropriately, like Sleeping Beauty) and expects to be told his/her story.

It is worth noting that the empowerment and sense of control that Dinah experiences depend on her ability as a storyteller. In a way, the fairy-tale characters play the part of children, eager to know more about their favourite stories but also ready to interrupt and correct the story they are hearing according to their innermost wishes, while the child character, Dinah, appropriates the traditionally adult storyteller role as well as the knowledge of fairy-tale plots and conventions. By negotiating with the fairy-tale characters the right to tell a story from another point of view, Dinah shows that fairy-tale rules of morality can and need to be bent at times, as in the version of the wicked witch story she tells the witch:

> 'Once upon a time,' said Dinah, 'there was a wicked...er wonderful witch!'
>
> 'That's more like it,' said the witch.
>
> 'She was very beautiful, this witch – very beautiful. She had a beautiful black dress and hat, beautiful black hair and fingernails, and a very pretty wart on the end of her nose. Her name was...'
>
> 'Esmerelda!' said the witch. The witch's own name was not Esmerelda, but she always wanted it to be. ...
>
> 'Well, there was the witch, and what she was doing was practising a few spells. ... Anyway, suddenly she heard a noise outside ... It was a horrid, naughty, little boy. ... So Esmerelda thought for a minute, and said to herself, 'I cannot stand for this. I'm going to teach that boy a lesson. What I am going to do is -' '
>
> 'Cook him in a pie and eat him up!' shouted the witch. ...
>
> Dinah paused again. She could feel the story slipping away from her.
>
> ...
>
> By this time the witch was sitting bolt upright in the bed. ... 'What's going on here? I'm offering a good story and all I get is aggravation.'
>
> 'You keep butting in, that's the trouble,' said Dinah. 'Whose story is it, anyway?'
>
> 'That's what I want to know!' The witch leant over the side of the bed.
>
> (Ahlberg, 1990 pp 20,21,24)

Not only do these texts provide the reader with gaps which, according to Iser (1972), leave space for interpretation ('one text is potentially capable of several different realisations, and no reading can ever exhaust the full potential, for each individual reader will fill the gaps in his own way, thereby excluding the various other possibilities' (1988, 216), he/she is actually encouraged to see the frame, or the palimpsest behind the tales, and therefore use it as a starting point to compose his/her own version of the story. Activating the implied reader's textual and intertextual competency in self-referential texts can result in an intellectual collaboration in the production of meaning so that transgressing the rules of realistic narrative 'might foster awareness of how a story works without intrusive didacticism' (Mackey, 1990, 181). Therefore, even if these more experimental texts do not appear to endorse any traditional moral teaching, the reader may learn how to read and how to write creatively and be empowered by the tools of the trade which the author and the narrator(s) have placed at his/her disposal.

To conclude: retelling or rewriting practices are a characteristic trait of the literary fairy-tale genre. If, on the one hand, revisions appear to point to the consolidation of a definitive set of values, on the other hand, they develop strategies to challenge and negotiate those same values, thus inviting the implied reader (or listener) to turn from passive recipient into a perceptive critic of outmoded or unrealistic standards of morality. The controversial question of the intrinsic aesthetic/ethical value of these revised fairy tales has been addressed by Maria Tatar. As she has conveniently and succinctly put it:

> How do we preserve the fairy tale canon even if we divest it of the 'wisdom' of another age, of cultural constructs that are irrelevant or inappropriate for the child to whom the tale is read? One obvious answer is to rewrite the stories so that they are closer to our own time and place. But such projects do not necessarily succeed in producing 'better' texts – they may end by reflecting the values of one class, ethnic group or other social segment of our own culture. (Tatar, 1992, 19)

Bibliography
Ahlberg, A (1990) *Ten in a Bed*. London: Puffin Books

Atwood, M (1995) *Alien territory*. In *Bones and Murder*. London: Virago

Auerbach, N and Knoepflmacher, U C (eds) (1982) *Forbidden Journeys: Fairy tales and fantasies by Victorian women writers*. Chicago: University of Chicago Press

Barthelme, D (1967) *Snow White*. New York: Atheneum

Carroll, L (1971) *Alice's Adventures in Wonderland and Through the Looking-Glass*. Oxford and New York: Oxford University Press

Carter, A (1979) *The Bloody Chamber*. London: Vintage

Carter, A (1990) Introduction. In A Carter (ed) *The Virago Book of Fairy Tales*. London: Virago

Clifford, L L (1882 /1993) The new mother. In Lurie, A (ed) *The Oxford Book of Modern Fairy Tales*. Oxford and New York: Oxford University Press

Cross, G (1990) *Wolf*. Oxford: Oxford University Press

De Morgan, M (1877) A toy princess. In J Zipes (1991) *Victorian Fairy Tales. The revolt of the fairies and elves*. New York and London: Routledge

Fromm, G. (1984) E. Nesbit and the happy moralist. *Journal of Modern Literature* 11, 45-65

Gatty, M (1851) *The Fairy Godmothers and Other Tales*. London: Bell

Granowsky, A (1996) *Giants Have Feelings, Too*. Austin: Steck-Vaughn

Haase, D (2004) *Fairy Tales and Feminism: New approaches*. Detroit: Wayne State University Press

Hearne, B (1988) Beauty and the Beast. Visions and revisions of an old tale: 1950-1985. *The Lion and the Unicorn* 12(2), 74-109

Honig, E L (1988) *Breaking the Angelic Image. Woman power in Victorian children's fantasy*. New York: Westport Connecticut, London: Greenwood Press

Iser, W (1972) The reading process: a phenomenological approach. New Literary History 3, repr. in D Lodge (ed) (1988) *Modern Criticism and Theory. A reader*. London and New York: Longman

Jackson, E (1998) *Cinder Edna*. New York: Mulberry Books

Joosen, V. (2005) Fairy tale retellings between art and pedagogy. *Children's Literature in Education* 36, 129-139

Keiser, M (1994) Fairy tale as sexual allegory: intertextuality in Angela Carter's *Bloody Chamber. The Review of Contemporary Fiction* 14, 30-36

Mackey, M (1990) Metafiction for beginners: Allan Ahlberg's *Ten in a Bed. Children's Literature in Education* 21, 79-187

Nesbit, E (1901) Fortunatus Rex and Co. In *Nine Unlikely Tales for Children*. London: Fisher Unwin

Nesbit, E (1975) *The Last of the Dragons and Some Others*. Harmondsworth: Puffin Books

Perrault, C (1999) *Perrault's Complete Fairy Tales*. (A E Johnson *et al*, tr). London: Puffin Books

Ruskin, J (1841) The king of the golden river, or the black brothers. In J Zipes (ed) (1991) *Victorian Fairy Tales. The revolt of the fairies and elves*. New York and London: Routledge

Scieszka, J (1992) *The Stinky Cheese Man and Other Fairly Stupid Tales*. New York: Viking

Stone, K F (1985) The misuses of enchantment: controversies on the significance of fairy tales. In R A Jordan and S J Kalčik (eds) *Women's Folklore, Women's Culture*. Philadelphia: University of Pennsylvania Press

Tatar, M (1992) *Off With Their Heads. Fairy tales and the culture of childhood*. Princeton: Princeton University Press

Waugh, P (1984) *Metafiction. The theory and practice of self-conscious fiction*. London and New York: Routledge

Wheeler, W (1995) Little Red. In E Datlow and T Windling (eds) *Snow White, Blood Red*. London: Signet

Zipes, J (1983) Setting standards for civilization through fairy tales: Charles Perrault and his associates. In *Fairy Tales and the Art of Subversion. The classic genre for children and the process of civilization*. New York: Routledge

Zipes, J (1991) Introduction. In J Zipes (ed) *Victorian Fairy Tales. The revolt of the fairies and elves*. New York and London: Routledge

Zipes, J (1994) *Fairy Tale as Myth. Myth as Fairy Tale*. Lexington: University Press of Kentucky

Zipes, J (2001) Cross-cultural connections and the contamination of the classical fairy tales. In *The Great Fairy Tale Tradition from Straparola and Basile to the Brothers Grimm*. New York/London: Norton

14

Changing frames: from theatre on the page to galleries as a stage

Elizabeth Hammill

The original words and pictures for children's books – particularly illustrations – are relatively new arrivals in British galleries. While the printed children's book has an exhibition history, shows of original material from first doodles, roughs or notes to finished artwork and text have been a rarity. Not any more. Over the past ten years, exhibitions from Seven Stories' pioneering shows to the British Council and Quentin Blake's *Magic Pencil* at the British Library, to Cambridge Fitzwilliam Museum's *Picture This!* have acted as catalysts – spotlighting and generating new perspectives and debate on the art of children's books and their makers, drawing record breaking audiences and revealing an eager readership for such shows.

Should we be surprised? I think not. Picturebooks are the primary literature of childhood, often providing our first experiences of visual art and of the collaborative narrative art-form that text and image create together. Picturebooks are invariably shared – by parent and child, grandparent and child, teacher and class – and, at their best, are multi-layered – challenging and engaging young and old alike. Fiction, too, is often shared. So when an exhibition of original work for such books is mounted, audiences of all ages come to discover old literary friends in new places, and to satisfy their curiosity about the creative process.

If meeting authors and illustrators bridges the gap between children and books in ways that no other experience can do, seeing original artwork or handwritten manuscripts can have a similar effect. Philip Pullman writes:

Nothing gives us such a powerful sense, both of personal connection and of sheer awe – this is the first time those words were ever written – as seeing the actual paper on which an author or an illustrator we love has made the first marks, the first tentative reachings-out towards what will later become known all over the world. (Pullman, 2002)

Such moments of discovery, of illumination, of connection may well take place these days within the framework of an exhibition and, more often than not, an exhibition about illustration. But exhibitions displaying illustration (or text, for that matter) present their curators with an unusual aesthetic, readerly and critical dilemma. A picture book is an art form whose singularity, possibilities, flexibility, drama and impact arise from the symbiotic play of words and pictures as they 'interact productively on each other' to create a narrative. 'The words come to life in the context, the environment, of the pictures and vice versa' (Lewis, 2001, 48). The *book* is the work of art.

Changing frames

What happens then if you demount an illustration and remove it from its original context to be re-framed and placed on a gallery wall as part of an exhibition? A frozen moment, a single frame, a still from a longer narrative is shown – one that may stand on its own as hang-on-the-wall art or one that may seem strangely adrift and alone. How will we respond to it as readers, particularly if we do not know the picture book of origin? How will we read it out of context, out of its story? What will we read it for? What will our experience of it on a gallery wall in the company of other such works bring to us as readers? What might we learn from 'changing frames'?

This depends on the viewpoint of the curator. Illustration in all its forms has often been 'relegated to step-child status in the arts' (Heller, 2007). For the Eric Carle Museum of Picture Book Art in the United States, 'literally deconstructing the book' and re-framing components of it on the gallery wall becomes a way 'to underscore that ... the art', like all fine art, can 'stand on its own' and invite an aesthetic response to images that, for beginning viewers, may be 'familiar and beloved' (*ibid*). An interpretative 'toolkit of questions', based on the 'visual thinking strategies' of museum educator Philip Yenawine and cognitive psychologist Abigail Hausen, invites young visitors to engage with art in meaningful ways: 'What is going on in this picture? What do you see that makes you say that? What more do you see?' (*ibid*). Children at the Carle are encouraged to become detectives and compare the art on the wall with the art in the published books, triggering discussions about artistic methods and how books are made and introducing them to language to talk about what they are seeing. The gallery and museum experience is designed to introduce young visitors to art in an empowering, non-intimidating way and to foster an appreciation of the visual world. Little, if any, text, however, is on show.

Exhibitions in Britain have likewise reinforced and celebrated the importance of the art of illustration. Shows such as *Magic Pencil* have both highlighted the intriguing possibilities of the picture book as an art form – a space where artists' imaginations may take surprising turns and new ideas, media and techniques are constantly being born to realise these, and showcased the richness, diversity, skill and experience of its creators. Such exhibits invite close inspection of detached pieces of artwork for what they reveal about their makers and their making – use of line, colour, shape, choice of medium and its effect, and page design – and for comparison with other work on show. The change in frame from picture book to gallery heralds a change in aesthetic meaning and perception – one that viewers may bring to future readings and one that may open up the visual world to them in ways that help them to understand and appreciate the artistry of the picturebooks they next encounter.

What distinguishes the evolving and boundary breaking Seven Stories' approach to exhibition design and curation from this more traditional approach are its roots in story, in the act of reading itself and in the creative process. To introduce what is unfamiliar, original material to new apprentice audiences – to de-construct and then freshly re-construct some of the ingredients in the making of a book – we have experimented with the nature of the frame into which we have moved them. Thinking about old literary friends in new critical ways has opened up surprising storylines. Creating exhibitions is like, or can be like, creating a picture book. If we are telling a story, then we can transform gallery walls from blank pages into stages where the interplay of newly re-framed words and pictures can become part of a bigger, ongoing dialogue with other work on show and with writers, illustrators and audiences. Galleries now become a kind of literary playground, a changing landscape for the imagination, one that can awaken viewers to the endless creative possibilities of playing with words and pictures and the ingredients of story.

But there is more to it than this. The experience of reading a book often occurs in a private meditative space amounting to an immersion in a virtual world; a space where we can travel anywhere, magically acquiring the ability to be 'outside over there' or 'inside under here' at once. When an author's or illustrator's world wraps round us like a cloak, we become lost in a book. Could this experience – this entry into the 'worlds' of reading – be recreated in a gallery?

Daft as a bucket: inside the world of Colin McNaughton

Let's look back at our first exhibition *Daft as a Bucket: Inside the world of Colin McNaughton* held at Newcastle's Discovery Museum in 1998. The circumstances of its creation were crucial to its realisation, success and our approach to subsequent shows. It was to be a pilot – a trial run for the Arts Council of what a centre such as we were proposing might achieve. It was to be my first job as an untutored curator, although, in retrospect, I can see how my particular experiences as a reader, children's bookseller, lecturer, critic, editor and lover of galleries and theatre opened my imagination to the creative and interpretative potential of such shows. Funding came from an Arts Council 'New Audiences' initiative. Families with little or no experience of either galleries or literary events were therefore a key target audience. The site was the magnificent Great Hall in the Discovery Museum, once a banqueting hall in the building's days as the headquarters of the Co-operative Society. It was a space that would require us to design a gallery environment within it and provide us with an exciting challenge in new literary territory.

Colin McNaughton was the perfect subject for such an exhibition. He had grown up on Tyneside, and his creative roots lay in the popular culture of his youth – in the comics, the Saturday morning cinema, the pantomimes and the street corner play. A local lad whose work had achieved international recognition, he was seen as an artist who 'makes popular culture in front of your eyes' – one whose picturebooks and verse collections played inventively with the 'crash! bang! wallop!' of the comic book tradition with its controlled graphic mayhem' and extended jokes; one whose work was underpinned by a mastery of line and of the interplay between what McNaughton called 'performing' words and pictures, and by a wry, playful interest in adult foibles (Alderson, 1998, 6). He was also, I might add, an old friend, the first illustrator I ever worked with – one who was prepared to risk his reputation with an untested new organisation and work together to create a show of words and pictures that would *play* in new ways to new audiences.

The notion of play was central to McNaughton's view of his work. Referring to his approach to creating fictional worlds, he said:

> I seem to be able to lose myself in a story the way children do when they're making up a game or story – they very naturally and easily suspend belief. They tap into the

joy of creating their own world – of getting lost in their imaginations. That's what I do ... When I'm making a picture book, I'm doing exactly what I did when I was seven years old and playing with my toys – when a shoebox was a skyscraper, my kitten was Godzilla and my lead soldiers were alive! (Hammill, 1998, 9)

Creating a picture book, for McNaughton, was like creating a piece of theatre – one where he was playwright, set and costume designer and an actor who got to play all the parts; one where the play and the drama were both on the page and at the *turn* of a page.

Following McNaughton and picture book logic (and our need to transform the Great Hall), we decided to set *Daft as a Bucket* inside scenes from the fantastical worlds of McNaughton's books, to create a graphic context from and for his work. Working in partnership with Foundation Art students from Newcastle College on what became a Centre-Course design project, we immersed ourselves in his books. We read, reread, discussed, remembered the pleasures of earlier readings, and discovered for ourselves how McNaughton played games with language, with stock characters, and with our expectations as readers. We met what he referred to as his 'repertory company of characters' and followed their over-the-page lives as they reappeared elsewhere in his work, and over a term and then a summer, watched as the students designed and built theatrical sets (*ibid*, 16).

Meanwhile McNaughton and I trawled through what proved to be an incredibly rich body of work. There were W H Smith notebooks where he played with visual and verbal ideas – rejecting some, developing others, dummies, character sketches, rough drawings, finished black and white drawings and finally painted artwork. We pondered what stories we could tell and how we might best show what this work revealed about him as a picture book maker, about the creative process, about his artistic choices. If we could lose ourselves in McNaughton's fictional and artistic worlds, we hoped that we could create a gallery experience that would not only entice our new audiences to do this too, but would also immerse them in the stories about different aspects of the artist's work that each world told.

Visitors entered the exhibition through a Giant's Library filled with McNaughton's books where the skirting boards were eight feet tall, bookshelves rose forty feet high and artwork hung, providing an overview of his development as a picture book maker since 1976. The scale of this room reflected McNaughton's interest in size – the smaller you are, the more you see and hear – and was designed to dramatically change visitors' perspectives and draw them out of the everyday world into the artist's world.

Exploring the quayside and deck of The Golden Behind from *Jolly Roger and the Pirates of Abdul the Skinhead* and *Captain Abdul's Pirate School,* visitors next met an ever expanding cast of pirates – from the Pirate at the entrance to Long John Silver, to Captain Abdul, Bully-boy McCoy and Walker the Plank, and found a treasure chest containing work by illustrators like Gilray, Ardizzone, Moebius, and the strip cartoonist Dudley D. Watkins who had inspired McNaughton. In an Outer Space populated by some decidedly quirky Aliens, visitors followed the creation of *The Aliens Are Coming!* from first idea to printed book. In the Horror House, nightmares became jokes, spoof and parody reigned, and the opportunity beckoned to join the school Casket-ball Team at Doctor Frankenstein's School for Little Monsters or to dine on the contents of Dracula's fridge. On the Weirdos' Poetry Street, each poem from limericks to ballads to a 'reptile rap' was shown to be a 'little playlet' where words and pictures needed to be read for it to make sense. And at Preston Pig's School House where Mister Wolf lurked outside, audiences watched how McNaughton charted the modern relationship between Pig and Wolf over five books and how he adapted features of the strip cartoon to his picturebooks.

These were the worlds of the books and inside them, we explored McNaughton's world as a picture book maker. In keeping with his use of bubble talk, the exhibition labels were speech bubbles where McNaughton spoke directly to his new audiences, giving them clues to reading, looking at or thinking about the work exhibited and showing how his mind and imagination worked – often with a light, humorous touch.

> Being a pirate and being a writer/illustrator are very similar jobs in that the main qualification needed for both is a refusal to grow up. The advantage of being a writer/illustrator is that I can play at being a pirate whenever I like ... Black and white pictures are the hardest to do because you don't have the colour to help you. If you look closely at the other pictures in the exhibition, you will see the lines. The drawing. Without them, my pictures would be like a person without a skeleton! These are called 'dummies'. No, silly, not the kind you give to babies! These dummies are pretend books. I make them to see how a story or idea will look in the form of a picture book. (McNaughton, 1998)

Running alongside the exhibition was a theatrical production of McNaughton's *The Last of the Giant Killers* – theatre on the page turned into theatre on the stage – as well as some live piratical theatre in the gallery with Jolly Roger, his mother, and Captain Abdul during afternoon school visits. McNaughton was resident every week-end giving readings and advice.

The Daft as a Bucket experience – and it was an experience – the essential Colin McNaughton experience – was a revelation. It amounted to a total immersion in the worlds of a particular picture book maker whose particular visual and verbal ingenuity on the page and over a body of work almost invited a theatrical exhibition framework. Framing, Nikolajeva and Scott tell us, is 'an extremely powerful visual element of setting. Frames normally create a sense of detachment between the picture and the reader, while an absence of frames (that is a picture that covers the whole area of a page or double spread) invites the reader into the picture' (2004, 64). Think of a gallery in this light, and the difference in mood, expectation and the nature of the possible engagement with this show, or this show in a traditional gallery, becomes apparent. Like the best picturebooks, *Daft as a Bucket* transported, enchanted, surprised, enlightened and inspired its audiences. But it did more. 'Only connect' E. M Forster wrote. Changing frames, we discovered, can change, extend and ignite reading lives and expectations of literary encounters, occasion new critical understandings and new readings, and inspire new writers and new illustrators.

Over the hills and far away

If *Daft as a Bucket* was an experiment in exhibition design and interpretation, determined by both the artist and the nature of the work to be displayed, our ensuing shows have played with design and form in similar ways – always attending to what the work to be shown suggests, to the story to be told, and to the reading experience to be offered. In another retrospective, *Over the Hills and Far Away: Tales from a Northumbrian Farm*, we invited visitors to walk into the work and world of Kim Lewis, picture book chronicler of life on a Northumbrian hill farm, and to 'experience' that life for themselves. Work here was mounted traditionally (we were in a traditional gallery) but placed around an iconic recreation of the hill farm setting and studio where Lewis created her picturebooks – a studio where gallery visitors were encouraged to become authors and illustrators themselves.

In keeping with a body of work rooted in place, in the cycle of the Northumbrian farm year and in what Lewis calls 'the small corners of country life for young children' (2003) when the landscape, animals and life about them are all new and the everyday and the ordinary are extraordinary, the show had an early years focus. In a sequence entitled *Days in My Studio*, Lewis spoke to us directly about how she makes her picturebooks:

> How do I find the right words to tell my story? How do I find the right pictures? How can I make the words and pictures work together to make a book? Is this the best way or is there a better way? (Lewis, 2003)

Her questions were answered with displays of notebooks, storyboards, alternative texts, photographs, artefacts, sketches, lithographs and finished artwork – all relating to the making of *Friends* (1997), a sensitive tale of anger and reconciliation in the lives of two young best friends.

In *Days on the Farm*, we journeyed through the farming year (and Lewis's books) in the company of Floss, the sheepdog, and her puppies, a picture book experience itself, for Lewis wrote a new autobiographical story which provided a textual framework for the artwork on show. Here we saw how Lewis turned her family farm and the people, places and animals she knew so well into pictures and words. It begins:

> This is a story of days on a farm over the hills and faraway from town. The farm is our family home where my husband works as a farm manager and my children and their friends grew up and played. Every day I look out at the wild, beautiful countryside and think: 'This is home' – a place full of stories waiting to be found and told – inside the barn, out in the fields or over a hill – just as the place where your home is has stories waiting for you to discover and tell. You only need to look and listen. (Lewis, 2003)

Over the hills and faraway was clearly a very different gallery experience from *Daft as a Bucket.* In keeping with the quieter nature of Lewis's work, it immersed viewers in a very different kind of literary world and opened them to the possibilities for story making that lie in our own everyday landscapes.

Incredible journeys – travel by book

More recently, we have played with the framing device in different ways to different ends. The framework for our first exhibition at Seven Stories, *Incredible Journeys: Travel by Book*, for instance, was created in a unique collaboration with four illustrators: Anthony Browne, Ted Dewan, Satoshi Kitamura and Jane Ray. What we explored together over a preparatory year and what we asked 'travellers' to the exhibition to consider were some key questions and ideas about acts of reading:

> What happens when we read?
>
> When we say that we are lost in a book, where are we, how did we get there and whose company are we keeping?
>
> Books can take us anywhere – beyond the boundaries of this world into a galaxy of possible worlds. Once there, we can try on other lives in other places in other times. Returning home, we can test once-upon-a-time in the here and now.
>
> Think of a book as a portal. Turn the page, step through and your journey begins...

Could we translate these questions into a gallery experience? How could we use the idea of worlds as a framework? Entering the galleries, journeyers found themselves in a black and white world of Words. Here the walls became pages on which were printed life-size works – mostly poems – about the wonder of words, written in a variety of voices by a range of contemporary poets – from Roger McGough to Michael Rosen, John Agard, Benjamin Zephaniah and Grace Nichols. A recording in one of the letter-shaped stools spelling LISTEN let visitors hear the verse on the walls spoken by the poets. The approach was light but it surrounded journeyers with words and invited them to stop, savour and think about language and its possibilities in new ways. Kitamura ingeniously wove alphabets and pens and other drawing implements – the ingredients and shapers of stories – around the poems, along with a host of playing, reading, musing cats to draw viewers in and on.

From the world of Words, travellers passed through a curtained portal into a theatrical dressing room, complete with dressing tables, mirrors and costumes where they met an assortment of popular, classic and archetypal picture book and fictional characters including Mr Benn, Meg and Mog, the Iron Man, Harry Potter, Paddington Bear, Tracy Beaker, Worzel Gummidge, Little Tim and Will and Lyra. Here they were invited to step into their shoes before stepping out into a sequence of possible story worlds: Our world, a world of Time Travel, designed by Jane Ray, a Topsy Turvy world with a topsy turvy installation designed by Ted Dewan, a Forest world set in a wood designed by Anthony Browne, and through a dragon's cave into a world of Quests and Challenges.

Framed inside these worlds, travellers discovered how a veritable who's who of children's writers and illustrators from the past seventy years, including J. K. Rowling, Philippa Pearce, Lucy Boston, David Almond, Quentin Blake, Diana Stanley and Angela Barratt, play with those key ingredients of storytelling – words, pictures, character, setting and time – to create their invented worlds. Passage through the exhibition followed the path of the reader – from words, characters, known reality, and as yet unknown reality – to alternative realities and other ways of seeing and thinking.

If the *Incredible Journeys'* experience sought to re-create or draw attention to the reading journey, it also provided curatorial opportunities to engage viewers in both learning to read and reading to learn from the work on show in ways that could influence future reading experiences. Through the careful selection, framing and sequencing of work displayed in these new world contexts, we pointed up, for instance, how illustrators look for meanings underneath an author's words and illuminate or envision these very differently; for this we used artwork from Anthony Browne's and Helen Oxenbury's highly individual interpretations of *Alice's Adventures in Wonderland.*

We explored how different illustrators use different batteries of effects to create the character, nature and atmosphere of a place – in this case, a forest. Framed by Anthony Browne's increasingly dark and surreal forest, blown up from the cover artwork for his *Into the Forest*, travellers moved from Axel Scheffler's mock scary forest for Julia Donaldson's *The Gruffalo*, to Helen Cooper's darkening, Rackhamesque forest in *Pumpkin Soup*, to Anthony Maitland's creepy, sinister forest which formed the original book jacket for John Gordon's *The Giant under the Snow*, to Angela Barratt's mysterious, atmospheric, fairy tale forest for *Snow White. Incredible Journeys* invited explorers to see beyond the horizons of their own reading experiences, to travel by book and to return home to test their new understandings of once-upon-a-time and its creation in their own worlds and their own reading.

This off-the-page and into life transfer of reading experiences served as a creative underpinning for the exhibition *We're Going on a Bear Hunt: Picturebook Adventures*, a show dedicated to the late Sebastian Walker, founder of Walker Books. Here, in another variant on the world frame, visitors were invited into three dimensional recreations of a key scene from ten different picturebooks – each offering ten different reading experiences and adventures. Here they discovered the urban fairies of Bob Graham's *Jethro Byrd, Fairy Child* as well as original artwork; built an igloo with stones washed up on Patrick Benson's beach for Russell Hoban's *The Sea-Thing Child*; joined the Large Family from Jill Murphy's *Five Minutes' Peace* for breakfast; or entered the bears' cave and cosied up in Big Bear's chair to hear Martin Waddell's *Can't You Sleep, Little Bear?*

The invitation both to play and to play with each story was irresistible, but there was more to explore too. Ten portable picture book paddles offered intriguing trails through the exhibition in search of: 'beginnings and endings, the story, characters, the art, special words and sounds, colour, aspects of the heart, twinkle, the physical book, and worlds and places'. Story ruled here and delighted, as did the beginnings of critical appreciation – however light-hearted the approach.

What have we learned about changing frames? For a curator, the act of reading now calls for a fresh perspective and way of thinking and approaching work critically. Whether you are reading for a retrospective or a group show, reading becomes focused in different ways. For instance, in a reading brief, written in the early stages of developing *Incredible Journeys*, I suggested that staff find two or three possible quotes and/or images which captured the essential quality of that book and which also related directly to the nature of the world the original work from the book would be displayed in – and to the nature of the reading experiences to be explored in that world. I reminded them that ultimately all the text and artwork in each world needed to work together to tell a story and to comment on one another.

Work to be shown becomes part of a larger canvas – one which will give clues as to its nature. As curators, like picture book makers, we play with the possibilities of what to show on the pages of the gallery walls and how to show it – hoping that the theatrical approach will allow visitors to find old friends in new places and to make new friends in their journeying, hoping that it will create 'the sorts of grand tour that might make sparks fly out of the brain' (Brennan, 2000, 21) hoping that it will send them away *dancing*, as one critic put it, to bring new readings to new books.

Bibliography

Alderson, B (1998) Pigs, Pirates, and Preposterous Pictures; Making Friends with Colin McNaughton. In E Hammill (ed) *Daft as a Bucket: Inside the world of Colin McNaughton*. London: HarperCollins

Brennan, G (2000) Exhibition: Tales for the Telling – a journey through the world of folktales. *The Times Educational Supplement*, October 6

Hammill, E (1998) Talking words and Pictures: Elizabeth Hammill and Colin McNaughton in conversation. *Op cit*

Heller, S (2007) Since When Did Children's Books Have a Museum? Interview with H. Nichols Clark. *Voice*, March (np) http://journal.aiga.org.content.cfm/

Lewis, D (2001) *Reading Contemporary Picturebooks: Picturing Text*. London: Routledge

Lewis, K (2003) Days in My Studio. Exhibition Text. Unpublished

Lewis, K (2003) Days on the Farm. Exhibition Text. Unpublished

McNaughton, C (1998) Daft as a Bucket. Exhibition Text. Unpublished

Nikolajeva, M and Scott, C (2001) *How Picturebooks Work*. Abingdon: Routledge

Pullman, P (2002) Bank of England Speech for launch of the Centre for the Children's Book Fundraising Campaign. Unpublished

15

Reading in a Digital Age: Using new technologies to navigate texts together

Anouk Lang

Given the speed at which developments occur in the field of technology, thinking about what it means to read in the digital age is somewhat daunting. As a bewildering and proliferating array of new practices arises, mutates and fades before the next wave, following the fortunes of an old technology as it intertwines with all these new media seems more archaically Sisyphean still. However, these rapid changes and transmogrifications of the act of reading may in fact be of assistance to those attempting to gain access to the complex of interior processes – intellectual, hermeneutic, social, psychological, ideological – that occur when individuals read, both on their own and with others.

Advances in technology have made public and permanent many interactions that would once have been conducted in private and ephemeral ways, something which provides clear ethnographic advantages. Scholars of computer-mediated communication (cmc) have taken advantage of this, and online communities are already widely studied for sociological, linguistic and other reasons, but in this chapter I want to focus on a narrower aspect of this kind of computer-mediated communication: the kind that occurs when people read together.

Howard Rheingold cites government and media-funded research in which users repeatedly demonstrate that they are more interested in interacting with other users than with simply accessing pre-packaged information (1993, 276-77). As Molly Travis puts it, 'Information alone cannot substitute for experience. Networkers want to chat, to debate, to collaboratively create a virtual world' (1998, 114). The reading practices generated by these new virtual spaces enable us to gain a clearer picture of the way readers engage with each other through the text, and with the text through their interactions with others.

The Transliteracies project at the University of California is one forum in which interest in the technological, social and cultural aspects of online reading formations is in evidence. Its working definition of 'online reading' points out that this new form of reading practice brings into visibility the negotiation that occurs between individual and social ways of reading: a digital environment not only 'alter[s] the way an individual reads with the enhancement of a standalone computer, PDA, or cell phone; it also brings back into prominence the historically important social, collective dimension of reading (as instanced by Web blogs or the Google search-engine technology that filters hits according to popularity or relevance in a community of referring Web pages)' (Liu, 2008). Transliteracies identifies as a topic of particular interest the 'currently underdeveloped' technologies and practices through which communal online reading occurs in pedagogical contexts.

Case study: Reading *In the Skin of a Lion*

In this chapter, I take as a case study an online discussion in which a group of 23 final-year undergraduates at a UK university were asked to discuss Michael Ondaatje's novel *In the Skin of a Lion* via an online forum on the virtual learning environment platform WebCT. I employ methods from corpus linguistics to analyse the textual record of the discussion, attending particularly to the social dynamics between the students, and I draw on the students' own feedback to explore the advantages and drawbacks of this online reading experience. The students were asked to post one comment of 500 words and one reply of an unspecified length to another person; they knew that participation in this discussion was compulsory and would count towards their class mark. After the discussion was over, they were given the opportunity to provide unstructured feedback on post-it notes which all of them did.

In this chapter, I examine the text of the discussion, the students' interactions and their reflective feedback, to investigate how the process of negotiating the meaning of this text unfolded, in what was for the students a fairly unfamiliar online environment. I also put forward some tentative conclusions about how best to manage and structure this kind of online communal reading from a pedagogical point of view. Finally, I consider what this case study might suggest about mediated reading more generally in terms of its radical potential to engage, connect and transform readers in ways as yet unobserved in face-to-face contexts.

The students were asked to choose a passage from the novel and write a post explaining why they had chosen it and offering some analysis of it. They were also required to respond to another student's posting, and encouraged to reply to those who commented on their own analysis. The discussion that resulted came to over 21,000 words. Upon reading through it, I observed a pervasive pattern of agreement among the students. A general sense of carefully constructed politeness and courtesy emerged from the over-formality of their language, which differed substantially from the face-to-face (f2f) classroom in which informal language was used freely.

To explore this further, I analysed the text of the discussion using the software package MonoConc Pro 2.2, a concordancing programme which facilitates the analysis of patterns within bodies (or corpora) of text. Baker (2006, 36-37) raises some of the issues that need to be taken into account when carrying out corpus analysis on computer-mediated communication, for example how to account for emoticons and whether or not to omit portions of text that appear more than once due to citation in the replies of other discussion participants. One of the advantages for the purpose of this study was the absence of avatars or emoticons on the message board, although this analytical simplicity may not have equated to a pedagogical advantage for the students. The question of whether to include cited text was also obviated as none of the students quoted each other at length.

Discursive patterning around agreement

I began by examining patterning around the idea of agreement (Table 1). There were eleven instances, all expressing agreement with other discussion participants. The one instance of 'disagree' was used to describe an event in the text.

October 2006 4:25 PM I certainly **agree** that this passage highlights the k

tle for territory', I completely **agree** in saying that I think Ondaatje wa

25 October 06 8:55 AM Yes, I **agree** – one of the key themes of the nov

nd the nun were the same – but I **agree** that Ondaatje treats women in a my

Date: 18 October 2006 5:57 PM I **agree** with what you're saying B about th

Date: 18 October 2006 5:04 PM I **agree** with T that there is a metaphor fo

han the natural world. Whilst I **agree** with P's opinion that Ondaatje has

imagery of the landscape, I too **agree** that this is crucial for the devel

g her about Ambrose and their **disagreement** over her leaving. Patrick desc

Table 1: Concordance lines for *agree* in online discussion corpus

Clearly the students felt a strong compulsion to express themselves in terms of agreement, which ran counter to their usual practice in class of dissenting robustly with me and with each other. It was as if, missing the behavioural resources to mitigate criticism of their peers, the students had to compensate by agreeing with each other and using each others' comments as inspiration for their own ideas, rather than as fodder for critique. The feedback responses suggested that critiquing others was felt to be perilous, with one student proposing a structural solution (*There was an element of nervousness in choosing who to post on initially – perhaps if students between [the two] groups were paired, the postings may have gathered momentum*). I wondered whether one student's oblique comment (*Prefer face to face ... [as] conversation allows for many differing opinions/analysis*) concealed frustration at the pressure to agree with others and subjugate the desire for discussion to the need for courtesy.[1]

It is necessary to point out that students did sometimes signal their distance from the points made by others, but without using the term *disagree*, and usually by preceding their dissent with praise or assent. Student M, for example, questioned student P's analysis by framing her disagreement as an additional point which 'agree[d]' with P's statement: *Whilst I agree with P's opinion that Ondaatje has written about the 'untold history of a nation', I would draw his attention to Linda Hutcheon's interview with Ondaatje ....* Another example is provided by student J's comment on a post by student L: *I thought your analysis was interesting, you looked at the ways in which a disguise was assumed by characters that wished to transcend social bounderies* [sic]. *I would question the success of these characters, did they achieve their objectives and escape their true identities? In Patrick's case, he failed in his disguises.*

However, there are very few examples of outright robust disagreement. I would argue that the defamiliarised context of the online discussion board helps to foreground the importance of other participants' feedback and the validation of participants' contributions to the discussion. One interpretation of the high incidence of the word *agree* is that participants recognised the importance of signalling to others in the group that they had been heard and understood precisely because they needed this kind of validation themselves.

It should also be noted that it can be entirely possible to have a productive online discussion in which students agree. One student, E, provides some analysis of an excerpt that two other students, N and T, also reported enjoying when they came across it in Ondaatje's novel. Both respond to E's posting to say that they agree with her and both then proceed take her points further. N relates the excerpt structurally to other parts of the novel and speculates about metaphorical possibilities of the images in the scene, while T extends one of E's ideas and relates it to another episode.

Interpersonal interaction and the digital 'rules of engagement'

This divergence between online discussion and f2f class discussion led me to wonder how the students were interacting with each other in other ways, so I then ran queries on personal pronouns in order to look at patterning of interpersonal interaction.

Pronoun	Number of instances relating to discussion (not text of novel)	Summary
I	137	many are used to express an opinion, as is seen from right collocates (*I think what's interesting about this passage; I too agree that this is crucial*)
me	15	many are used in to *me* (4) and *for me* (7) constructions, in order to hedge (*seemed to **me** to embody*)
my	22	many draw attention to subjective interpretation, eg analysis, opinion, interpretation (*what originally drew **my** attention towards this passage; in **my** opinion it allows for*)
we	39	mostly referring to the (imagined) reader of the novel (*Later **we** are told; **we**, as readers, are unable to see*)
us	11	mostly referring to the imagined reader (*used by Ondaatje to inform **us** that her story is yet to be told; also from **us**, the readers*)
our	5	again mostly referring to the imagined reader (*this may increase **our** sympathy towards Patrick*) though is more ambiguous – could also be the class group
you	30	mostly referring directly to another individual or their comments (*as you quite rightly point out*), some as the generic third-person pronoun (*it is now not just what you are reading, but how you are reading it*)
your	10	mostly referring to the comments of others (*I thought **your** analysis was interesting*)

Figure 2: Summary of pronoun use in online discussion corpus

From this summary of the concordance findings (Table 2), it can be seen that in this context, the discussion participants were most comfortable talking about their own interpretations, which they were nonetheless careful to hedge. They were somewhat less willing to invoke a community of imagined readers in which they were themselves included, and the least willing of all to directly address and talk to their classmates. This can be seen in the graphs below (Tables 3 and 4):

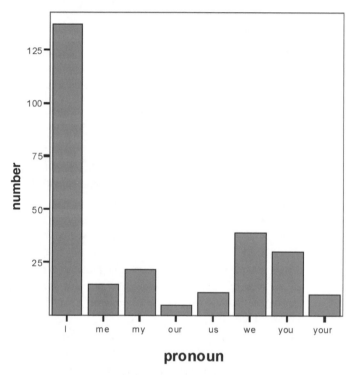

pronoun

Table 3: Use of personal pronouns in online discussion corpus

References to *I, me and my* (total 174) are about the individual her/himself, usually expressing an opinion

References to *we, us* and *our* (total 55) are predominantly *not* about the class but about the imagined reader

References to you and your (total 40) are mostly directed at other members of the group

Even allowing for the fact that each student was asked to provide a longer post at the outset – when they did not yet have any interlocuters to address as 'you' – it can be seen from a qualitative reading of the discussion that the students were cautious about speaking to or about the other discussion participants.

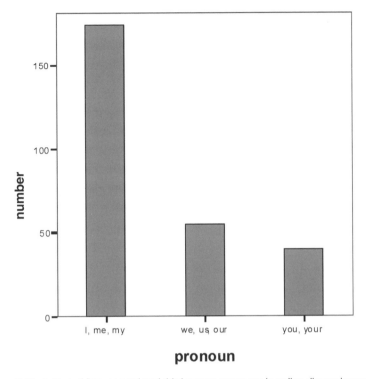

pronoun

Table 4: Use of first, second and third person pronouns in online discussion corpus

This is also supported by the feedback comment on nervousness about choosing who to respond to. While there is a limit to what this pronoun data can tell us, as it only addresses the linguistic behaviour of students rather than their holistic reading experience, I would cautiously posit that it reveals the uncertainty students felt while interacting with each other in this mediated context. It is interesting that this ambiguity resulted in increased courtesy: users of messageboards will be aware that anonymity most often results in less, rather than more, courtesy in interpersonal interactions. In this case, the students not only knew they were being monitored but also knew each other in a f2f context. What is interesting is that this evidently did not make them feel as if they had the freedom to use the same informal language as they would in the classroom, where they were also monitored.

Biber *et al* have demonstrated that pronoun use in English is around five times higher in conversational language as it is in academic prose, while academic prose contains roughly twice the number of nouns as conversational language (2002, 93). Academic prose thus has a higher lexical density, and therefore usually contains more informational content, while there is generally more interpersonal interaction in conversational language.

However, as current pedagogical thinking moves increasingly towards active learning, with the recognition that discussion and interaction are more productive learning environments than the presentation of large amounts of information for students to absorb passively (see for example McKeachie, 1999, 44, 209), it would seem that online discussions that move towards the more conversational, pronoun-heavy and thus interactive and apparently less substantive discussions provide better learning experiences than those in which students are prompted to generate formal and lexically dense contributions more in the nature of academic essays. Indeed, in their feedback students reported dissatisfaction with having to absorb these large blocks of expository prose (*huge sea to wade through and too long/much to read*).

It is perhaps not surprising that the students produced formal, essay-type prose, given that offline production facilitates the careful crafting of language, and that they were aware that their work would be assessed. But this suggests that in unfamiliar mediated contexts in which students are unsure of the social rules of engagement, instructors have to help move students away from a lexically dense essay-style mode and towards a more discursive mode, where they must engage critically with the ideas of others and not simply articulate their own. It is evidently a strength of offline production – in which there is time to compose and edit one's language rather than producing it on the spot – that it enabled the students to take as much time as they needed to produce well-reasoned and creative close analyses of the text, and to track down the textual examples needed to support their own assertions about the text. I would argue, however, that this mode may be best kept for assessed essay writing rather than the communal reading and discussing of a text that not only comprises the backbone of the academic teaching of literature, but can be seen developing organically in online forms.

If we accept that it is desirable to discuss, argue and enter into dialogue in the process of reading together, then the potentially solitary aspect of posting on an online discussion board is something that requires careful scaffolding to overcome. The instructor should model the kind of interaction sought. In this discussion, directly addressing students and posing rhetorical questions to them succeeded in influencing some of their own language use as they entered into dialogue with one another. In the very first thread to appear on the board, I posted a reply which was deliberately informal, friendly and dialogic in the attempt to get the students to respond in kind, and indeed this had the effect of changing the initial poster's language dramatically (see Table 5).

Table 5. Exchange between student J, student L and class instructor

Post number and author	Text of post	Features of post
1 L [student]: excerpt from initial post	*... This passage foreshadows this breakthrough in communication: 'even a silent daughter could put on the cloak and be able to break through her chrysalis into language'. Another animal figure of speech, this time alluding to the possibilities gained by adopting the 'skin' of another – the cloak of animal skins. Of course this directly links to the book's title but also to the necessity of wearing another animals' hide, only then can one 'break into language'. Perhaps Ondaatje is suggesting obliquely that the only way a minority community with little power or influence, such as immigrants and/or the working class, can communicate is through wearing the skins of the powerful. ...Indeed, the working-class Harris whom Patrick confronts explosively in the last part of the novel has power because he has integrated himself into the lifestyles of the rich. He has left his working-class roots behind. he can only control and wield authority (over those he grew up amongst) when he is wearing the 'cloak' of the powerful – the ruling class. ...*	■ formal register ■ no personal pronouns ■ no interpersonal engagement ■ specialised lexis
2 Class instructor: reply to L	*Thank you, L, for getting our discussion off to a fine start. These are very helpful observations here about some of the themes of /In the Skin of a Lion/ which allude to the critical readings. Your analysis of the idea of skins/surfaces/moss was useful to me in suggesting the significance of all that imagery in the book around the theatre and the mutability of identity (I love that wonderful image where the dyers are showering at the end of the day's work and all of a sudden the dye slips off their skin like clothing falling away). I wonder the extent to which Ondaatje is questioning whether it is possible to have a stable*	■ direct interpersonal engagement ■ interlocutor addressed by name ■ higher use of personal pronouns resulting more informal tenor ■ use of nonstandard grammar ■ specialised lexis

Post number and author	Text of post	Features of post
	identity, or whether this is desirable politically? – think of Harris whom, as you say, achieves power and control only by leaving behind his working-class roots.	
3 J [student]: reply to L	*I thought your analysis was interesting, you looked at the ways in which a disguise was assumed by characters that wished to transcend social bounderies [sic]. I would question the success of these characters, did they achieve their objectives and escape their true identities? In Patrick's case, he failed in his disguises, as you mentioned he had no affinity with any particular community or group and he was only comfortable 'in his own skin' towards the end of the novel when he explains the situation (his life and history) to the innocent child.*	■ direct interpersonal engagement (including questioning) ■ personal pronouns used to maintain more informal tenor ■ specialised lexis
4 L: reply to J	*I think they do achieve something – look at Harris – he's rich and wealthy though perhaps a betrayer to his roots. However, he seems to enjoy his wealth. Do you think Patrick actually disguises himself? Or merely fails to communicate...*	■ direct interpersonal engagement continuation of the rhetorical questioning ■ use of non-standard grammar ■ informal register ■ lexis not particularly specialised

By the end of this exchange L and J – students in separate classes and degree streams – do in fact seem to be communicating with each other, and the interpersonal tenor and discussiveness has begun to approach that of a f2f interaction much more closely than the initial posts. In threads where I did not intervene, the tenor tended to remain relatively formal, the communication stilted and the interaction correspondingly superficial. This suggests that even for a generation often categorised as entirely comfortable with online social spaces, these students need assistance in learning how to interact with others in an online learning environment and mediated reading formation.

Indeed, in their feedback there is evidence of uncertainty and anxiety around this interpersonal domain:

> *I did not get a response until after the people who wrote their analyses got a response so I was unsure as to whether people understood me*
>
> *Definitely prefer face to face as online is quite impersonal and not as exciting*
>
> *I find it easier to understand class discussion when talking face to face*

Students also reported their desire for more guidance from the class instructor to scaffold and structure the exercise:

> *It might have been [?enhanced] if you, [class instructor], had given more prompts or questions about novel to which we could've responded. Made whole thing more structured and focused?*
>
> *It might be a nice idea to post up some headings of general themes/questions that people could contribute to as a discussion*
>
> *needed more mediation*

These comments suggested the need to buttress the discussion beforehand and follow it up afterwards in the more familiar setting of a f2f class until the social and behavioural norms of the online context were established. Indeed, the interactive aspect to engagement with internet technology may be the most important, as suggested by the comments of Rheingold and Travis. Bargh and McKenna (2004, 579) cite research indicating that in business contexts, negotiations that involved internet-mediated interactions proceeded more smoothly if they were preceded by non-internet-mediated contact. It seems likely, then, that the kind of textual negotiations occurring in shared online reading would also be improved by prior face-to-face contact.

Benefits of reading in an online environment

If online interaction was imperfectly negotiated by the students and experienced as a barrier to discussion, there were also benefits to the learning environment which the students recognised in their feedback. The flexibility of the messageboard structure meant that students could take more time to understand something, if they needed (*I find it easier to understand class discussion when talking face to face*), and could also choose the path they navigated through the discussion (*It was good to be able to dip in and out of discussions*). These benefits on the comprehension side of the online discussion were accompanied by advantages in terms of self-expression: those who found it more difficult to contribute-because of a lower level of mastery of f2f social dynamics or a non-native speaker level of English, for example-found it easier to explain themselves:

> *I liked the online discussion as it is an easier way for me to express opinions on what was being read*
>
> *I can better express my opinion online. In fact it is difficult to understand or express arguments in oral discussions*
>
> *I don't mind either class / WebCT based discussion as long as I get given a chance to speak*

One student recognised that it might be a learning medium more suited to the less confident (*I am quite confident contribut[ing] to class discussion so maybe online benefits introverted people*).

A further benefit was that due to offline production of the contributions, the quality of the input was perceived to be higher. Students stated that it was helpful to hear everyone's views (*it helped to hear views from other people; I enjoyed reading everyone's pieces and looking at the different responses*), and in fact two feedback responses tied these elements together:

> *It was interesting to see what other students were thinking and sometimes it can be easier to write your thoughts than articulate them clearly in a class discussion*
>
> *The online discussion was good as it meant you could give a full explanation, and you were able to organise your thoughts rather than being put on the spot*

The online learning environment, then, provided some students with a context in which not only was posting easier than verbal interjection, but in which written language is easier than spoken language to produce under pressure, and to process (*I did think it was useful to have written records so you could fully absorb text*). Having a permanent record of the discussion was mentioned as useful in the feedback, and this was clearly contingent on the pedagogical context in which the discussion occurred:

> *useful as it is more permanent than a face to face discussion (– revision purposes)*
>
> *the online aspect means that it's a resource that can be referred to whenever (it's possible to lose paper, but you can't lose the internet)*
>
> *It was good to have a written record of discussion*

To assist the group in their revision, I compiled the entire discussion into one document after the discussion ended. I examined the download statistics to see who among the 23 students had viewed it. There were seventeen visits, with the average time per visit 2 hrs 36 minutes, making a total of 44 hrs 16 minutes overall across all the students. This suggests that almost three-quarters of the class did at least set out to use it as a resource for learning or revision.

The main strength of this online discussion appeared to be the forum it provided in which students could take extra time to produce well-reasoned and creative close analyses of the text, and could support their own assertions with textual examples. This is something that is important in literary studies, but it is difficult to do quickly in a verbal context as one often needs time to flick through the text to find the exact quote or reference. Usually this kind of careful preparation goes into written work that is seen by assessors rather than others in the class, and the indications from these students is that seeing these more polished analyses from their peers was helpful. The principle disadvantage was the forced and disjointed nature of the interpersonal communication: some interactions were stilted, and some questions which were asked did not get answered. My efforts as the class instructor to model a less formal and more interactive approach were picked up by students writing in the same thread, but not to any great degree by students who posted their contributions later, something which further suggested that some students may not have bothered to read all the threads.

Challenges of reading in an online environment

There was not much continuity at all between the postings, despite my efforts in later comments to draw students' attention to points of resonance, with the effect that the entire text read less like a communal discussion and more like a collection of different analyses. The level of interaction between the students remained fairly superficial, and this was something that the students themselves noted and commented on as a negative feature in their feedback on the online discussion. In what I have posited as an intermediate stage of familiarity with cmc discussions in an academic context (for both teachers and students), teachers should ideally contribute to as many of the discussion threads themselves as is practicable, to model the appropriate register of language and level of engagement with the contributions of others, and to reassure students that their points have been heard.

The need to buttress the discussion, before and afterwards, by giving the students questions to discuss beforehand, and then following this up afterwards in the more familiar setting of a face-to-face class, are further suggestions for consideration. Compiling the discussion threads into one document that can be downloaded and taken away is appreciated, especially as it can be useful as a revision resource. In view of this, teachers should also carefully consider the amount each student is required to write; reading the entire discussion should not become so much of a burden that students do not bother attempting it.

Towards a transformative reading experience

Clearly the kind of reading I have been discussing here is a very specific type: that undertaken in a higher education context by undergraduates who can be considered to some extent professionalised readers. They have been taught a range of reading strategies that are likely to differentiate their reading practices from other groups of readers without this specialist academic training. This context, moreover, foregrounds the difficulty of identifying a single ideal model of online textual discussion.

What I have been using as a baseline of sorts in this discussion is resemblance to a certain type of class interaction valorised within the UK higher education system: participation from all members of the group, evidence of focussing on and engaging with the content of others' comments, and dissent as well as agreement. With the technology still in flux, and teachers and students at different levels of familiarity with it, we are evidently a long way from agreeing on what constitutes an ideal online discussion, and we cannot assume the same principles hold in online pedagogical contexts as for offline.

However, the model of reading which the above analysis assumes – reading as the process of making meaning from a text, both individually and in a communal setting – is one that I think is nonetheless applicable to other contexts outside academic and educational settings, in which value may not always be articulated in terms of a set of aesthetic features but rather in terms of social meaning. Considerations of how to analyse and enhance the reading experience of this group of student readers, then, are also pertinent to readers engaged in other mediated reading formations.

Scholars continue to search for evidence of the transformative potential of reading: its power to effect change, particularly outside the domain of educated middle-class readers who habitually occupy centre stage within the discipline. Impressive work has been undertaken in this area, most notably by Janice Radway, whose seminal study of romance readers (1984) searched for evidence that these women were using their reading as a way of resisting the patriarchal structures that constrained them, and by Elizabeth McHenry in her analysis of the role of African-American literary societies in raising the consciousness of African-Americans and helping to spur them to collective action (2002, 17-18). Jonathan Boyarin noted in 1993 that scholarship had begun to dissolve the stereotype of the isolated lone reader, demonstrating that 'not only is all reading socially embedded, but indeed a great deal of reading is done in social groups' (1993, 4), so it seems more important than ever to understand the processes that are occurring in new social contexts as these take shape in virtual space, and to attend to the ways in which reading is able to foster transformation through them.

The burgeoning democratisation of online spaces for reading together is perhaps one of the most fruitful frontiers along which to pursue this work. Travis, for example, gestures towards the radical potential of mediated reading formations, seeing them as expanding the communicative possibilities between individuals, and increasing the facility with which they can reflectively respond to both literary texts and to the comments of others. Conversations of this kind can be sustained over a long period of time and between people from different cultures and countries. As Travis sees it, 'encountering cultural 'others' who talk back and reading contestatory multicultural literature would likely effect the self-interrogation and cultural discomfort (friction) necessary for the reader to perceive her subject position in relation to others. The long-range goal of such experience would be the reader's ability to avoid responding to cultural difference as a threat' (1998, 16).

Much as I share Travis's enthusiasm for this putative ideal mediated reading encounter, I do not think that we are quite at this utopian point yet, if my research is any indication. This discussion suggested that it was precisely this encounter with the 'other' that was rendered difficult by the online context, and it was this interactional element which had to be scaffolded by the instructor in order for students to begin to engage with each other's readings rather than solipsistically presenting their own interpretations and considering those of others only relatively superficially.

Travis is clear that potential for change is predicated on a thoroughgoing engagement with the other, something which the act of reading is well positioned to supply as it is an empathetic act. Textual interpretation involves 'a temporary fusion with the other, followed by separation/differentiation and active interpretation' and if 'the merging leaves the interpreter unchanged, then the radical potential of such fusion is lost – both in aesthetic terms and in interpersonal terms' (1998, 12).

It is encouraging, then, that at least in this small case study, students could be seen changing their mode of interaction when other ways of reading were modelled for them. To find ways of modelling reading practices so as to facilitate imaginative, authentic and transformative encounters with others, while simultaneously avoiding the perils of prescriptively imposing reading practices that serve to reinforce hierarchies of value, is the continuing challenge for those of us who model, and ourselves mediate, the act of reading to our students.

Notes

1 Interestingly, this finding of a pervasive pattern of agreement is replicated among students from a very different context to those in this study. In four online discussions over a twelve week period, first year students at the University of Hong Kong studying for a Bachelor of Nursing discussed the topic of eating behaviours and eating disorders among adolescents in the context of an Academic English course. In these discussions, the patterning around the lemma agree was even more marked than for the UK students: there were 136 instances of *agree* or *agreed,* but only one instance of *disagree* (and the disagreement was with a claim made by an article rather than by another member of the class). This did not mean that the students did not have opinions of their own; reading each use of *agree* in context makes it clear that they would frequently add new information or expand upon the point being made. It is, however, interesting to observe that non-native English speakers at a different point in their academic careers and in an entirely different disciplinary context appear to feel the same compunction to explicitly signal agreement in their contributions to an online forum. I am grateful to Lisa Cheung for sharing this corpus of online discussion with me.

Bibliography

Baker, P (2006) *Using corpora in discourse analysis.* London: Continuum

Bargh, J A and McKenna, K Y A (2004) The internet and social life. *Annual Review of Psychology* 55, 573-90

Biber, D, Conrad, S and Leech, G (2002) *Longman student grammar of spoken and written English.* Harlow, Essex: Pearson Education

Boyarin, J (1993) Introduction. In J Boyarin (ed) *The ethnography of reading.* Berkeley: University of California Press

Liu, A (2008) Transliteracies Research Project. http://transliteracies.english.ucsb.edu/category/research-project/ (accessed October 2007)

McHenry, E (2002) *Forgotten readers: recovering the lost history of African American literary societies.* Durham: Duke University Press

McKeachie, W J (1999) *McKeachie's teaching tips: strategies, research and theory for college and university teachers* (10th ed). Boston: Houghton Mifflin

Radway, J (1984) *Reading the romance: women, patriarchy and popular literature.* Chapel Hill: University of North Carolina Press

Rheingold, H (1993) *The virtual community: homesteading on the electric frontier.* New York: Addison-Wesley

Travis, M A (1998) *Reading cultures: the construction of readers in the twentieth century.* Carbondale: Southern Illinois University Press

16

Teachers as Readers in the 21st Century

*Teresa Cremin, Eve Bearne, Marilyn Mottram
and Prue Goodwin*

Introduction

Since the inception of the National Literacy Strategy (NLS) in England and Wales (DfEE, 1998), concerns have been voiced about the ways in which children's literature has been positioned and may be used in the classroom. In particular, the practice of relying upon extracts, downloaded or purchased, has been heavily criticised (Dombey, 1998; Frater, 2000; Sedgwick, 2000; King, 2002). Writers too have articulated their concerns that their works are being subjected to inappropriate levels of analysis and that, as comprehension and assessment are seen to dominate over reading and response, this may lead to reduced pleasure in the text and adversely influence children's desire to read (Powling *et al*, 2003, 2005).

There has also been a sense that teachers' own creative uses of literature have been subjugated to a centralised system for teaching literacy (Goouch and Lambirth, 2005; Grainger *et al*, 2005; Marshall, 2001; Martin, 2003) and that their confidence in knowing and using children's literature may be limited, particularly by lack of time to read personally for pleasure (Kwek *et al*, 2007; Arts Council England, 2003).

In addition, comparative UK research by Sainsbury and Schagen (2004), who collected data on children's attitudes to reading at the onset of the NLS in 1998 and again in 2003, revealed a decline in reading for pleasure across this period. They also found that although the majority of children still report enjoying reading stories, their desire to do so had markedly decreased, for example from 77 per cent to 65 per cent in 10-11 year olds and a decline in the percentage of boys of this age group who say they enjoy reading from 70 per cent in 1998 to 55 per cent in 2003.

In response to these concerns and the findings from the 2001 Progress in International Literacy Study (PIRLS) (Mullis *et al*, 2003; Twist *et al*, 2003) that children in the UK read less independently, and find rather less pleasure in reading than many of their peers in other countries, various surveys and reports have been produced, including *Reading for Purpose and Pleasure* (Ofsted, 2004) and the NLT survey Young Children's Reading Habits, (Clark and Foster, 2005). In particular, Ofsted perceived that some schools had not given sufficient thought to promoting children's independent reading or building on children's preferences and were concerned to note that few schools successfully engaged the interests of those who, whilst competent readers, did not choose to read for pleasure.

Overall in the NLT survey, despite some enthusiasm for reading, it was clear that secondary school pupils and boys were rather more inclined to report negative attitudes than the primary aged learners and the girls. The more recent PIRLS study, undertaken in 2006, continues to show that children in England have less positive attitudes to reading than children in most other countries (Twist *et al*, 2007). This report states that: 'Of particular concern is the 15 per cent of children in the sample for England who had the least positive attitudes, a significant increase from 2001' (Twist *et al*, 2007, 33).

This decline in children's enjoyment in reading is not unique to England but nonetheless represents a challenge for the profession. Recently, an English Arts Council project *Literature Matters* (2004-6), designed to help ensure Initial Teachers Education (ITE) students develop a rich working knowledge of children's literature through liaison work between ITE institutions and the Schools' Library Service, has been shown to lack sustainability (Bailey *et al*, 2007). The Training Development Agency found that ITE students in England have a limited knowledge of children's multicultural texts. Furthermore, it has been argued that the emphasis on synthetic phonics in England as a result of the Rose Review (Rose, 2006), has the potential to lead to a more disconnected and atomistic approach to teaching reading, particularly in the early years, one which profiles decoding at the relative expense of reading for meaning and developing pleasure in the process.

Additionally, it has been shown that effective teachers of reading in the primary phase need much more than knowledge of the skills and cueing systems which young readers employ; they also need an extensive knowledge of children's literature (Medwell *et al*, 1998). Yet at present the extent of their knowledge in this area is unknown for, while studies of children's attitudes to reading and knowledge of literature have been undertaken (Whitehead, 1977; Hall and Coles, 1999; Clark and Foster, 2005), no studies have systematically documented teachers' knowledge and use of literature.

The research design

In response to the context outlined above, the United Kingdom Literacy Associations' (UKLA) children's literature Special Interest Group (SIG) believed it was timely to undertake research into teachers as readers and ascertain their knowledge and use of children's literature in the primary classroom. There is also some evidence that teachers do not make significant use of children's and school librarians or libraries (Ofsted, 2004) so this research provided an opportunity to consider the working relationships between teachers and librarians and look for ways of developing innovative partnerships.

As a consequence the Phase 1 research sought to explore primary teachers':

- personal reading habits and preferences
- knowledge of children's literature
- reported use of children's literature in the classroom
- involvement in local area /school library services.

Linking into UKLA networks, the research team collected questionnaire responses from 1,200 primary teachers in eleven Local Authorities (LAs) in England. Approximately 50 per cent worked in Key Stage 1 (children aged 5 – 7) and approximately 50 per cent in Key Stage 2 (children aged 7 – 11) with varying lengths of teaching experience. There were also some responses from student teachers in five different ITE institutions. The LAs represented a spread of inner city, rural and suburban areas reflecting a broad range of socio-economic status. The questionnaire was piloted, adapted and introduced to teachers on continuing professional development short courses.

Each Local Authority had a designated co-ordinator who completed context sheets and administered the questionnaire. The LA co-ordinators made efforts to administer the questionnaires at generic courses for classroom teachers rather than on courses specifically intended for literacy co-ordinators. This meant that the research team could gain evidence of a more general picture of teachers' knowledge and experience of children's literature. The questionnaire on reading would be completed and returned on the same day to ensure a high response rate and a wealth of data from a range of authorities in different parts of the country, thus increasing the validity and reliability of the findings.

Both qualitative and quantitative information about teachers' views, knowledge and practices with regard to reading was sought; the former has been subjected to categorical analysis, the latter has been inputted and analysed by a research assistant making use of the quantitative software package SPSS (no. 13). The data indicated connections and relationships between the three strands of the research, namely the teachers' personal reading habits and preferences, their knowledge of children's literature and their reported use of such literature in the classroom. Information was also gathered about length of experience and the age phases taught.

Teachers' personal reading

The questionnaire began with four questions about personal reading preferences and when respondents had last read a book for pleasure. These were followed by two questions about use of libraries. In terms of current reading, 73.2 per cent had read for pleasure during the last month and 20.2 per cent during the last three months. Five per cent had read for pleasure during the last six months and 1.6 per cent over six months ago (See Table 1). Popular fiction, including so-called 'chick-lit', thrillers and crime novels, was the most frequent choice (40%). Autobiography and biography (14%) and other post 1980s novels (14%) were the next most popular categories and 6.5 per cent had recently read children's fiction. The lowest recorded categories (2.5% and under) were: newspapers and magazines; lifestyle/health; religious/spiritual; academic; educational; practical/factual; travel; short stories; poetry; and plays.

Table 1: Teachers' personal reading: responses to When did you last read for pleasure?

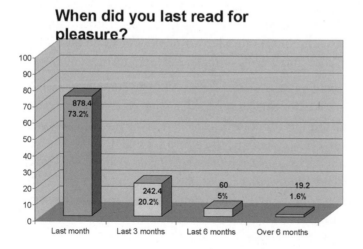

There was a different picture in response to the question about the most important book ever read. The highest percentage recorded (17%) was for religious/spiritual books with 12 per cent for significant recent novels (post 1980s) in second place. Following these, high scoring categories were: nineteenth century and earlier classics (11%); children's fiction (11%); autobiography and biography (9%); twentieth century American classics (9%) and European classics (5.5%). Smaller percentages were recorded for: allegorical books (4.5%); lifestyle/health (3.5); academic, educational and practical/ factual books scored just over 2 per cent, but all other categories, including popular fiction, poetry, plays and travel scored less than 2 per cent.

In terms of favourite childhood reading, the overwhelming majority of respondents recorded popular fiction. Enid Blyton and Roald Dahl were by far the most mentioned authors. Ten per cent of favourite childhood books were nineteenth century classics such as *Black Beauty* (Sewell) (with 23 mentions), *Heidi* (Spyri) (19 mentions), *Little Women* (Alcott) and *What Katy Did* (Coolidge) (13 mentions each). Relatively high numbers were also recorded for twentieth century classics such as *The Lion, the Witch and the Wardrobe* (Lewis) with over 50 mentions, *The Hobbit* (Tolkein) (16), *Swallows and Amazons* (Ransome) (15) and *Winnie the Pooh* (Milne) (14). Nine per cent of the total were picturebooks, with *The Very Hungry Caterpillar* (Carle) topping the list with 13 mentions.

Very few indeed (1.5%) named poetry as their favourite childhood reading although this may, in part at least, have been a function of the question which referred to a favourite 'book' as a child, triggering perhaps a memory of a narrative. Nonetheless this response is in line with the limited mention of poetry in the question on recently recorded reading and is reinforced by the extremely limited knowledge of children's poets known to these teachers. It is no surprise, perhaps, that popular or series fiction was so pre-eminent, but the connection between teachers' favourite childhood reading and the texts they currently offer in the classroom is worth considering.

Teachers recorded several sources of finding books for their own reading. Bookshops – local (mentioned by 80%) and on-line (36%) were the most popular, although friends were mentioned as a frequent resource (56%). In contrast, libraries were not recorded as a frequent source of getting reading material (34%). Some respondents noted other routes to finding reading material, including advertising, Richard and Judy recommendations and magazine/newspaper reviews. Some did not respond to this question.

Overall, a mixed picture of teachers' preferences and practices emerges. Memories of favourite reading as children and current reading for pleasure are dominated by popular fiction although the sample as a whole reflects a wide range of reading, including children's and crossover fiction. There is a clear emphasis on affective content, as evidenced by choices of autobiography and biography, many of which were about people who suffered indignity, emotional, political and physical deprivation and triumphed over adversity. However, when choosing their most important book, the respondents discounted popular fiction in favour of religious, spiritual, allegorical and exemplary books. These were not only the Bible (mentioned over 200 times) but also, for example, works with themes of morality and justice, including very recent as well as twentieth century fiction. It is not possible to assess how far the demographic had an influence on these figures.

The responses included many classics – both from Europe and North America – which the teachers would have studied in school when they were pupils, including a few mentions of plays and poetry which had made an impact. This bears out the importance of teachers studying literature with children as well as simply reading for pleasure.

Since the great majority of the respondents had made time for their own reading pleasures within three weeks of answering the questionnaire, it seems that for these teachers at least, settling down with a book remains a pleasure. In addition, it is clear that ENJOYMENT of popular fiction is balanced by the satisfaction of reading which prompts thought and reflection. For more discussion of teachers' reading habits and preferences, see Cremin *et al* (2008a).

Teachers' knowledge of children's literature

Three questions asked the respondents to name six 'good' children's writers, six poets and six picturebook authors. The term good was explained as referring to writers whose work the teachers had found both valuable and successful with primary aged learners. The responses indicate that a relatively small number of authors are well known to primary practitioners; quite a few listed in this category might be more readily seen as picturebook makers. However, 64 per cent of the teachers named five or six writers. Forty six per cent named six. Dahl gained the highest number of mentions by far (744). The nearest four were: Michael Morpurgo (343), Jacqueline Wilson (323), J. K. Rowling (300) and Anne Fine (252). Others which attracted over a hundred mentions were: Dick King Smith (172), Janet and Alan Ahlberg (169), Enid Blyton (161), Shirley Hughes (128), C.S. Lewis (122), Philip Pullman (117), Mick Inkpen (106) and Martin Waddell (100).

It is questionable whether the teachers' knowledge is diverse enough to enable them to make informed recommendations to young readers. It could be argued that their repertoires represent a primary canon of significant children's authors, most of whom are likely to be well known to parents as well as grandparents. The dominance of these writers places in shadow the myriad of writers, such as Chris D'Lacy (1 mention only) Geraldine McCaughrean (10) Darren Shan (8) Jonathon Stroud (1) and Eva Ibbotson (1) whose work, more directed at older readers, deserves to be introduced to the young. In addition, it is surprising how few writers of novels for older readers are included in terms of range and diversity, for example, no mention is made of Morris Gleitzman or Marcus Sedgwick. Given the current popularity of fantasy novels, there are few authors of this genre noted, for example there is only one record made each for Philip Reeve and William Nicholson.

The data suggest that naming six good poets was not such an easy task. Fifty eight per cent of the respondents could name only one or two poets, including 22 per cent who named no poets at all. Only 10 per cent named six poets. Once again, some of the named poets might also be seen in the other categories (eg Ahlberg and Dahl). As might be expected, there was a predominance of poets mentioned whose poetry might be seen as light-hearted or humorous. In the top twenty in order of numbers of mentions, the last two were women poets. The highest number of mentions was Michael Rosen (452) with five others gaining over a hundred mentions: Alan Ahlberg (207), Roger McGough (197), Roald Dahl (165), Spike Milligan (159) and Benjamin Zephaniah (131). After these, three poets were mentioned more than fifty times: Edward Lear (85), Ted Hughes (58), A. A. Milne (57).

The data for poetry indicate that the teachers in the survey leant towards the more humorous or light hearted poets (eg Rosen or Milligan) or towards the work of particular poets whose work may well be studied under the NLS category of 'classic poetry' (e.g. Causley, Lear, Stevenson or Milne). In a sample of 1,200, very few women poets are mentioned; the highest numbers are: Grace Nicholls (16), Christina Rosetti (11), Eleanor Farjeon (9), Judith Nicholls (8), Pam Ayres (5), Floella Benjamin (3), Sandy Brownjohn (3), Sharon Creech (3), Carol Ann Duffy (3), Jill Murphy (3), Jackie Kay (2), Valerie Bloom (2) and Wendy Cope (1). This is a matter of concern, but may reflect trends in anthologising or in the world of poetry more generally. Furthermore, with the notable exception of Zephaniah, very few black poets received any mentions.

Unlike the picturebook category few teachers named any poetry collections, suggesting more use of anthologies or perhaps that the covers and titles of poetry books are less memorable than their fictional counterparts. The apparent lack of knowledge of poets may indicate that teachers tend to select poetry for its capacity to teach particular language features rather than enjoying it for its own sake. The recent Ofsted survey on poetry also supports the view that too limited a range of poets is known by primary phase teachers who, it is suggested, rely upon a very narrow range of specific poems, many of which they were taught in school (Ofsted, 2007).

In this category, the repeated mentions which the Ahlbergs receive and indeed Mick Inkpen, Shirley Hughes and Colin McNaughton suggest that much of the well known work, whilst poetic in nature, is found within the pages of picture fiction. This question preceded that on picture fiction list so it is unlikely answers were influenced by it. Indeed the 150 plus mentions that Dahl received as a poet are presumed to relate to his collection *Revolting Rhymes* and need to be placed alongside the evidence of 'over dependence' on Dahl found in the fiction section.

Well over half the sample (62%) were only able to name one, two or no picture fiction creators, 24 per cent named no picture fiction authors/illustrators, whilst 10 per cent named six. Some of these picturebook makers were also named as 'authors' in the first list. The highest number of mentions by far was for Quentin Blake (423) with four others being mentioned over a hundred times: Anthony Browne (175), Shirley Hughes (123), Mick Inkpen (121) and Alan Alhberg (146). There were also 302 specifically named books rather than authors.

In response to the question about picture fiction, it is noticeable that some of the picturebook makers were also named as 'authors' in the first list. In terms of multiple mentions, a relatively small group of the myriad of authors/ illustrators who are publishing for teachers today are mentioned. The second highest category noted is the many books whose titles are offered but whose authors have not been recalled. These were very varied and included for example *A Piece of Cake* (Jill Murphy), *Pumpkin Soup* (Helen Cooper), *Can't You Sleep Little Bear?* (Martin Waddell), *We're Going on a Bear Hunt* (Michael Rosen), *Owl Babies* (Martin Waddell), *Catkin* (illustrator P.J. Lynch) as well as a fairly large number of titles of traditional tales, eg *Goldilocks and the Three Bears* and *Jack and the Beanstalk*. In addition, there was a relatively large number of authors of other kinds of books inadvertently mentioned in this category, for example Rowling, Fine, Jigsaw books, Graham Greene.

Perhaps unsurprisingly, many of the picturebook makers mentioned create texts targeted at children in the early years or KS1 (eg Carle, Inkpen, Butterworth, Donaldson). There are fewer mentions of named picturebook makers/illustrators who offer texts for KS2. For example, there was negligible mention of the work of Gary Crew (4), Marcia Williams (3), Philippe Dupasquier (2) Shaun Tan or Neil Gaiman (1 each) and no mention at all of David Wiesner or Colin Thompson. The visual world which young people live in deserves attention in classrooms and many complex picturebooks offer challenging reading for all ages. It would also appear that a relatively small number of more recent authors/illustrators are noted, although Lauren Child receives 22 mentions. The work of Blake stands out as well known – whether this is through texts such as Zagazoo or Clown or his illustrations of Dahl (*The Twits, The Giraffe and the Pelly and Me* and *Revolting Rhymes*) is unknown.

In summary, the data presents issues of concern about teachers' over-dependence on a relatively narrow range of very well known writers, and their limited knowledge of poets and picture fiction creators. The high numbers for Dahl, Morpurgo, Wilson, Rosen and Blake may be related to how and where teachers access material that they use in the classroom. It is likely that if teachers are not reading from beyond the class library they may only be able to name those whose work they have been reading aloud over time. It also seems likely that the NLS (DfEE, 1998) requirement to study 'significant' children's authors may have influenced the knowledge indicated here, especially as the focus appears to fall on key authors in each category. Additionally, the media profile given to the top five authors mentioned in the survey, three of whom have been Children's Laureates, may also be influential, as may the teachers' childhood favourites, many of which appear to be relied upon and revisited years later in the classroom.

Since 86 per cent of the teachers indicate that they rely on their own interest and knowledge of children's books for decisions about classroom reading, the relatively limited range indicated is a matter of concern. In addition, although the teachers' personal reading indicates knowledge of global literature, this is not reflected in their classroom choices. For further discussion of teachers' knowledge of literature from this work, see Cremin *et al* (2008c).

Teachers' use of library services

Questions about library use indicated that 52 per cent of the respondents use the local library facilities for school, mostly for borrowing books for classroom use but also for professional and personal reading. Fourteen per cent had visited the local library with a class within the last three months and 6 per cent within the last six months. The largest percentage (60%) had not taken children to visit the local library for over six months and 18 per cent recorded

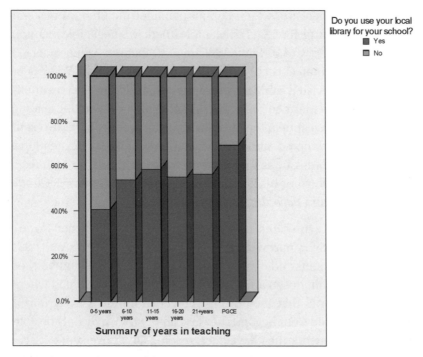

Table 2: Graph for question: *Do you use your local library for school?*
By number of years in teaching

never visiting the local library. Teachers with fewer years of teaching experience in the classroom were less likely to use library services. Sixty two per cent of those who had taught for up to five years reported not using the local library for school purposes (See Table 2).

Overall, there is some basis for concern about links between teachers and their local library services. Although the figures will have been influenced by local conditions and arrangements between the local authority and the library services, the overall figures, drawn from a range of LAs, indicate at best infrequent visits and not much reliance on librarians in developing activities or selecting materials for the classroom. This is a serious under-use of valuable services and expertise. For further information about the teacher use of libraries see Cremin *et al* (2008b).

Teachers' use of literature in the classroom

There were six questions which sought information about teachers' use of children's literature in their teaching. The practice of reading aloud to a class for pleasure remains a popular activity, with 70 per cent of the respondents reporting having read a book aloud during the previous month or reporting currently reading a book aloud to the class. Nine per cent had last read aloud over six months ago or never. Forty five per cent of Key Stage 2 teachers had either only read a complete book to their class within the last three or six months or had never done so and reading aloud diminishes considerably in older classes. Teachers who are new to teaching tend to read whole books more frequently to their classes than more experienced colleagues. Picture-books were by far the most frequently read to the class with 35 per cent of the response. In terms of novels, fantasy (20%) and mystery/adventure (14%) predominated, with smaller percentages for fairy tales (5%), short stories (4%), war stories (4.5%), school stories (4%) and poetry (3%). Non-fiction and 19th century classics only represented 1 per cent each of the totals, with about 6 per cent books unclassified (See Table 3).

Although there were quite positive responses with regard to the reported frequency of reading aloud for enjoyment, the figures indicate that teachers in their early years of teaching read aloud most frequently and teachers with longer experience less frequently. Also, it seems that this practice declines with older classes, which is of particular concern since, as children become more independent as readers, they continue to need encouragement, support and enthusiastic introductions to the work of quality writers as well as

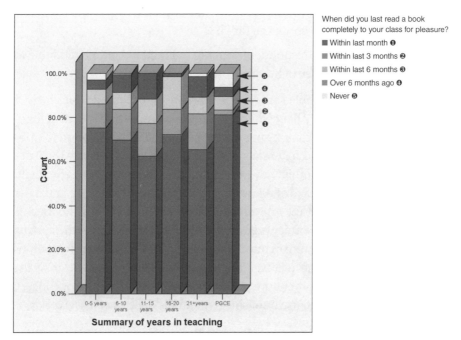

Table 3. Question *When did you last read a book completely to your class for pleasure?*
By number of years in teaching

the experience of engaging with demanding and emotionally satisfying literature.

In deciding which books to use in the classroom, many teachers used several criteria, the highest category being personal interest (85%) with children's recommendations being another factor (64%). 31 per cent take guidance from the literacy coordinator in their school and 21 per cent use librarians' recommendations. This is in contrast to their practices with regard to sourcing their personal reading and it would seem that different practices drive the teachers personally and professionally. It is intriguing to speculate on this difference and Phase II of the project has attempted to explain this anomaly.

One more open-ended question invited teachers to comment on their use of children's literature in the classroom. The replies were analysed according to the following categories:

- *holistic approach* where literature is seen as offering imaginative, creative and text-analysis purposes as well as being used as the basis for teaching reading and writing rooted in meaningful contexts

- *functional approach* where literature is used to teach skills at word or sentence level, or for teaching reading

- *partial approach* where respondents adopted a mixed approach but were not explicit about the range of activities

- *unspecific* where respondents did not or could not offer a rationale to underpin their use of literature in the classroom.

Eleven per cent of the whole sample offered no response to this question. Of those who did respond, 27 per cent took a holistic approach; 22 per cent functional; 28 per cent partial and 22 per cent were unspecific. In relation to publishers' prepared materials for literacy, these are used daily or weekly by 26 per cent of respondents, monthly by 7 per cent and infrequently by 38 per cent. There was a high percentage of nil responses to this question (27%), and 2 per cent explicitly stated that they never use publishers' materials. It thus seems that about half of the respondents adopt a wide-ranging approach to enjoying and using children's literature in the classroom. However, that raises questions about the other half. The relatively high number (almost a quarter of the sample) noting the use of literature as purely functional is a matter of concern as are the 26 per cent who use publishers' materials daily or at least weekly.

Respondents saw the importance of literature in the classroom as developing the imagination (top priority) and engaging the emotions (second). The role of literature in promoting reading and developing knowledge were ranked

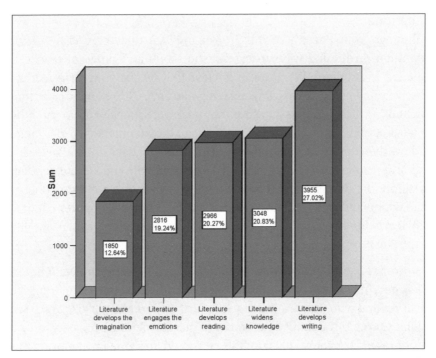

Table 4: Responses to the question asking for ranking of five statements about the value of literature (NB The lower the score, the higher the ranking)

third and fourth with the role of literature in developing writing rated as having the least importance (See Table 4).

In recognising the deep imaginative value and emotional engagement which literature can offer, the survey's respondents clearly seek such satisfactions, sustaining themselves as adult readers. However, their apparently limited knowledge of children's authors suggest that some tensions and difficulties exist for these primary phase professionals, who may be able to source their own reading habits successfully, but are not in a strong position to support younger learners in developing their preferences. Whilst the teachers in this survey may find time to read at home, the diminishing frequency of sharing literature as children grow older suggests that they may be finding it difficult in school to prioritise reading for pleasure.

The lowest rating of the role of literature in developing writing further suggests that the teachers did not necessarily see the important links between reading and writing. This raises the question of whether there is a tendency to divorce literature from pedagogy. Has literature become a mere tool for teachers to employ in the context of reading instruction, a resource for shared and guided reading?

Implications

The findings from Phase I of the project indicate that there is room for development in finding ways to extend the scope and range of teachers' knowledge of children's literature. It is clear that teachers are avid readers themselves, and enjoy fast-paced, engaging narratives. It is equally clear that many books which teachers treasure the most were introduced to them by their teachers. If their enjoyment of reading can be extended to a wider range of authors then this can only be beneficial for future readers whose diverse interests and reading preferences deserve to be both honoured and extended. In addition, the data suggest that teachers' knowledge of children's poetry, picture fiction and global literature needs considerable development, if they are to teach for the 'maximum entitlement' and develop readers for life (Martin, 2003).

Recent work about identities and reading suggests that the choice of books and teachers' mediation of them has a profound effect on 'how [children] see themselves and who they want to be' (McCarthey and Moje, 2002, 237). (See also Silin, 2003.) At the same time, teachers' literate identities are becoming a focus for research (Moore, 2004) and there should be scope for exploring this further.

It is also clear that the findings have implications for the education of future teachers as well as the continuing professional development of those already in post. The Department for Education and Skills, the National Literacy Strategy and the Qualifications and Curriculum Authority have agreed, with Arts Council England (ACE) and the Poet Laureate Andrew Motion, a 'Literature Entitlement':

> Every child has the right to read and write creatively and we believe that creativity should become a central part of formal education. This enriches the curriculum for the foundation stage and in schools. (ACE, 2003, 3)

If this is to be achieved, then more needs to be done to support teachers in providing a wider and richer experience of children's texts and building new partnerships with parents and librarians. These are key aims in Phase II of this work, *Teachers as Readers: Building Communities of Readers* (2007-8) which is a professional development project designed to develop children's pleasure and enthusiasm for reading through enriching and extending primary teachers':

■ knowledge of children's literature

- confidence and skilful, reflective use of such literature in the class-room
- relationships with librarians and parents.

This project will be documented as a series of case studies drawn from the five Local Authorities involved: Barking and Dagenham, Birmingham, Kent, Medway and Suffolk. It is hoped that in supporting teachers' development as readers, and in enhancing their understanding of the reading process and pedagogic practice they will become more effective 'Reading Teachers': teachers who read and readers who teach (Commeyras *et al*, 2004) in the 21st century.

Note: The authors would like to acknowledge the grant awarded by the Research Committee of the UKLA which made this work possible, and the time so generously given by the 11 Local Authority Research Co-ordinators, as well as Ruth Rogers from Canterbury Christ Church University, who was also a member of the team.

Bibliography

Arts Council England (2003) *From Looking Glass to Spy Glass: a consultation paper on children's literature.* London: Arts Council

Bailey, M, Hall, C and Gamble, N (2007) Promoting school libraries and school library services: problems and partnerships. *English in Education* 41(2) 71-85

Clark, C and Foster, A (2005) *Children's and young people's reading habits and preferences: the who, what, why, where and when.* London: National Literacy Trust

Cremin, T, Bearne, E, Goodwin, P and Mottram, M (2008a) Primary teachers as readers. *English in Education* 42(1) 1-16

Cremin, T, Bearne, E, Goodwin, P, and Mottram, M (2008b) Teachers' reading and links with libraries. *Library and Information Update* 7(6) pp40-43

Cremin, T, Mottram, M, Bearne, E and Goodwin, P (forthc, 2008c) Exploring Teachers' Knowledge of Literature. *Cambridge Journal of Education*

DfEE (1998) *The National Literacy Strategy Framework for Teaching.* London: DfEE

Dombey, H (1998) Changing literacy in the early years of school. In B. Cox (ed) *Literacy is not Enough.* Manchester: Manchester University Press and Book Trust

Hall, C and Coles, M (1999) *Children's Reading Choices.* London: Routledge

Frater, G (2000) Observed in practice, English in the National Literacy Strategy: some reflections. *Reading* 34 (3) 107-12

Grainger,T, Goouch, K and Lambirth, A (2005) *Creativity and Writing: Developing Voice and Verve in the Classroom.* London: Routledge

Goouch, K and Lambirth, A (2006) Golden times of writing: the creative compliance of writing journals. *Literacy* 40(3) 146-152

King, C (2001) 'I like group reading because we can share ideas' – the role of talk within the literature circle. *Reading, Literacy and Language* 35(1) pp32-6

Kwek, D, Albright, J and Kramer-Dahl, A (2007) Building teachers' creative capabilities in Singapore's English classrooms: a way of contesting pedagogical instrumentality in *Literacy* 42(1) 71-78

McCarthey, S J and Moje, E B (2002) Identity Matters. *Reading Research Quarterly* 37(2) pp228-238

Martin, T (2003) Minimum and maximum entitlements: literature at key stage 2. *Reading Literacy and Language* 37(1) 14-17

Marshall, B (2001) Creating danger: the place of the arts in education policy. In A. Craft, B. Jeffrey and M. Liebling (eds) *Creativity in Education.* London: Continuum

Medwell, J, Wray, D, Poulson, L and Fox, R (1998) *Effective Teachers of Literacy: A Report of a Research Project Commissioned by the Teacher Training Agency.* Exeter: University of Exeter

Moore, R (2004) Reclaiming the Power: literate identities of students and teachers. *Reading and Writing Quarterly* 20(4) 337-342

Mullis, I V S, Martin, M O, Gonzalez, E J and Kennedy, A M (2003) *PIRLS 2001 International Report.* Chestnut Hill, MA: Boston College

National Literacy Trust (2005) *Children's Reading Habits.* London: National Literacy Trust

Office for Standards in Education (Ofsted) (2002) *Reading for Purpose and Pleasure.* London: Ofsted

Office for Standards in Education (Ofsted) (2004) Conference Report by Phil Jarrett, Ofsted, Subject Conference July 2004

Office for Standards in Education (Ofsted) (2007) *Poetry in Schools: a survey of practice 2006/7.* London: Ofsted

Powling, C, Ashley, B, Pullman, P, Fine, A and Gavin, J (eds) (2003) *Meetings with the Minister.* Reading: National Centre for Language and Literacy

Powling, C *et al* (2005) *Beyond Bog Standard Literacy.* Reading: National Centre for Language and Literacy

Rose, J (2006) *Independent Review of the Teaching of Early Reading.* Nottingham: DfES Publications

Sainsbury, M and Schagen, I (2004) Attitudes to reading at ages nine and eleven. *Journal of Research in Reading* 27(3) 373-386

Sedgwick, F (2001) *Teaching Literacy: A Creative Approach.* London: Continuum

Silin, J G (2003) Reading, writing and the wrath of my father. *Reading Research Quarterly* 38(2) 260-267

Twist, L, Schagen, I and Hodgson, C (2003) *Readers and Reading: the National Report for England (PIRLS).* Slough: NFER

Twist, L, Schagen, I and Hodgson, C (2007) *Readers and Reading: the National Report for England (PIRLS).* Slough NFER

Whitehead, F (1977) *Children and their Books: the Final Report of the Schools Council Project on Children's Reading Habits, 10-16.* Basingstoke: Evans /Methuen Educational

Woods, P (2001) Creative literacy. In A Craft, B Jeffrey and M Liebling (eds) *Creativity in Education.* London: Continuum

The United Kingdom Literacy Association

Teachers as Readers Questionnaire

We're very grateful for your help with this survey. The background sheet will give you full details of the research project.

Local Authority: _____ Date: _____

Year group you currently teach: _____ Years in teaching: _____

Responsibility in school: _____

1. What was your favourite book as a child? _____

2. What have you read recently for your own pleasure? _____

   Please indicate when this was:
   ☐ Within the last month
   ☐ Within the last 3 months
   ☐ Within the last 6 months
   ☐ Over 6 months ago

3. What do you think is the most important book you have ever read?

   _____

   _____

4. How do you usually get hold of books for your own reading?

   You may tick more than one.
   ☐ Library
   ☐ Bookshop
   ☐ On-line bookshop
   ☐ From friend/s
   ☐ Other (please specify) _____

5. Do you use your local library for school? Yes/No *Delete as appropriate*

   If yes, in what ways?

   _____

   _____

6. When did you last visit your local library with a class?
   ☐ Within the last month
   ☐ Within the last 3 months
   ☐ Within the last 6 months
   ☐ Over 6 months ago

7. What was the last book you read completely (or with small cuts) to your class for pleasure, not with specific objectives in mind?

   _____

   When did you read this? _____

8. How often do you read aloud to your class?
   ☐ Daily
   ☐ Weekly
   ☐ Monthly
   ☐ Infrequently

9. List 6 'good' children's book authors

10. List 6 'good' children's poets

11. List 6 'good' children's picture book authors/illustrators

12. How do you decide which children's books to use in your classroom?

You may tick more than one.
- ☐ Personal interest/knowledge
- ☐ Children's recommendations
- ☐ Library service
- ☐ Literacy coordinators' recommendations
- ☐ Other (please specify) _____

13. Do you import books on to the IWB (interactive whiteboard)? Yes/No *Delete as appropriate*

Please give details _____

14. How do you use literature (books, poems, picturebooks) in your literacy teaching?

15. Do you use publishers' prepared materials in teaching literacy?
- ☐ Daily
- ☐ Weekly
- ☐ Monthly
- ☐ Infrequently

If so, what do you use them for?

16. Rank the following statements in order of importance (1 is most important.)

Literature is important because
- ☐ it develops reading
- ☐ it develops writing
- ☐ it widens knowledge
- ☐ it engages the emotions
- ☐ it develops the imagination

Sign (if you wish): _____

17

And what do you think happened next?

Eve Bearne

Several threads permeate this book: that reading is very much to do with identity; that reading is a transformative act, having power not only to transform the here-and-now to what-might-be, but also transforming us as we develop as readers; that helping children become committed and lifelong readers is a matter of engaging hearts and minds. This commitment starts in the home and is sustained through enlightened experience in school. Which leads to another key theme – the much debated matter of how best to teach reading. Again, this often starts in the home, although it is easy to forget this in the exhaustive and exhausting amount of talk about how reading should be taught in school. Another important theme is the importance of valuing what children bring to school as they are introduced to the wider repertoire of texts offered throughout their formal education. Underlying all these threads is the matter of just what reading involves and implies – the texts, the practices and, indeed the acts of reading.

Jane Johnson, the inspiration for this book, gives wise guidance on all of these matters, but it is one particular aspect of her approach to reading which is my starting point for looking to the future. Jane Johnson knew about multimodality – that it is both to do with the reading material and an approach to teaching reading. Jane Johnson's children learned that reading involved all the primary modes of representation and communication: the play of gesture and movement, images, speech and writing. The reading materials which Jane Johnson produced for her children have very close parallels with the multimodal texts which make up the reading repertoire of twenty-first century classrooms. However, while there are strong continuities between these texts and practices of the eighteenth century and now, there are also significant differences, particularly related to developments in technology. I shall take two examples, one quite a large-scale research project into children's on-screen reading and the other a focused curriculum development project about multimodality piloted in one classroom, to explore what might happen next in reading practices and pedagogy.

The introduction of digital technology into everyday life has not only made it easier and quicker to send and receive messages but has changed the form of those messages. One of the most significant changes has been to shift written language, or print, out of its position as the principal public means of communication. We are now very familiar with reading material where pictures and design features accompany – and sometimes outweigh – print. All forms of public texts are more image-based. Of course, newspapers and magazines have carried images for a long time but now financial and commercial documents also use images and designed text to get their messages across and information texts of all kinds are more visually presented.

Sound, too, is taking a more prominent position, either as spoken text accompanying presentations or as background sound in visual texts. The screen, with its icons, pop-ups and familiar layout is ever present as a means of keeping in touch with friends, dealing with tasks for work, finding bargains or tracing our ancestry. PowerPoint™ presentations are an expected part of industry and commerce and DVDs are distributed in all kinds of places – at conferences, as newspaper giveaways and even by estate agents showing properties to potential buyers. Although we can be sure that print remains a major means of communication, the digital revolution has implications for reading pedagogy.

Children take the highly visual and designed environment for granted. From their earliest years they are surrounded by texts which combine images, words and sound, on screen and on paper, in the home, in the street and in school. This means that they bring a wide experience of texts to their school work, expecting to read images as well as print. The multimodal texts which children encounter at home and in the social environment combine elements of gesture, movement, posture, facial expression; images: moving and still, real or drawn; sound: spoken words, sound effects and music; and writing, including colour, font and typography. These texts are realised in paper-based forms like books, picturebooks, comics, magazines and leaflets which combine print, typographical features, colour, and design or layout. Screen-based texts such as DVDs, film, television, video, computer games and internet sites bring together image, movement, speech, music, sound effects, colour, image, layout and print.

These texts require some shifts in the ways in which reading is taught. Many of them – on paper or on screen – are read radially rather than in the linear left to right sequence required of the traditional printed word. On-screen texts are designed to be navigated differently and often invite interaction with a single screen as well as by moving between screens reached by hyperlinks. In terms of content, much of the new screen-based reading landscape is made up of hybrid kinds of text which make different reading demands from those encountered in books, magazines, comics and advertising material (Kress, 2003). In addition, there are issues of authorship and provenance to be considered. Screen-based texts: blogs, chatsites, websites and wikis do not go through a process of editorial scrutiny and any site can present 'information' which is sometimes little more than unconfirmed assertion. This means that attentive and critical readership is even more important as part of the young reader's repertoire. My first example, taken from a wide-ranging research project, clearly shows this need for critical reading.

Reading on screen

The *Reading on Screen* research (Bearne *et al*, 2007) sought to investigate whether the skills needed for reading paper-based texts are substantially different from reading screen-based texts. A group of researchers – teachers, local authority literacy advisers and lecturers in higher education institutions – carried out a variety of projects in four different areas of England.[1] They collected evidence through surveys and questionnaires, pupil journals, videos of children interacting with screen texts, observation of practice and interviews with teachers, practitioners and children. The research investigated the skills and strategies children use as they read texts on screen and attempted to identify teaching approaches which will support the new range of reading. For this chapter I have selected some key aspects of the findings.

Several of the projects began by surveying children's home experience of digital technology or their home-based reading both on-screen and off. Since one of the research questions was to identify the skills and strategies needed for on-screen reading, it seemed sensible to find out about children's existing funds of knowledge (Moll *et al*, 1992). There have already been some substantial research projects about children's use of media and digital technologies in the home (Marsh, 2004; Rideout *et al*, 2003) but this research sought to link home and school on-screen reading. Another matter of interest to the researchers was to establish as far as possible if there was any substance to the often-heard concern that on-screen texts threaten to elbow books out of the reading repertoire. What would evidence of home-based reading suggest?

Surveys in different areas and with different age groups showed a rich variety of home-based text experience, both screen-based and on paper. Unsurprisingly, perhaps, for independent leisure reading there was a generally higher preference for screen-based texts, particularly popular children's internet sites, rather than paper-based texts. Evidence from children as young as five showed sophisticated expertise in on-screen reading, even where homes did not have computers. Friends, other family homes, internet cafes and school clubs provided opportunities for children to access on-screen texts. DVDs and videos also contributed to awareness of screen conventions.

However, there was evidence that screens are not – at least at the moment – replacing the book. In fact, the data suggested that reading on screen often boosts reading paper-based texts. From the earliest years there was evidence of children seeking books and magazines based on their chosen home-based screen reading. There was no marked lack of interest in sustained book reading but an awareness from the children surveyed that they could gain different reading satisfactions from different types of text. Responses from older students suggested that they used computers at home both for work and leisure and made considered choices about whether books or screen will best serve their purposes in reading. Some small groups of students were interviewed about their home uses of ICTs and one group of older pupils (from a boys' secondary school) explained how they used the computer for work and social purposes:

> I *use it for coursework, to write up drafts. And I use Messenger services to talk to my friends* (Ben).

> *...for games. Sometimes I look up stuff, like if it's science homework* (Josh).

When asked whether they prefer researching on screen or from books, they responded:

> *I like both ways, but I think I prefer ICT because it's easier to refer back and go between them quicker. The computer is most effective because it's easier to save, easier to understand, and you could go on the internet to get more information if you needed it* (Alan).

> *When it's on paper it doesn't seem to make as much sense. On the screen you can hyperlink to what it means, this is helpful. It seems sort of harder to follow in print ... unless it's a novel* (Mohan).

> *On the computer screen it's harder. You can't get easy on the chair, with a book you can just like take it anywhere. On the computer it's harder, you've got to search it up (if you're looking for information), so if you're doing about snakes, if it's a book you can just get a book about snakes* (John).

I just enjoy reading a book. With the computer you get a picture, what they think it says, instead of seeing a forest you can imagine what the forest looks like... they might have leaves, mine might not. With a book you can imagine (Amos).

These responses echo some of the findings from the 10 and 11-year-olds' surveys and observations. While computers and other screens feature highly as leisure preferences, when it comes to everyday use for work, books also had their place in the text landscapes of the young people in this survey.

Implications for teaching

Many of the teachers who opened their classrooms to the research were already embracing the opportunities – and demands – of digital technologies. However, it would be wrong to suggest that this is typical. The teachers involved with this project were already more likely to be assured in their use of the technologies. The nursery practitioners and Early Years teachers who regularly include word processing, internet searching and children's involvement with the interactive whiteboard (IWB) were committed to an open and inclusive approach to children and digital technology.

The IWB has afforded teachers opportunities to teach reading more systematically by the use of software tools like highlighters and focusing tools. There was evidence of teachers being more explicit about how texts are constructed and extending the repertoire of available texts by importing video clips, images and pre-prepared screens. They demonstrated and encouraged a range of navigation strategies for children to find their way through hypertext, particularly using the wealth of internet information texts now available. However, the research also highlighted some problems.

The data from the different projects showed that children's home experience and fluency in finding, trawling, navigating, scanning and reading screen-based texts can be transferred to reading of all kinds of texts. But there were questions about how much children's reading was being extended and challenged in schools. Online reading involves texts which offer new challenges for teaching, for example, interactive texts and documentary video texts which appear on interactive websites. Not only is the content more fluid, and even perhaps ephemeral, but the structure of such texts involves different reading choices from those of paper-based texts.

For those reasons, if for no other, teaching critical reading is necessary for internet (and other) on-screen texts. This is particularly true when teaching multimodal texts. School classrooms and curricula generally lack models of on-screen multimodal texts. Gaps between home and school experience and between teachers' and pupils' screen-based text experience mean that some teacher-chosen reading CDROMs do not match children's on-screen reading expertise or preferences. Overall, the research showed variation in teachers' own levels of experience with digital technologies, the features of screen-based texts and the analytical processes involved in reading them.

Evidence about children's and students' home uses of computers and other screen-based texts suggests a wealth of experience from a very early age but there is a danger that children's expertise and experience with screen reading is not being acknowledged and valued in the classroom. At the same time, while computers, data projector screens and interactive whiteboards offer new opportunities for shared and collaborative reading, there are issues of inclusivity (and exclusivity for children who have perceptual problems with reading). While visual and interactive texts can help some children engage more with the world of print, electronic multimodality has increased the complexity of classroom reading for some pupils with learning difficulties and may further marginalise children who are already disadvantaged by print. Rosemary Anderson (2005) notes that the introduction of some digital technologies into the classroom can disadvantage children who experience specific learning difficulties or dyslexia. She points out:

> The greatest demands of all occur when pupils are overwhelmed with huge amounts of text as they try to navigate internet websites which may have numerous hypertext links. Because the pupils tend to work on laptops with partners who are more able, and therefore more confident than they are, they often take on the role of assistant or apprentice, and although they may appear engaged with a task, in effect they may at times be no more than passive observers. (Anderson, 2005, 137)

There is often an assumption that using computers in the classroom offers greater opportunities for inclusion of children with different learning needs. But Anderson's research suggests that there are implications for reading pedagogy of using screen-based texts with children who experience particular literacy difficulties.

Despite the problems, however, the future looks promising. The *Reading on Screen* research project showed that many children are expert in navigating hypertext on screen, selecting content and commenting on their choices even from a very young age. Their reading repertoire – at home at least – is often extensive. The book is not dead, nor even on the way out, as some may have feared. Young readers continue to gain satisfaction from paper-based texts as they extend their range with a variety of on-screen texts. Future reading provision will need to help children to discuss purposes of different types of reading and reading material so that they can make even more informed decisions about book and screen reading choices. Teaching critical reading is necessary for internet (and other) on-screen texts and, indeed, for texts of all kinds.

Asking questions of the text

My second example picks up the theme of critical readership. In Newham, an inner city borough of London, the Ethnic Minority Achievement (EMA) team developed a project designed specifically to include multimodal texts in the reading and writing repertoires of bilingual and multilingual children[2]. This was a very rich project but I can only show a small part of it here. As a pilot project, Jane Bednall (EMA adviser) worked with Leanne Cranston, a year 5 teacher, on a five-week project designed to support bilingual readers in reading complex texts by developing the sophisticated inference and deduction skills involved in reading multilayered texts. Jane Bednall explicitly wanted to develop critical literacy:

> Through our work in supporting teachers to develop more culturally inclusive ways of working we have identified some key learning processes that we want to encourage: visual literacy; critical literacy (questioning how texts come about: *who made this text? how I am being influenced by it?*); enquiry-based questioning for learning and cross-cultural awareness. (Bednall and Cranston, 2008, 19-20)

She identified a clear connection between multimodality and the ability to read critically:

> ...in developing strategies to facilitate bilingual learners, developing critical literacy is teaching multimodally – using all four modes of: sound or talk; gesture and movement; writing; and images. What's needed is explicit discussion and teaching about how the different modes contribute to making meaning. (*ibid*)

There was a further aim – to create a classroom environment of openness, recognising and celebrating cultural diversity. One thread in the multimodal project was to understand how children's reading experience is influenced by their cultural experience. And, equally, to consider how their own experience shapes their understanding of the text, so that they feel comfortable to share that experience in the classroom.

The project involved the children keeping portfolios of their work so that they could return to ideas and build on them. In the first few sessions the emphasis was on becoming familiar with multimodal texts and how authors and artists have made meaning in multimodal ways: hieroglyphs, cave paintings, aboriginal art, story scrolls and music and dance. Teacher modelling suggested how authors use different devices to engage the reader, including font style, size and colour, characters' posture, the combination of words and images. The children annotated double page spreads, asking questions of the pages. Mazeeda and Labiba read a double page spread from Colin Thompson's *The Paperbag Prince* with a large block of text on the left and on the right hand page an image of an odd looking man surrounded by rubbish and facing the reader. They were keen to discuss:

> *Why is the man ignoring the action?*
> *What is the dump?*
> *What are the birds doing and why are they there? Why is one bird chirping?*
> *What's in the cupboard?*
> *Why is the text so long?*

The children's use of questions afforded opportunities for the teacher to explain something about reader response – that there may be no hard-and-fast answers and that the children's opinions were valued.

After this introductory work, the class read and re-read the chosen book *The Red Tree* by Shaun Tan, looking for mood created by colour, posture and gesture and the meaning carried by the words. The theme of the book is a sense of isolation and this is powerfully evoked by the images and text. Parthik's comments show how the children learned to read this complex text. He chose a particular double page spread which shows a cityscape with high rise buildings and aeroplanes surrounded by a collage of fragments of newsprint in different languages. Amongst the oppressive buildings the text reads simply 'Without sense or reason' with a very small image of the girl on a ladder towards the bottom right. Parthik analysed the design, and the use of colour, posture and words:

> *It's bloody and angry, the people are at war. It seems like children are separated from mothers, people shouting and screaming, war between countries...*

> *The words match with the picture. There's no sense and nobody listening to her. The facial expression shows that she's sad and the body language shows that she's the only person on earth. She doesn't have a mouth to speak.*

After reading and analysing the whole book, the children then created poems using ideas taken from their earlier annotating of double page spreads from the book. They used different artistic techniques, particularly the use of inks and black and white tree drawings as a basis for collage double page poems. Following the theme of isolation, despair and renewed hope of *The Red Tree*, the children planned and wrote poems based on emotions. They used digital photography to capture a sense of how body language and actions reveal mood. Language then became a focus as the children made their own poems composed of statements about their feelings. The children's critical reading allowed them to write in role as a desolate person, drawing on their own feelings as well as those of the girl in the book. However, they made a clear distinction between the girl's feelings and their own.

Figures 1 and 2 show poems by Mazeeda and Aniqa Begum. Although the words in Mazeeda's poem capture a sense of isolation and despair, she is a cheerful person and deliberately shows herself smiling and raising a small image of herself up high, indicating the hope which is a feature of the end of *The Red Tree*. Her final question 'Can I get out of this?' is answered by the hope expressed in the central image on the left. Aniqa Begum uses line to evoke a sense of being trapped. She encloses her central figure with a swirling background which captures a sense of confusion and is interwoven with repeated words and phrases: *you can't get out, regret, why? disconnected* (on the right hand image this is even written backwards). But, just as in Pandora's box, there is also hope.

Figure 5: Mazeeda's poem. (see extract on page 228)

I am so confused, as confused as a never ending maze
I am a lost piece of a puzzle of happiness
I am trapped with locked doors everywhere I turn....
I have not done anything to people
But they are still against me
I wish I had my own world with kind and generous friends in it
Life is dull with no light
I am so tiny that nobody notices me
What will happen in the future? Can I get out of this?

Figure 6: Aniqa Begum's poem with an extract printed below

I'm never happy or excited.
Life is so unfair.
Why is the world a ball of hatred?
When are the tears going to stop falling from my eyes?

Life is not to be lived.
Why does my heart not beat but I still live?
Can't I just live in another world instead of living here?

At the end of the project, the children were interviewed to assess how far the original aims of the project – to help children read beyond the literal – had been achieved. When asked how they would explain to a younger reader how to read a complex picturebook, their explanations of the process showed sophisticated understanding of how these texts work:

> *Tania*: Look at the pictures carefully. If they can't read they *have* to look at it really carefully and look at the colours and what the person is doing – the facial expression and the body language. You have to look at the picture and the colours and the person's face really carefully to ask yourself a few questions: *How is the person feeling? What sort of state is he or she in?* or maybe a few more questions. But I think that they should look at the picture really carefully... the colours and the face represent something.

> *Rashida*: You connect with the picture and put yourself in that person's shoes and ask yourself: 'How would you feel if you were that girl?' Connect with the picture and look at the emotion under the picture...

> *Parthik*: ... and compare it when you're in her shoes and when she's in your shoes, ... how she's reading you in the book and when you're reading her in the book...

The future – continuity and change

These insights bring us back to the continuities permeating the book as a whole. In the first place, that reading is very much to do with identity. Rashida's sense of connectedness shows her identification with the emotions of the girl in *The Red Tree*. Parthik takes it further, showing the transformative nature of reading as he indicates his feeling that there is a kind of exchange between the book and the reader – a merging of selves. In writing about reading and identity, McCarthey and Moje (2002) suggest that reading should support 'how [children] see themselves and who they want to be'. Who children will become as readers depends to a large extent on the adults who share with children the satisfactions of engaging with different kinds of texts. The *Reading on Screen* research showed how home reading – on-screen and off and supported by friends and family – provides a strong basis for children developing confident readers' identities but it also warns that their experience in school may not extend or challenge their reading repertoires sufficiently.

The wealth of text experience shown in the large-scale research and the depth of understanding shown by the children in Newham re-introduce the theme of valuing what children bring to school as they are introduced to an increasingly wide range of texts. In terms of screen-based texts there are some problems, however, as teachers may not be as confident with the range of texts and technologies as their pupils are. Despite this, there is some suggestion that teachers may not give themselves enough credit for what they do know about digital texts (Graham, 2008). I would argue that the future of reading depends not only on valuing what children bring to the classroom in terms of reading experience but also valuing teachers' knowledge of different kinds of text. The Teachers as Readers research, reported in Chapter 16 of this book, strongly indicates that teachers read avidly and persistently for their own pleasure. I wonder how often, in the hustle and bustle of trying to teach the reading curriculum, they share these pleasures with their pupils.

It is clear that multimodal texts are not recent inventions. However, there has been an explosion in different types of multimodal texts, particularly digital texts, over the past twenty years or so. Production processes have made design a significant feature of books and prompted a flowering of complex, challenging and beautiful picturebooks. Their texts work through the intricate and varied relationships between word, image and design. While children may be able to probe their deeper meanings, they gain the greatest satisfactions if they can discuss them fully, noticing how colour, posture, design and words combine to make meaning.

The greater availability of DVDs and the now ubiquitous computer screen equally demand that children are able to discuss the intentions of directors, as shown in their editing, camera angles and shot choices as well as the use of music and sound effects. The internet extends the reading repertoire by the sheer mass of material which comes largely unmediated to the reader.

The two examples in this chapter indicate very clearly that there is an urgent need not only for extending the reading repertoire to embrace screen texts while continuing to value print, but that there needs to be some extension of pedagogy if the readers of tomorrow are to be able to make discriminating choices. Young readers need to be given greater experience of critical reading and analysis of texts. At the same time, teachers and children benefit by having a vocabulary for discussing and analysing multimodal texts – on screen and on paper. This allows for explicit teaching of how to read images, sound, design, posture and movement as well as words.

In thinking about what might happen next, perhaps the last word should go to some of the young readers who have come to understand something about the complexities of multimodality. They remind us that reading is not only about texts, but about an approach to teaching. It is about openness, an attitude of trust and a very clear sense of the exciting adventure of lifelong reading. When they were asked to give advice to teachers about how best to support readers, Parthik and Rashida had no doubts:

Parthik: Get them active. Read more books that have pictures in them. Make them understand that this is what you mean by multimodal texts and this is what you learn in school.

Rashida: Don't keep us so tied in ... be adventurous. Keep an open mind and heart ... be sensitive really.

Notes

1 This work was made possible by a grant from the Qualifications and Curriculum Agency

2 For a full account of this project see *English 4-11* (the professional magazine published jointly by the English Association and The United Kingdom Literacy Association) March 2008, 19-26

Bibliography

Anderson, R (2005) Coping with Classroom Reading as a Dyslexic Pupil in the Middle Years of Schooling. Paper presented at the United Kingdom Literacy Association conference. University of Bath, July 2005

Bearne, E, Clarke, C, Johnson, A, Manford, P, Mottram, M and Wolstencroft, H (2007) *Reading on Screen.* Leicester: UKLA

Bednall, J and Cranston, L with Bearne, E (2008) The most wonderful adventure ... going beyond the literal. *English four to eleven* 32, 19-26

Graham, L (2008) Teachers are digikids too: the digital histories and digital lives of young teachers in English primary schools. *Literacy* 42 (1), 10-18

Kress, G (2003) *Literacy in the New Media Age.* London and New York: Routledge Taylor Francis

Marsh, J (2004) The Techno-literacy practices of young children. *Journal of Early Childhood Research* 21, 51-66

McCarthey, S J and Moje, E B (2002) Identity Matters. *Reading Research Quarterly* 37 (2) 228-238

Moll, L, Amanti, C, Neff, D and Gonzalez, N (1992) Funds of Knowledge for Teaching: Using a qualitative approach to connect homes and classrooms. *Theory into Practice* 31, 132-141

Rideout, V J, Vandewater, E A and Wartella, E A (2003) *Zero to Six: Electronic media in the lives of infants, toddlers and preschoolers.* Washington: Kaiser Foundation

Tan, S (2006) *The Red Tree.* London: Lothian Books

Thompson, C (1992) *The Paperbag Prince.* London: Julia McRae Books

List of contributors

Evelyn Arizpe is a Lecturer in Children's Literature at the Faculty of Education, University of Glasgow. She has taught and published widely in the areas of literacies, picturebooks and children's literature. She is co-author, with Morag Styles, of *Children Reading Picture: Interpreting visual texts* (Routledge, 2003) and *Reading Lessons from the Eighteenth Century: Mothers, Children and Texts* (Pied Piper Press, 2006). She has a particular interest in Mexican children's books and her current research involves immigrant children, picturebooks, literacy and culture.

Eve Bearne is a highly respected teacher, lecturer and writer. She has published several distinguished books about language and literacy, as well as co-editing many volumes on aspects of children's literature. Her research interests while at the University of Cambridge Faculty of Education have largely focused on issues relating to children's production of multimodal texts and gender, language and literacies. She is currently responsible for Publications for the United Kingdom Literacy Association.

Janet Bottoms was a Lecturer in English at Homerton College, Cambridge, and a member of the Subject Studies team in the University of Cambridge Faculty of Education. Her professional interests are in the area of Shakespeare, Renaissance Drama and the late 18th/early 19th century. She is completing a full-length study of the history of Shakespeare in education, as well as contributing to conferences and leading workshops on using his drama in primary schools and in the home. She has also published a number of articles on William Godwin's Juvenile Library and the work of Charles and Mary Lamb.

Valerie Coghlan is Librarian at the Church of Ireland College of Education in Dublin. She has a particular interest in visual literacy and in Irish children's literature. She has published widely on these topics, and recently co-edited *Irish Children's Writers and Illustrators 1986-2006* (CBI/CICEP, 2007) with Siobhán Parkinson, *Divided Worlds: Studies in Children's Literature* (Four Courts, 2007) with Mary Shine Thompson, and with Clare Bradford *Expectations and Experiences: Children, Childhood and Children's Literature* (Pied Piper/IRSCL, 2007). She organised the highly successful IRSCL Conference in Dublin in 2005 and is currently president of IBBY Ireland.

Peter Cook is a Senior Lecturer in the Faculty of Education, Anglia Ruskin University, and a Fellow of the Higher Education Academy, London. He taught for ten years in Africa and the Middle East, and has degrees in English and Art Education. He has published work on the Romantic poets, and has presented papers at many international conferences. His most recent publication is 'Go Ask Alice: the Image of the Child in the Sixties Counterculture' in *What Do You See? International Perspectives on Children's Book Illustration,* Cambridge Scholars Press, 2008.

Teresa Cremin is Professor of Education (Literacy) at the Open University. Her work involves research, consultancy and writing about creative teaching and learning and the professional development of teachers as readers, writers and artistically involved creative professionals. Teresa is President of the United Kingdom Literacy Association (UKLA) and co-coordinator of the BERA Creativity SIG. She has published widely including: *Teaching English: A Creative Approach* (2009, Routledge), *Creativity and Writing: Developing Voice and Verve in the Classroom* (2005, Routledge) and *The Routledge Falmer Reader in Language and Literacy* (2004).

Prue Goodwin *is* a freelance lecturer in literacy and children's books and works with trainee teachers at the University of Reading. She runs courses on language and literacy development, acts as a consultant to publishers of children's books, researches literacy development in schools and has edited four books on literacy learning. Prue has lectured internationally and is involved in many national initiatives concerning literacy and children's literature in the UK. She has edited several books including *Understanding Children's Books* (Sage, 2008).

Judith Graham still works occasionally in the Faculty of Education in Cambridge. Her earlier teaching experience was in London schools, University of Greenwich, Roehampton University and the London Institute of Education. Margaret Meek supervised her thesis on picturebooks which was published by NATE as *Pictures on the Page* (1990) and they worked together on *Achieving Literacy* (Routledge, 1983). Further publications include *Cracking Good Books/Picturebooks* (NATE, 1997, 2000), *Reading under Control* and *Writing Under Control* with Allison Kelly (David Fulton, 2007, 2003) and *Historical Fiction: Capturing the Past* with Fiona Collins (David Fulton, 2001).

Elizabeth Hammill is the initiator and co-founder of Seven Stories, the Centre for Children's Books. As Artistic and Collection Director, she laid the foundations for the Centre's novel approach to exhibition design and interpretation in groundbreaking exhibitions. She was instrumental in developing its growing collection of original manuscripts, artwork and other materials by modern British authors and illustrators for children, drawing on her earlier experiences as a primary teacher, children's bookseller, editor, critic and lecturer. She has written distinguished articles for *Signal* and other publications and was awarded an OBE in 2007 for services to literature.

Shirley Brice Heath, linguistic anthropologist, is the author of the classic *Ways with Words: Language, life, and work in communities and classrooms* (Cambridge University Press, 1983). Heath has taught at universities throughout the world, most notably Stanford University and Brown University, and as Visiting Research Professor at Kings College, University of London. Of emphasis in her research are the long-term effects for learners of immersion in both the arts and sciences as companions in building effective learning environments. With Shelby Wolf, she published a series on visual literacy and learning through drama, arts and science project-based work (2004, 2005). She co-authored *On ethnography: Approaches to language and literacy research* (Teachers College Press, 2008) with Brian Street.

Marilyn Mottram has taught in a variety of contexts including schools, nurseries and HE institutions. She is currently an Adviser with Birmingham local authority where she works on curriculum design and development projects with schools and educational settings across the city. She is passionate about school-led action research and about offering space for teachers to be researchers of children's learning. Her own recent research considers the implications of the personalisation agenda on the language and practice of literacy teaching as it currently operates in England.

Anouk Lang is a postdoctoral research fellow in the Department of American and Canadian Studies at the University of Birmingham, where she works on the AHRC project Beyond the Book: Contemporary Cultures of Reading in the UK, USA and Canada. She holds a PhD in English from the University of Cambridge, and her research interests include postcolonial studies and world literatures, comparative modernist studies and the impact of technologies on reading practices. She is currently editing a collection on contemporary cultures of reading.

Karlijn Navest is a doctoral student in the VICI research project 'The Codifiers and the English Language: Tracing the Norms of Standard English', led by Professor Ingrid Tieken-Boon van Ostade at the University of Leiden. She wrote the entry on Robert Lowth (1710-1787) for the *Encyclopedia of Language and Linguistics, 2nd edition*, and is one of the contributors to *Grammars, Grammarians and Grammar-Writing in Eighteenth-Century England* (Mouton de Gruyter, 2008). She is currently completing her PhD thesis on John Ash (1724-1779) and the rise of the children's grammar.

Geraldine O'Connor is a Lecturer in Education at the Church of Ireland College of Education in Dublin. She lectures on a range of professional development courses relating to history, geography and science education. She is a member of the board of CICE Publications and was a consultant editor of *Slates Up! School and Schooling in the Nineteenth Century* (2005). Geraldine is the education officer for primary history at the Irish National Council for Curriculum and Assessment (NCCA) and a member of the Irish Association for Social Scientific and Environmental Education (IASSEE).

Francesca Orestano is Associate Professor of English Literature at the State University of Milan. Her research interests include connections between literature and aesthetics on the Gothic and the Picturesque, and visual culture between the 18th century and Modernism. Publications include *Gothic Modernisms* (2000); two collections of essays, *Le guide del mattino: alle origini della children's literature*, with Carlo Pagetti (Milano, CUEM, 2004) and *Tempi moderni nella children's literature: storie, personaggi, strumenti critici* (Milano, CUEM, 2007). She is responsible for the website http://users.unimi. it/childlit in cooperation with scholars in the universities of Padua, Salerno, Turin, Venice, the first website devoted to the study of children's literature in Italy.

Vivienne Smith teaches in the Department of Childhood and Primary Studies at the University of Strathclyde, where she prepares students to be primary teachers and carries out research into children's reading, literature and critical literacy. She has published a number of articles and chapters in edited books, including, most recently, 'Gatty's Tale: or Virtue Restored' (*English in Education*, 2008, 42:1) and 'Learning to be a reader: promoting good textual health' in Goodwin (ed) (2008) *Understanding Children's Books*.

Margaret Meek Spencer is Reader Emeritus at the Institute of Education, University of London. She is the author of many publications including *Learning to Read, On Being*

Literate, How Texts Teach What Readers Learn and *Information and Book Learning*. For 25 years she was the book-review editor of the *School Librarian* and received the Eleanor Farjeon Award for services to children's literature. Later, she was a founder member of the Executive Committee of the National Literacy Trust. Her continuing concern is to link children's reading, at each stage in their schooling, with the best books written for them.

Morag Styles is a Reader in Children's Literature and Education at Cambridge. She writes, lectures and organises conferences internationally on children's literature, poetry, visual literacy and the history of reading. She is the author of *From the Garden to the Street: 300 Years of Poetry for Children* (1998), Advisory Editor for *The Cambridge Guide to Children's Books in English* (2001) and co-editor, with Evelyn Arizpe, of *Children Reading Pictures: Interpreting Visual Texts* (2002) and *Reading Lessons from the Eighteenth Century: Mothers, Children and Texts* (2006). She has organised exhibitions at the Fitzwilliam Museum, Cambridge and the British Library.

Laura Tosi is Associate Professor in English Literature at the University Ca' Foscari in Venice. Her research includes Elizabethan and Jacobean drama, women's studies, postmodernist fiction, and children's literature. She has written books on Ben Jonson (Milan, 1998), John Webster (Pisa, 2001) and has edited and translated a collection of Victorian fairy tales (Venice, 2003). Her latest book is on the literary fairy tale in England (*La fiaba letteraria inglese*, Venice, 2007). She is a member of the editorial board of the website http://users.unimi.it/childlit/ (Children's Literature in Italy). Her current research is focused on the folklore sources and Victorian adaptations of Shakespeare's plays for children.

Victor Watson was Head of English at Homerton College, Cambridge, and has been the Chair of Seven Stories – the Centre for Children's Books in Newcastle, where he is still a Trustee and Chair of the Collection Committee. He is the author of *Reading Series Fiction* (Routledge, 2000), co-author of *Coming of Age in Children's Literature* (Continuum, 2002), with Margaret Meek, and the editor of *The Cambridge Guide to Children's Books in English* (CUP, 2001). He has been assembling a collection of children's annuals from 1880 to 1980 which he hopes will find a permanent home at Seven Stories.

David Whitley is a Lecturer in English at the Faculty of Education, Cambridge University, where he has taught literature (both adult and children's) and film for a number of years. He has published articles and chapters on Aesop's fables, poetry, fantasy writing and animated film. His book on environmental themes in animation, *The Idea of Nature in Disney Animation* (2008), was published in the Ashgate Studies in Childhood series.

Index

Also from Trentham

Art, Narrative and Childhood
edited by Morag Styles and Eve Bearne

...offers readers a cosmopolitan and entertaining overview of the interactions between children, images and texts ...will be used and enjoyed well into this new millennium. **Times Educational Supplement**

... breaks new ground in thinking about reading text and image. ... a valuable addition to the libraries of all educators... **British Journal of Educational Studies**

What determines the nature and style of the literature and pictures produced for children? And how do children respond? *Art, Narrative and Childhood* reviews current conceptions of visual texts and explores what will be understood as visual literacy in the future.

Drawn from a distinguished international conference in Cambridge in 2000, the contributions range from Aboriginal visual narratives to European artists' sketchbooks to children's 'classics' such as *Alice in Wonderland*, new 'classics' and media texts. The enduring appeal of humour is discussed, as manifest in comics, poetry and popular fiction such as the *Dr Seuss* books. Children's voices are also here, offering sophisticated views of pictorial texts and revealing new possibilities about what reading might come to mean.

This authoritative and fascinating book will interest the creators, producers and consumers of children's literature and those who study it worldwide.

2003, ISBN 978 1 85856 263 6
186 pages, 228 x 145mm, £17.99

Trentham Books Limited
Westview House, 734 London Road, Oakhill,
Stoke-on-Trent, Staffordshire, England ST4 5NP
Tel: +44 (0) 1782 745567/844699
FAX: +44 (0) 1782 745553
www.trentham-books.co.uk